The Velvet Chancellors

A History of Post-War Germany

TERENCE PRITTIE

FREDERICK MULLER LIMITED
LONDON

First published in Great Britain 1979 by
Frederick Muller Limited, London NW2 6LE

British Library Cataloguing in Publication Data

Prittie, Terence
    The velvet chancellors.
    1. Germany, West – Politics and Government
    2. Prime ministers – Germany, West
    I. Title
    943.087   DD259.4
ISBN 0–584–10461–8

Typeset by Computacomp (UK) Ltd, Fort William, Scotland.
Printed in Great Britain by Biddles Ltd, Guildford, Surrey.

Contents

Illustrations

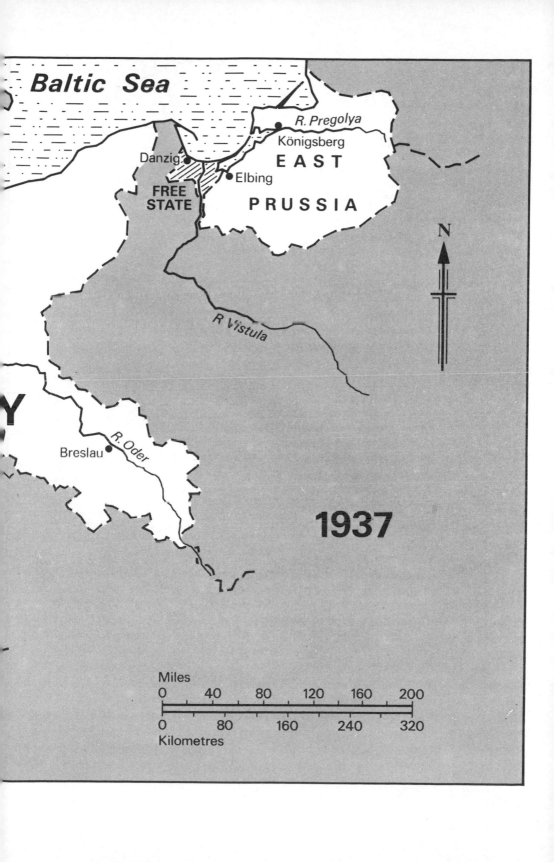

Baltic Sea

R. Pregolya

Königsberg

Danzig

EAST

FREE
STATE

Elbing

PRUSSIA

R. Vistula

N

Y

R. Oder

Breslau

1937

Miles
0   40   80   120   160   200

0   80   160   240   320
Kilometres

North Sea

Flensburg

Kiel Canal

Kiel

Hamburg

Bremen

R. Ems

R. Weser

Osnabrück

Hannover

G E R

Dortmund

Essen

Düsseldorf

R. Rhine

Cologne

Aachen

BONN

R. Mosel

Koblenz

Frankfurt

Trier

Würzburg

Mannheim

Saarbrücken

Karlsruhe

R. Rhine

Stuttgart

Ulm

Freiburg

Bodensee

M A N Y

Nuremberg

Regensburg

Augsburg

Munich

BERLIN

(West)   (East)

N

1961

Miles
0   40   80

0   80   160
Kilometres

Dedication

To those who have worked for a better understanding between the German and British peoples, and in particular to good friends whose special contribution was an encouragement to my work – Karl Günter von Hase, John Paice, Lance Pope and Herbert Sulzbach.

Author's Note

Some might think that the word "velvet" could hardly be applied to the five post-war West German Chancellors. Konrad Adenauer had an instinctive power of command and an often acid wit. Helmut Schmidt, especially in earlier years, could be caustic, rigorous, even rough. Willy Brandt, essentially a "man of the people", was often devastatingly direct and outspoken.

But all five post-war Chancellors have, in their different ways, represented the antithesis of that "blood and iron" tradition embodied in Otto von Bismarck and, even more, of the philosophy and exercise of total, brutal and unrestrained power practised by Adolf Hitler. Bismarck played the leading role in making Germany the mightiest country in Europe. The five "velvet" Chancellors have, between them, done something of far more lasting value: they have given the great bulk of the German people real freedom and real hope of a fair and settled future.

CHAPTER ONE

From Glory to Ruin

There has never been a country called, quite simply, "Germany". This is part of the paradox and tragedy of German history. A great people has enjoyed unity for only a brief period in its history, and then under false colours, as a "Reich" or pseudo-empire. That period lasted only three-quarters of a century and ended in 1945, leaving Germany apparently more irrevocably divided than at any previous time in its history.

In 1871 Bismarck, Germany's "Iron Chancellor", founded the German Reich out of the Kingdoms of Prussia, Bavaria, Saxony and Wurtemberg, eighteen grand-duchies, duchies and principalities, and the three "free cities" of Hamburg, Bremen and Luebeck, and Alsace-Lorraine. Four years earlier he had taken the first step in this direction by creating a reasonably cohesive North German Confederation, under the leadership of Prussia; prior to that, the 1815 Congress of Vienna shelved a real solution of the German question by its bequest of a loosely bound-together German Confederation of 39 states.

Bismarck's achievement in 1871 seemed to amount to the re-creation of the medieval Reich, dating back to the Emperor Charlemagne and claiming to be the successor of the Roman Empire. That medieval Reich had been headed by a Holy Roman Emperor, whose authority was supposedly derived from God and who was expected to assume the moral leadership of European Christendom. In such misty concepts was German sovereignty obscurely founded. In place of them, Bismarck, the total realist, sought to create a unified State (*Einheitsstaat*), solidly based on Prussian leadership. Austria, the only possible rival for leadership of the German people, was resoundingly defeated on the battlefield in 1866; France, the only European power capable of frustrating Bismarck's aims, suffered the same fate in 1870. Bismarck calculated boldly and ruthlessly, but always in the knowledge that he must have allies in the diplomatic field in order to change the European balance of power and place a dynamic German people in the position of European continental leadership. So his 1863 convention with Russia safeguarded Prussia's exposed eastern frontier. He treated defeated Austria with leniency, and divided it from France by playing on rival aspirations in Italy. He exploited the vague plan of France's Emperor, Napoleon III, to annex Belgium, in order to keep France and England apart. Bismarck may not have been the man to make real friends for Germany, but he built alliances with superb diplomatic skill.

Bismarck gave the Reich an Emperor, the King of Prussia, Wilhelm I; an army, Prussia's; and a philosophy, his own. It has become conventional to criticize Bismarck, the flawless diplomat, as a politician steeped in the traditions of the past, so short-sighted that he was utterly unable to appreciate the social consequences of the industrial revolution and the strength of the rising tide of European liberalism. But he knew German history, and drew his own lessons from it. Germany had been everlastingly rent by civil war and threatened by foreign invasion. Such episodes as the unimaginable horror of the Thirty Years War and the unparalleled shame of total conquest by Napoleon were in no way isolated in German history. German impotence to prevent them was bound to produce a reaction sooner or later; and the stage was set for this reaction by the Congress of Vienna, which handed the Rhineland to Prussia and brought what had been a relatively small East German state onto the borders of France and the Low Countries and into the heart of Western Europe. Prussia, suddenly, straddled the German people, from the Memel to the Maas, and found itself in control of Europe's potentially greatest workshop, the Ruhr.

Bismarck gave Germany an Emperor because mere kingship seemed hardly enough; the Emperor was to be the symbol of German power and glory. His sword and buckler was to be the Prussian Army, itself the symbol of those wholly admirable Prussian virtues – courage, discipline, obedience, selfless service and absolute loyalty. One British historian has referred to "the extraordinary position of ascendancy which the military caste maintained in the Kingdom of Prussia and the German Reich for very little short of a century and a half".[1] The Army's loyalty was to the Emperor; he was its commander, and every officer and soldier pledged his personal loyalty to him. The Army stood ready at all times to do the Emperor's bidding; he was entitled to declare a state of emergency and order a *Staatsstreich* – in effect, an official "coup" – whenever he chose to do so. This nearly happened on at least two occasions between 1871 and 1914.

Bismarck's political philosophy was a more complex matter. Certainly, he made forthright enough statements. There was, for instance: "Not by majority decisions and resolutions will the great issues of our time be settled, but by blood and iron."[2] He talked of the "muddy wave of parliamentarianism",[3] and quoted Virgil when indicating his readiness to undermine constitutional government – "If I cannot bend the High Ones, I shall move the underworld." He successfully blocked constitutional reform, for his aim was that Prussia should dominate the other 24 German states and that the monarch should rule Prussia. Thus, right down to 1917, the Reichstag could not secure the dismissal of the Chancellor save through the King of Prussia (who was also Emperor), while the three-tier voting system gave the *kaisertreu* Conservatives, loyal to the Emperor, solid control of the Prussian Parliament. Prussia, in turn, controlled the Bundesrat, or Federal Chamber, which initiated bills for the Reichstag, or all-German Parliament. In the 1870s he fought a *Kulturkampf*, or "cultural war", against the Roman Catholic Centre Party, and his legislation deprived thousands of parishes of their priests and dispatched many of the clergy to prison. In the 1880s he turned his attention to the Social Democrats, outlawing socialist societies, restricting the press, prohibiting meetings, and committing political opponents to prison on the spurious charge of "agitation".

At the same time, Bismarck introduced universal suffrage, the secret ballot, and the most progressive and beneficial social legislation of any country in Europe. He carried on government by a unique mixture of bluff, deceit, opportunism, enlightenment and cynicism. His Germany, according to one historian, was dominated by "the cold but living hand of Prussia, the kingdom which dips one wing of the eagle in the Niemen and the other in the Rhine",[4] and "the state of soldiers and officials". Efficiency was Bismarck's eternal watchword: he succeeded in presiding over an industrial revolution which came late but was of truly dynamic force, and over an unprecedented expansion of German power and prestige. He was backed by the Prussian military caste and the Prussian landed aristocracy, the *Junkers*; they supported the salient characteristics of Prussian hegemony – "exceptionally bold leadership, systematic arming and disciplined manpower".[5]

There is a school of thought which believes that the seeds of future chaos and collapse were already being sown before and during Bismarck's era. Thus, one British writer: "National Socialist theory is almost entirely derived from the common elements in traditional German thought during the past hundred and fifty years. For that line of thought which leads from Herder to Hitler is traditionally and typically German."[6] Ernst Moritz Arndt was propagating the lunatic myth of German racial purity, and Friedrich "Turnvater" Jahn proclaimed that "The purer a nation, the better; the more mixed, the more like bandits." Anti-semitism was already rife; the *Junker*, Ludwig von der Marwitz, accused the Prussian Government of creating a "Jewish state", because it proposed Jewish political emancipation. An openly proclaimed Anti-Semitic Party was active from the 1870s onwards, and in 1893 actually won 342,000 votes and 16 seats in the Reichstag. The composer, Richard Wagner, called the Jew "the plastic demon of the decay of humanity" and "a repulsive caricature of the German spirit". Much earlier, Georg Friedrich Wilhelm Hegel defined his theory of "the State as power", and called the State "the image and reality of reason" and "the reality of the moral idea". To this prosaic interpretation was added the hysteria of Friedrich Nietzsche, in such phrases as "The masters of the globe shall replace God and shall acquire the deep and unconditional confidence of those over whom they will rule", and "I am not a human being; I am dynamite".[7] Interestingly, nationalists like Arndt, Jahn, Paul de Lagarde and Houston Stewart Chamberlain were, as apostles of German "dynamism" and Prussian "hardness", unfriendly to the West.

Bismarck may have honestly believed that political evolution was impossible in his day. The Germany which he had unified had to be held together. There is more reason to blame his successors for the tragedies of the twentieth century, two world wars, two terrible defeats, and the final and apparently lasting division of the country between two different European and world systems. The record of misrule by Kaiser Wilhelm II and his Ministers, from 1890 to 1914, is indeed a sorry one. Out of glory and prosperity, they created ruin. The dream of German greatness, of a genuine and indeed beneficial German role in Europe, was shattered.

Yet it need not have happened. A balanced description of the Germany of the time comes from Golo Mann:[8]

> The Germany of the Kaiser, of the Admiralty, of the General Staff, of Krupp, of self-righteously nationalist Professors, snarling bemonocled lieutenants, was also the Germany of the *Simplizissimus*, that wonderful satirical paper ... with a freedom and wit which one can only study with nostalgia today, for that kind of serene and solemn humour seems to have gone forever. It was the Germany of the great Social Democratic Party of Bebel and his friends, of Einstein and Planck, of Gerhart Hauptmann ... of Max Reinhardt's theatre, which contributed so much to the success of Ibsen and Bernard Shaw, perhaps more than their own nations did at the time. In any case, the Germany of the Kaiser must have been a country pleasant to live in and many foreigners chose to live there, in Munich and Dresden and elsewhere. Why it did not last, why the end was so miserable and so miserably stupid, for this one would have to go back to the beginning for an explanation, to the original sin of founding the new union in a French neighbour's royal palace instead of peacefully and democratically at home, to the feeble Bismarckian compromise between the old authority by the grace of God and the liberal bourgeoisie – the bourgeoisie who betrayed their ideals in order to get a small share of power from the monarchy, the feudal aristocracy and the military, who in their turn remained in command and excluded the democrats and the Social Democrats from national responsibility. That was the law under which the new Reich began ...

What, in more precise terms, went wrong? Certainly, the deliberate exclusion of the Social Democrats from government, and the gradual decline of German liberalism, meant that the government was strangely unrepresentative, a matter of expertise and manipulation rather than an expression of the true will of the people. The Social Democratic vote climbed steadily; in 1898 it was 27 per cent, in 1903, 31 per cent, and in 1912 nearly 35 per cent. By then, the party was Marxist in theory only and not in practice, and stood essentially for social reform.[9] The Social Democrats were deprived of the chance of sharing political responsibility: this was the negation of democracy. A partly bemused, partly dazzled public accepted the Kaiser's "personal" rule; their eyes were fixed on far horizons, on dreams of German greatness, of hugely increased armed might, of virtual hegemony in Europe, and the beginnings of an overseas colonial empire. This was an era of dangerous German mirages – of a Prussian-controlled domain stretching from the Baltic to the Black Sea, of the union of the two "fighting races", the Germans and the Turks, on the Bosphorus, of the Berlin to Baghdad Railway and even a German "Raj" in India and tropical Africa. It was the era of expansionist organizations like the Navy League, of student duelling societies whose members prepared themselves for the battlefield, of industrial pressure groups calling for, above all, strong government – thus, Gustav Krupp von Bohlen und Halbach, writing to the Kaiser, urged that there should be less social legislation, since the Social Democrats claimed credit for it and picked up support among the "semi-educated" masses.[10]

The lack of really representative government left the Kaiser and his advisers free to pursue a foreign policy which certainly made a major contribution to the outbreak of world war in 1914 – even though war-guilt cannot be laid exclusively at Germany's door. The dynamic Kaiser,Wilhelm II – so pathetically intent, according to Gustav Krupp, on proving that he was not a coward[11] – dominated his Ministers. Caprivi, Chancellor from 1890 to 1894, toyed with the idea of alliance with France and England. His successor, Prince Hohenlohe, wanted to draw England away from France, but was frustrated by the Kaiser's animosity towards his uncle, the Prince of Wales and future King Edward VII. Bernhard von Buelow took his place, and sought to revive the alliance with Russia – Bismarck's "reinsurance treaty" with Russia had been abandoned as soon as he fell from power. From 1909 Bethmann-Hollweg was Chancellor; more bureaucrat than statesman, he was helpless to compete against the Kaiser's "substitute diplomacy", which took the form of seeking to exploit family relationships instead of leaving statesmen to get on with their job. These were two decades of fumbling and futile diplomacy. The "Triple Alliance", with the Austro-Hungarian Empire and Italy, continued in existence, but there were serious doubts about Italy's credentials as an "ally". The "Entente Cordiale" between England and France, in 1904, came as a shock, and led to persistent talk of "encirclement" in Germany.

The "Entente Cordiale" seems, rather, to have been essentially a defensive reflex on England's part. On three separate occasions, at least, England had indicated a desire for understanding with Germany. In 1901 England offered formal cooperation; the offer was ignored. In 1906 England cut down its programme for building battleships from four to three, and in 1907 reduced this to two. Naval programmes had become the principal source of enmity between England and Germany. In 1908 the German Ambassador in London, Count Paul Metternich, sent a memorandum to Berlin, advising that the Liberals at Westminster were strongly inclined towards a naval agreement with Germany; the Kaiser personally minuted "By no means" in the margin of the memorandum.[12] Metternich was well-informed: a proposal came shortly afterwards from the future Liberal Prime Minister, David Lloyd George, then Chancellor of the Exchequer, for a meeting with Chancellor Buelow to discuss a slowing-down of the naval arms-race. Buelow declined and issued an instruction to the German Press in August 1908 to stop writing about a possible Anglo-German naval agreement.

These British offers need not for one moment be regarded as "proof" of altruism and goodwill. England was desperately worried by the totally new German challenge to her naval supremacy. By 1900 this was barely apparent; but the head of the Reich Navy Office, Admiral Alfred von Tirpitz, had already tabled his plans and secured the Kaiser's tacit support. Tirpitz was a brilliantly successful naval officer, a specialist in the development of the torpedo and keenly aware that expert gunnery was the chief means of overhauling England in actual striking power.[13] He foresaw a period of intensive naval construction which would give the German fleet, involved only in the North Sea and its Atlantic approaches, the possibility of local superiority over an English fleet which had to guard English imperial interests all over the world. A man of formidable intellect and single-minded determination, von Tirpitz was the author of a whole series of German Navy Bills, and the protagonist of supplementary estimates designed to force the pace of naval construction to a point when England would, without striking a blow, surrender her supremacy of the seas.

From 1900 onwards, German Navy Bills steadily stepped-up the rate of building of naval vessels. Tirpitz argued, early on, for a so-called "iron budget", which would be approved for periods of up to six years ahead – and so eliminate the need to seek too frequent Parliamentary approval. His reasoning was, from his point of view, sound: the "German people did not understand the sea".[14] Altercations in the Reichstag could only be counter-productive; Tirpitz was able to note that his tactics succeeded and that "the Reichstag did not give me much trouble".[15] He continued to increase the rate of naval construction, reaching a total of four battleships a year in 1907, when England was down to only two. He had the increasing support of the Kaiser, who announced himself as "The Admiral of the Atlantic".[16] Both Tirpitz and the Kaiser were blissfully unaware of the diplomatic consequences of this foray into the high seas of the world. Ludwig Dehio explains: "We found ourselves embarked upon the road to world war. We, and we only, threatened the vital nerve-centres of British world power."[17] Tirpitz's own explanation of his marvellously executed programme (for the German Navy was able, in little more than a decade, to mount a frightening challenge to England's peerless Navy) was abstruse. He claimed that all of its objectives were defensive. They were "to put a definite stop to the Anglomania of certain circles [in Germany], and to arouse our nation to build a fleet", and to "attempt to keep German a population that was not increasing in our colonial settlements, but in the workshops at home".[18] Winston Churchill took a very different view. First he quoted Tirpitz as writing: "It was a question of our keeping our nerve, continuing to arm on a grand scale, avoiding all provocation and waiting without anxiety until our sea-power was established and forced the English to let us breathe in peace." Churchill's own comment was: "Only to breathe in peace! What fearful apparatus was required to secure the simple act of respiration!"[19]

There are no rights and wrongs in such differences of opinion. Fearing a threat to England's use of the sea on which she depended, Churchill wrote that the Tirpitz programme was "a dangerous, if not a malignant design".[20] Tirpitz's argumentation is more involved. He was to become an apostle of "total war", commending the sinking of the *Lusitania* in May 1915.[21] His afterthought was that, for "Prusso-Germany", the only recognizable objectives were "material power and the devotion of the individual to the State, not cloudy phrases about the brotherhood of peoples".[22] And he would eventually declaim against "that old pirate state, England", which had "again succeeded in letting Europe tear herself to pieces", against Belgium, which did not deserve "a legendary martyr's crown", against his own people in which "a strain of self-destruction runs like a thread of blood through the thousand years of our history".[23]

In a letter written in November 1914, Tirpitz suggested his own epitaph. He wrote: "After the war I shall join the Socialists and look for lamp-posts, a lot of them!"[24] He did nothing of the kind.

Tirpitz's contribution to the First World War should not, perhaps, be exaggerated. His naval programmes were bound to align England with France and Russia. His emphasis on seizure, in war, of the Channel ports reinforced the intention of the German General Staff to attack France by way of the long "right hook" through neutral Belgium. Much has been made of the "immorality" of attacking Belgium; more to the point is the reflection that Britain regarded the ports of the Low Countries as her own "front line". The Kaiser's own contribution to the outbreak of war was less tactical than psychological. There was his dispatch of a warship to Morocco, the *Panther*, in 1911 and his demand for a French cession of the Congo to Germany. But it was his wilder utterances which did more to create misunderstanding and fear. He told the *Daily Telegraph* that he alone stood between Germany and England in preventing war. He talked of a blood-bath, or a foreign war, as means to get rid of the Social Democrats, "who spell extreme danger to the life and property of our citizens".[25] This primed equally dangerous talk in military and press circles of war serving a dual purpose – as a cure for social ills and a preventive necessitated by the huge military build-up of the Entente Powers which was assumed to be under way. Proclaiming that he ruled "as the instrument of the Lord", the Kaiser created an atmosphere of deep and sincere apprehension.

Golo Mann believes that "In 1914 the almost non-existent German leadership had lost the political game, and went to war almost in despair".[26] This was not the mood of a large section, perhaps a big majority, of the German people. They believed that Germany was indeed being "encircled", that the "Russian bear" menaced European civilization and that France was animated by an undying spirit of revenge for the hurt inflicted upon her in both 1815 and 1870. The spirit of Germans marching to war was, as one Rhinelander put it to me, that of "*ein grosses Halali*" – a great blast on the hunting horn. The Kaiser proclaimed "Now I no longer know parties, only Germans", and even the unwarlike Social Democrats hastened to vote war-credits. One finds one of Germany's greatest writers, Thomas Mann, defending his country's action as an expression of the profundity of the German soul, "which may appear disturbing, worrying, alien, yea, offensive and wild, to the feeling and judgement of other and less profound people, partly because of its indispensable and missionary qualities". A British comment was: "British Imperialists had made fairly outrageous claims for themselves in their time, but most of them tied up closer to the matter in hand than Thomas Mann to the invasion of Belgium."[27] Was there, as one German historian suggests, "mass hysteria" in 1914?[28] Certainly, the language of men like Thomas Mann and the Kaiser suggests this.

Yet the peace treaty which ended the First World War was wrongly based on the principle of Germany's total war-guilt. And this was pinned on the German people as a whole, not simply their rulers. Admittedly, a mass of evidence could be produced to show that blame was more widely spread. Even German "moderates" seemed to have lost their reason. Thus Gustav Stresemann, very much a man of peace a decade later, was one of the National-Liberals who called on the Chancellor in August 1914 with these "war-aims" – cession by France of the ports of Dunkirk and Calais and of the coal-mines of Briey and Longwy; the partition of Belgium, with Flanders, Liège and Hainault becoming German provinces and Antwerp a "free city" of the Reich; annexation in the East of the Baltic provinces up to the gates of Petrograd.[29] Two years later, Matthias Erzberger, of the unwarlike Roman Catholic "Zentrum" party, called for the annexation of the whole of Belgium and the French Channel ports, of both the French and Belgian Congo, and the creation of satellite states in the Baltic provinces, Poland and the Ukraine.[30] But even statements of this kind do not add up to the war-guilt of a nation. On the Allied side, there had been failures which contributed to war, too. Plenty of Frenchmen had been preaching the *guerre à l'outrance* – the war of pre-emptive attack; Russia proclaimed a pan-Slav "right" to "protect" the Balkans and had designs on Constantinople; England was as sure of her God-given right to rule the seas as any German in his belief that his country must seek hegemony on the European Continent.

So much has been written about the Treaty of Versailles that it need only be touched upon here. Obviously, it was a tough peace. Its worst feature was attempting to saddle the German nation with the odium of war-guilt. Germany was called upon to pay unrealistically large reparations – another psychological blunder, for, in the event, Germany received about three times as much in loans as was paid out in reparations. The total annexation of all Germany's colonial territories was a harsh measure; they had played next to no part in the European war. Cessions of German territory in the East were obviously hard to bear for the German people, although they were mainly based on ethnic grounds, the detachment of Danzig from the Reich was clearly inequitable and the plebiscite in Upper Silesia was mismanaged. One informed British view, long after the event, points up the most serious flaw in the Treaty of Versailles:

> Germany sought peace because she was defeated in the field, on the Western Front. Nevertheless, the Germans sought to negotiate a peace. The Allies did not permit this. At the Armistice in 1918, and again at Versailles in 1919, they merely presented their terms for signature; in other words, they exacted unconditional surrender. But unconditional surrender must be explicit and acknowledged. The Allies did not make it explicit; the Germans did not acknowledge it. Legends of a "stab in the back" grew up in Germany.[31]

The Treaty of Versailles was one of the heavy burdens which the Weimar Republic, set up at the end of the war, had to bear. The "stab in the back" legend, born in the last days of the war, when the sailors at Kiel were mutinying and a peace movement was beginning to gain impetus, was another; it was given additional if unintended weight by no less a figure than the Republic's first President, Friedrich Ebert, who greeted the returning soldiers in Berlin's Unter den Linden on 11 December 1918 with the words: "I salute you, who return unvanquished from the field of battle." The leaders of the Republic were to be saddled with the problem of *Erfüllungspolitik* – the policy of fulfilment of the peace terms. They were the unwilling executors of Versailles, which was denounced by an increasing number of Parliamentarians and by the bulk of the German people.

There was another, deeper reason why the democracy of the Weimar Republic was likely to fail. According to Theodor Heuss, later to be the first President of the Federal German Republic, "Germany never conquered democracy for herself. Democracy came to Germany in the wake of defeat. But because it was not taken by storm, it could not develop its own myth nor acquire its own know-how."[32] Sir John Wheeler-Bennett put it more bluntly: "The change of regime from Empire to Republic did not come as a result of any long-planned revolutionary movement. It did not represent any basic change of heart on the part of the German people themselves. It was brought about without any deep-seated conviction."[33] It is doubtful whether the Republic ever had the full support of a majority of the German people – although a Parliamentary majority was found in its early years for the "policy of fulfilment" and for a democratic form of government.

All sorts of other factors combined to doom the Republic. The searing xenophobia caused by defeat and disgrace contributed to a "spiritual nihilism"[34] and to serious internal disturbances which aroused next to no interest in the outside world. There was the separatist movement in the Rhineland, transient Soviet Republics in Saxony and Bavaria, bloody *putsches* in Berlin, Munich and other cities, carefully organized murders of men like Erzberger and Walter Rathenau (the Centre Party Vice-Chancellor in 1919–20, and the Foreign Minister in 1921–22 respectively). There was hunger, unemployment, and inflation which became disastrous when the French marched into the Ruhr in 1923 in order to enforce collection of reparations "in kind". This led to German resistance, to the printing of money on a gigantic scale and to the collapse of the currency – between 1921 and 1923 the value of the mark fell from 63 to the dollar to 4,200,000,000,000 to the dollar. Meanwhile the Allies occupied a substantial slice of territory along the Rhine, and a state of "unofficial" war simmered on the eastern frontier with Poland. The Weimar Republic was blamed, largely because it was available as a scapegoat, and a familiar note was struck when Professor Max Lenz of Hamburg University proclaimed in one address: "Iron and blood has created our Reich. Iron and blood must decide whether we could breathe freely in the world, or would have to live henceforth in servitude and misery."[35]

Yet the Weimar Republic enjoyed a short and almost miraculous "springtime" from 1924 to 1929, which held out hope that Germany might after all settle down as a peaceful and stabilizing factor in Europe. The currency was reformed and stabilized. Under Gustav Stresemann's guidance as Foreign Minister, Germany received substantial foreign credits, signed the Locarno Pact with the Western Powers, was accepted into the League of Nations and achieved a degree of understanding with France which won both Stresemann and his French opposite number, Aristide Briand, Nobel Peace Prizes. "Stresemann's successes," Ludwig Dehio wrote, "must be understood in terms of the solid gold foundations of American loans" (under the Dawes and Young Plans).[36] There was more to it than that: his "Europeanism" may indeed have been based on an unwavering determination to secure the return of Danzig and of German territories ceded to Poland and Belgium; he was not above secretly violating the Versailles Treaty through military collaboration with the Soviet Union, and he may have remained a nationalist at heart – but diplomatic skill and human understanding and reason have an intrinsic value. Stresemann brought Germany back into a European community already shorn of Communist Russia and Fascist Italy. The future, momentarily, looked bright.

Why did the Weimar Republic fail? The Treaty of Versailles was one reason; there were many others. The Weimar constitution sought to be perfectionist, but in the electoral field proportional representation opened the way to a wild proliferation of political parties. Expertise might still have been enough to form stable government coalitions, but there was one insuperable obstacle: the elections of June 1920 were the last in which parties supporting the policy of "fulfilment" – Socialists, Left-Liberals and Roman Catholic Centre – commanded a majority in the Reichstag. No single party was ever in a position to govern, until the Nazis destroyed Weimar democracy. The two political leaders, who might have overcome this difficulty, failed for different reasons. Stresemann, worn out by endless bickering, died just one year too soon – in 1930 one of his dearest dreams was realized, the evacuation of the Rhineland by the Allied armies, five years sooner than laid down at Versailles. Heinrich Bruening, according to his own account, failed – in racing parlance – almost at the post. His plans to secure the revision of the Treaty of Versailles and restore the monarchy, with President Paul von Hindenburg as Regent, died still-born. His decision to govern by decree, well-meant as it was, sounded the death-knell of the Republic.

Bruening, moreover, took over the reins of government at a time of world economic crisis. Naturally, Germany's still recovering economy was badly hit; between 1930 and 1932, unemployment rose from 1,200,000 to 6,700,000, and every third worker in the country was out of a job. The *per capita* income of those who were working was only 60 per cent of, for instance, that of the British working man – and the 1920s and 1930s are depicted in British history as a black period of social deprivation.

As with the Treaty of Versailles, as with political instability, the economic "depression" was blamed on the Weimar Republic. It enabled the Nazis, who began as a party of the "right", to pick up working class as well as middle class support and become a mass movement. And the Nazis had powerful allies ready at hand – political nationalists who bitterly resented Versailles, big industrialists ready to jettison all political principles in return for the restoration of *Ruhe und Ordnung*, peace and quiet, and thousands upon thousands of decent, patriotic citizens who genuinely believed that their country needed a period of strong government. The popular demand for scapegoats extended beyond the politicians, and the Jews seemed an appropriate target. Anti-semitism, of course, was nothing new in Germany, but it existed elsewhere without turning into a deadly cancer – one historian has pointed out that Cecil Rhodes and Rudyard Kipling believed in British "racial superiority", that Hilaire Belloc and G. K. Chesterton were unashamedly anti-semitic, that Charles Dickens and Edmund Burke depicted Jews as parasites, while even Chaucer repeated the "blood-libel" of Jews allegedly drinking the blood of Christian infants and Shakespeare created in Shylock a crazy caricature of the Jew.[37] So it was with anti-semitism; so it was with the iconoclasts who dragged down the Weimar Republic.

A minor contributory factor was the rivalry between Prussia and the Reich, although a Social Democratic Minister of the Interior for Prussia, Carl Severing, might have saved the Reich in July 1932, when a general strike could have averted the dissolution of the Prussian Government. Then there were such idealistic misconceptions as government *by* the people, through referendum, and "gravitational" centralism, when Germany was still a country of provinces with widely varied identities – it was significant how many political leaders, Cuno, Bracht, Luther and Adenauer among them, were called to Berlin from the provinces.[38] There may, too, have been a lack of political talent which prompted this. There was certainly a notable failure to capture the hearts and minds of the young and to canalize that urge towards European and even world citizenship which expressed itself in the *Wandervögel*, the bands of young people travelling far and wide to learn about countries other than their own.

Behind all these considerations – perhaps, indeed, overriding them – is the sombre thought that the German people as a whole were still not ready for democracy. The Empire had given them unity, and with it, glory, glamour and sheer might, redolent in the brilliance of the Kaiser's entourage, the lilt and sparkle of Prussian march-music, and the powered discipline of the jack-booted, stamping soldiers in field-grey uniform. Weimar had so little of this kind to offer, so little *élan* and elegance. Weimar, admittedly, produced a remarkable cultural renaissance which made Berlin, for a time, the artistic capital of the world. The films of Fritz Lang, the plays of Brecht, the theatre of Piscator and Reinhardt, the paintings of Paul Klee, the revolutionary new architecture of Gropius – here was an almost bewildering plethora of creative talent. Yet German intellectuals remained strangely apart from the rest of society, unwilling to involve themselves. Once bitten, twice shy? One should recall that the sole notable demonstration of their feelings during the War had been the memorandum of 8 July 1916, supporting the most extreme pan-German war-aims and signed by 1,314 intellectuals, including 352 university professors.[39] It seemed to be an article of faith with the intellectuals of the Weimar era that – with the exception of the small "Tat Kreis", named after the newspaper *Die Tat* and led by Hans Zehrer and Giselher Wirsing – they should have nothing to do with politics. Nor did their work and thought impinge on the masses.

Somehow German society seemed to remain incomplete, un-fused, just as German politics remained a mosaic of provincial and sectional interests. The German genius remained "compartmented", at least to a greater degree than happened in other European countries. The man in the street remained, on the whole, convinced that politics were strictly for politicians and a matter of expertise outside his own grasp. Of course, the practice of democracy has not been fully perfected in any country in the world; but in the Weimar Republic it was experimental and was never accepted by the majority of the nation.

One view was that "No nation is inclined to swifter changes of mood and mind, because no nation is as profoundly disunited as the Germans".[40] These words were written in 1943, and their relevance has waned. But the Nazi Party came to power only after years of struggle, and by constitutional means (significantly, neo-Nazi parties in Germany, Britain and elsewhere currently make much of their readiness to win power only by popular vote – when this is exactly what Hitler proclaimed). The swiftness of change came thereafter, and the German people may have been unduly blamed for their failure to appreciate the significance of what was happening, and take appropriate action to stop it. The "Enabling Act", giving Hitler sweeping emergency powers, was passed by the Reichstag on 24 March 1933, when the Nazis and Alfred Hugenberg's Nationalists held only 51 per cent of the seats. On 2 May, the Trade Unions were dissolved. On 27 June, Hugenberg was discarded from the Cabinet. On 7 July, the Social Democrats were officially deprived of their Parliamentary seats, but the party had already been dissolved on 22 June and the Communists had been excluded from the Reichstag in March and most of their leaders arrested. On 14 July, all parties other than the Nazis were outlawed. Finally, on 2 August, President Hindenburg died, and Adolf Hitler took over the offices of President, Chancellor and Head of the Armed Forces. So prompt was Nazi planning that the law combining these offices under one person had actually been enacted by the Cabinet on the preceding day.[41]

In a period of just over three months, all vestiges of German democracy were destroyed and the total dictatorship of Hitler and the Nazi Party created. The precision and sheer bewildering speed with which all this was done overwhelmed a German people which was ill-equipped to offer real resistance, even if a clear majority had been prepared to do so. And this was not the case; those few who resisted were heroic individuals, and their resistance was crushed with the greatest ease.

The truth was that Weimar democracy had long since ceased to exist, before Hitler came to power. Its last chance went when President Hindenburg summarily dismissed Bruening on 30 May 1932. There followed the Chancellorships of Franz von Papen and Kurt von Schleicher, men who had no belief in democracy and who governed by Presidential decree and dickered intermittently with plans to introduce a type of "Presidential democracy", in which the Reichstag could be dismissed at the President's whim. All semblance of truly representative government vanished while Papen and Schleicher schemed unsuccessfully to split the Nazi Party and create a new power-block out of right-wing conservatives, dissident Nazis and the *Reichswehr* (Army). The destruction of representative government enabled Hitler to become Chancellor in January 1933 without a popular mandate – the Nazis won 230 Reichstag seats out of 608 in the July 1932 elections, and only 196 out of 584 in those of November 1932. Even in March 1933, the Nazis captured only 288 out of 647 seats, and were dependent on the 53 Hugenberg Nationalists for their slender Parliamentary majority. It has often been pointed out that a majority of the German people never voted for Hitler in a free election; but it may be equally apposite to remember that there was not a majority of the German people prepared to oppose him.

The reasons for Hitler's success are interwoven with those for Weimar's failure. But Hitler's qualities, good as well as bad, were utterly exceptional. Ludwig Dehio suggests that he was the "pre-requisite" to the Second World War – "Germany could not conceivably have raised herself to such dizzy heights yet again without the aid of some Satanic genius."[42] "Satanic genius" he certainly was. He canalized the frustrations of the German middle-class – Nazism has been called "the extremism of the middle".[43] He exploited the tradition of Lutheran Protestantism, of service to the State and obeisance to strong secular authority. He traded on national disgust with the terms of the Treaty of Versailles, and on national resentment. He and his minions, Josef Goebbels, Julius Streicher and Alfred Rosenberg in particular, embellished the myth of the Jew as the enemy of Christian civilization, a myth embedded in German memory. For one of Germany's greatest historians, Treitschke, believed that "the Jews are our misfortune" and the Nazis were able to evolve their concept of the Jew, via Treitschke, out of the racist bigotry and bestiality which had dominated most of medieval Europe.

At the same time, Hitler and his party were able to capture German youth. It was idealistic, impressionable, above all, malleable. It could not fail to be affected by the brutalization of political life – and the young have their own ready reactions of cruelty and callousness. Hitler exploited German youth's idealism, its adventurousness, its desire for leadership, its group solidarity and self-importance, its innate patriotism and its simple pleasures – sport, music, travel, communal activity. (One should point out that the Governments of the East German Republic have taken this last leaf out of the Nazi note-book.) By 1929, when they were polling little more than 5 per cent of the votes in a Reichstag election, the Nazis were securing the support of nearly one-third of the students in university elections. German and European youth became more cynical after the end of the Second World War; but charisma is still instinctively admired. Hitler possessed that quality in abundance.

Literally hundreds of books have been written about the Nazi era, about the *Glanz* or glitter which it restored to German life, its cults of German grandeur, racial "purity" and organized hatred, and its use of what one member of the German Resistance to

Nazism called "a combination of terror and habit"[44] – which led the vast majority of the German people into accepting the Nazi regime with such docility. In retrospect, the Nazi era seems like a black nightmare, but a nightmare shot through with brilliant flashes of light. Satan is conventionally portrayed as a hideous creature, with horns and a tail. But Lucifer was a fallen angel, with an angel's beauty. What was good about Nazism was paraded before the eyes of the German people; what was evil was, as far as possible, kept out of sight.

The miseries inflicted upon Germany by the Nazis were beyond computation. The Hitler–Stalin "Robbers' Pact" of 1939 handed half of Poland to the Soviet Union, ensured that Stalin would "push Poland west" in 1945 up to the Oder-Neisse Line, and encouraged a Soviet expansion into Central Europe which has left only a fringe of free European communities along the Atlantic and Mediterranean seaboards. The vice-like grip which the Nazis established in Germany itself resulted in the Allied demand for unconditional surrender – and it took total defeat and total foreign occupation to uproot and destroy Nazism. Hitler's personal belief in the *Götterdämmerung*, the twilight of the Gods, encouraged the immensely courageous and utterly pointless last-ditch defence of the Fatherland, which left the Russians occupying more than half the country, from the Niemen to the Elbe. By making enemies on every side (and not a single real friend) Hitler made certain that Germany would be divided when war was over – for there would never be the slightest chance of Four Power rule working successfully.

The Nazis left Germany's cities in ruins and German citizens in a state of stupor. For the first time for well over a century, Germany was no longer a Great Power and there was no German State with the potential or claim to become one. The kernel of Germany, Prussia, had ceased to exist altogether. The division of Germany, moreover, would become absolute when Cold War broke out between the Soviet Union and the Western Powers and the interzonal frontier between the two parts of Germany became the frontier between Eastern and Western Europe. The losses in German life were appalling. In one sector of the community, they were irreplaceable; the members of the German Resistance against Nazism, students, churchmen and workers as well as soldiers, were butchered for their beliefs, for their probity and moral courage. How desperately badly such people were needed, when war ended and a new Germany had to be created out of the ruins of the old!

Oddly, one potential benefit emerged out of the Nazi catastrophe – "Hitler's rule and its collapse ... greatly changed the structure of German society and made it more homogenous. The deep ideological and class differences of the Weimar period disappeared."[45] That apart, Germany staggered to defeat in 1945, in despair. For of one thing any thoughtful German could be sure: the Nazi armies, and the butchers of the SS who marched in their wake, had left a legacy of deep and bitter hatred behind them, from Norway's North Cape to the Isles of Greece, and from the gates of Moscow and Leningrad to the Pyrenees – hatred not just of Hitler and his works, but of all things German, of the very name of their once respected, proud and powerful country.

1. Sir John Wheeler-Bennett. *The Nemesis of Power*. London, 1953.
2. Graf Otto von Bismarck, addressing the Finance Committee of the Reich Chamber, 1857.
3. Sir Stephen King-Hall & Richard Ullmann. *German Parliaments*. London, 1954.
4. J. A. R. Marriott. *The Evolution of Prussia*. Oxford, 1917.
5. Ludwig Dehio. *Germany and World Politics in the Twentieth Century*. London, 1959.
6. Rohan Butler. *The Roots of National Socialism*. London, 1941.
7. Hans Kohn. *The Mind of Germany*. London, 1961.
8. Golo Mann. *Upheaval and Continuity*. Edited by E. J. Feuchtwanger. London, 1973.
9. Wolfgang Abendroth. *Upheaval and Continuity*.
10. V. R. Berghahn. *Germany and the Approach of War in 1914*. London, 1973.
11. Ibid.
12. Ibid.
13. Ibid.
14. Grand Admiral Alfred von Tirpitz. *My Memoirs*. London, 1919.
15. Ibid.
16. Ibid.
17. Ludwig Dehio, op. cit.
18. Grand Admiral Alfred von Tirpitz, op. cit.
19. Winston Churchill. *The World Crisis*. London, 1927.
20. Ibid.
21. Grand Admiral von Tirpitz, op. cit.
22. Ibid.
23. Ibid.
24. Ibid.
25. V. R. Berghahn, op. cit.
26. Golo Mann, op. cit.
27. Rebecca West. *Sunday Telegraph*, 26 March 1978.
28. Wolfgang Abendroth, op. cit.

29. Hagen Schulze. *Frankfurter Allgemeine Zeitung*, 6 May 1978.
30. Hans Kohn, op. cit.
31. John Terraine. *History Today*. London, December 1978.
32. Kurt Sontheimer. *Upheaval and Continuity*.
33. Sir John Wheeler-Bennett, op. cit.
34. Fabian von Schlabrendorff. *The Secret War against Hitler*. New York, 1965.
35. Hans Kohn, op. cit.
36. Ludwig Dehio, op. cit.
37. Julius Braunthal. *Need Germany Survive?* London, 1943.
38. Sir Stephen King-Hall & Richard Ullmann, op. cit.
39. Hans Kohn, op. cit.
40. Julius Braunthal, op. cit.
41. William Shirer. *The Rise and Fall of the Third Reich*. New York, 1960.
42. Ludwig Dehio, op. cit.
43. Martin Broszat. *Upheaval and Continuity*.
44. Fabian von Schlabrendorff, op. cit.
45. Kurt Sontheimer, op. cit.

CHAPTER TWO

Darkest Germany

May 1945 was "zero hour", Germany's "historical caesura", a moment unforgettable for the whole German people.[1] The German historian who expressed this view had ample justification for it. In 1919 German armies had marched back into the homeland in perfect order. Germany's cities and industries were intact – hardly a shell had landed on German soil, and the few Allied air-raids had been of a kind and on a scale which merely drew crowds onto the streets to watch something scarcely more than a fireworks display. In 1919 a modestly-sized strip of German territory, up to and in places just over the Rhine, was occupied by the enemy. The Treaty of Versailles, so bitterly denounced by virtually the whole German people, returned Alsace-Lorraine to France – from whom these provinces had been taken less than a half century earlier – handed West Prussia and Posen over to Poland, and ceded the Eupen-Malmèdy district to Belgium and a small slice of North Schleswig to Denmark. Germany remained intact, undamaged and, in the eyes of most of its citizens, undefeated.

How different was the situation in 1945! In the first place, the armies of Nazi Germany had been totally defeated, and the "unprecedented event"[2] took place of the entire German armed forces laying down their arms and becoming prisoners-of-war. It would be followed up by German soldiers – as well as members of the Nazi Government and of the black-shirted SS and the secret police (Gestapo) – being put on trial as war-criminals. On 7 and 8 May an Act of unconditional surrender was signed, in Rheims with the Western Powers and in Berlin-Karlshorst with the Soviet Union.

In the second place, Germany no longer had a Government. Admiral Doenitz formed a temporary administration, following Hitler's suicide, on 1 May 1945. It lasted just three weeks. On 23 May the Allied High Command announced that the Admiral, and the other members of "the Doenitz Clique", had been taken into custody as prisoners-of-war. Doenitz himself would subsequently stand trial and be sentenced to 10 years' imprisonment as a war-criminal.

Germany was totally occupied. The nature of occupation was described in the baldest terms in the US policy directive, Joint Chiefs of Staff Memorandum 1067 – Germany was "not to be occupied for the purpose of liberation but as a defeated enemy nation". This defeated, occupied country was condemned to pay reparations on a scale, agreed at the Potsdam Conference which opened in July 1945, which made the allegedly tough terms of the Treaty of Versailles pale by comparison. Reparations were to be paid out of current production and in the shape of plant and machinery taken from all key industries – the victor nations did not intend to repeat the mistake of Versailles in assessing reparations in meaningless monetary figures. The removal of plant and machinery served an additional purpose; it would enable German industrial production – under the so-called "Level of Industry Plan" which was also agreed at Potsdam, in March 1946 – to be reduced to about 50 per cent of 1938 figures. Even this was regarded as magnanimous by the victors; for there had been an earlier "Morgenthau Plan", devised by the US Secretary for the Treasury, Henry Morgenthau, which envisaged depriving Germany of all heavy industry and turning it into a land of cow-pastures.

It was very soon obvious that Germany would stay divided – certainly between the Soviet-occupied eastern half and the "zones" of Allied occupation in the west, and possibly between those western zones as well. It was France's veto which put paid to the somewhat illusory project for a centralized German administrative authority in the autumn of 1945, and France was initially a more outspoken protagonist of Germany's division than the Soviet Union. The French rejected a second proposal for German participation in central offices set up by the occupying powers, and refused to join with Britain and the United States in setting up an overall Economic Council.

France demanded the detachment of the Ruhr from the rest of Germany, or – as an alternative – the total destruction of its industries, and went ahead unilaterally in detaching the Saar and linking that area economically with France. A far more serious truncation was taking place at the same time in the east. The Soviet Union coolly annexed half of the German province of East Prussia, and handed the rest of Eastern Germany up to the Oder and Neisse rivers to Poland. This was "compensation" for the Soviet annexation of the whole of Eastern Poland. In due course, Belgium and Holland were emboldened to put in territorial claims of their own, admittedly of a minor nature, while the old Reich capital of Berlin was itself divided into four "sectors" and quickly ceased to function as a unified city. Germans, with reason, began to fear that their whole country would be carved up.

Some of these Allied actions affected Germans in intensely personal ways. Military occupation brought requisitioning of homes, livestock and movable goods on an enormous scale. The only compensation offered was in the shape of Reichsmark notes which the Allies, the Russians in particular, were printing in huge quantities and which were becoming increasingly worthless. Allied troops behaved in varying ways. In the Soviet Zone, the Red Army at first ran riot. Its looting was accompanied by every kind of brutality; countless Germans were maimed, murdered and raped. In a single day, a Berlin hospital treated 230 cases of rape,[3] and a German lawyer described how his daughter was raped eighteen times after Russian soldiers captured her when trying to cross the river Elbe.[4] The French were relentlessly hostile, the British more studiedly aloof and unfriendly. In the US Zone soldiers were readier to fraternize when at length allowed to do so – indeed the incidence of venereal disease in American garrison towns rose by 20 per cent after the "non-fraternization" order was withdrawn. A comic note is struck by the story of the Dean of the Theological Faculty at the University of Marburg, who "reported that, walking down a narrow street, he would certainly have been struck by troops in a passing lorry, had they not at that moment been distracted by a girl".[5] The Mainzer Landstrasse in Frankfurt was famed for its nightly car-crashes; the reason was that it was lined with German prostitutes, and American military vehicles continually cannoned into each other as their drivers' attention wandered.

After the first orgy of Red Army violence was over, American troops were the worst disciplined too. They drove out at night with spotlights to hunt rabbits and even deer, and fished with the use of hand-grenades which blew their prey to the surface. They drove trucks and tanks habitually over planted fields. While the black market flourished in all western zones of occupation, it reached spectacular proportions in the US Zone. Thus one lieutenant arrived in Germany in November 1945, "with a stated goal of $12,000 profit in the cigarette league. He reached his target in four months".[6] And one GI returned home carrying $25,000, after sending back another $15,000 in advance – all this on a monthly pay check of $64.[7] Cigarettes, coffee and chocolate were the most saleable articles on the black market; a single cigarette fetched seven Reichsmarks, and four or five pounds of coffee would buy a Persian carpet.

The British occupiers had a more modest track record, but carried out some outstanding black market operations. Two British Air Marshals were reported to have flown loot to an island in the Greek archipelago – one of their hauls being a collection of ducal carpets worth over £50,000.[8] One of their juniors converted his black market earnings into jewellery, which his wife took by air to Bermuda. A common practice among American and British personnel was to convert cigarettes into Reichsmarks, and re-convert the Reichsmarks into sterling, finally sending the proceeds home. A thousand cigarettes could produce "savings" of £350, for an outlay of £3, in this way. As one American writer put it, "This oblique raid on the Treasury amounted to more than $300 million, before the Army called a halt, with currency control measures."[9]

Even the presence and behaviour of enemy soldiers was no more than incidental in comparison with the human and material losses caused by war. More than three million Germans were killed during the Second World War, and at the end of it there were seven million more missing or prisoners-of-war. About two and a half million of the prisoners in Russian hands would never return home (one must recall that the Germans for their part treated their Russian prisoners with appalling brutality and killed off three-quarters of them – the estimate usually given is five and three-quarter million Russians taken prisoner by the Germans, of whom one million survived, three million definitely died in captivity, and the remainder simply "disappeared" – presumably having been killed even before they could reach POW camps in Germany). Germany lost over three million homes, which had housed nine million people. There were over a million war-cripples. At least eight million refugees poured in from the lost eastern territories and Czechoslovakia, and from farther afield – from German communities in Rumania, Hungary and the three little Baltic States which had been swallowed up by the Soviet Union.

These people returned to a Germany which had suffered destruction on a scale which could not be imagined, until one had seen it. General Lucius Clay, the US Military Governor, wrote back to Washington: "Retribution is far greater than realized at home ... Our planes and artillery have carried the war direct to the homes of the German people."[10] His was a lone voice among Allied administrators, who generally concluded that the Germans were responsible for their own woes, and would have to live with them. Every major city had suffered bitterly, most of them – sad to relate – as a result of the policy of saturation bombing of city centres pursued by the Chiefs of the British Royal Air Force, against the advice of those who rejected the sacrifice of so many hundreds of airmen's lives. The results were spectacularly hideous.

Thus, Cologne. It had been the first target for a British thousand bomber raid, and Konrad Adenauer, returning to his native city six months before the war ended, felt physically sickened by the destruction.[10] The French writer, André Gide, drove through Cologne after the end of the war and was so horrified that he stayed only a quarter of an hour and asked to be driven out again at once. Over 60 per cent of its houses had been totally destroyed, and another 30 per cent rendered temporarily uninhabitable. Yet Cologne was largely a "garden-city", and spread over the biggest area of any German city save Berlin – only one-third of it was built-up.

In other Rhineland and Ruhr towns damage was appalling – Essen was pockmarked with "holes" several hundred yards square and in Düsseldorf one could "date" air-raids according to the amount of vegetation growing in the ruins – but in Cologne the destruction "was catastrophic. Even its streets had disappeared; mountains of rubble had piled up in them and turned them into lunar landscapes, over which ran the meandering paths made by the feet of the thousands who returned to search for their homes in the ruins. All the bridges over the Rhine had been destroyed and all public services had ceased to function. The pre-war population of Cologne was three-quarters of a million; when the United States Army moved in it was about 32,000."[11] On a relatively miniature scale, but even more poignant in its way, was the damage suffered by the nearby small market-town of Jülich. In the winter of 1944–5 the river Roer, on which Jülich sits, was for long months the front line between the American and German armies. The Americans pounded the main part of the town, on the east bank of the river, into rubble. On 1 December 1944 the population of a previously thriving town of 12,000 inhabitants was officially listed as – zero. Later it became known to the American and British troops who travelled the Brussels–Cologne road on convoy duty as "the town of three houses".[12] One of them was occupied by a solitary British official and his staff; the other two were on the outskirts of the place. Destruction may be gruesomely imposing; total obliteration is far more awesome, more moving.

For sheer extent of devastation, of course, Berlin was unique. It was battered beyond recognition. Willy Brandt, who was to become its Governing Mayor, called it "a no-man's-land, on the edge of the world, and with every little garden a graveyard, and above this, like an immovable cloud, the stink of putrefaction".[13] The strange smell of the ruins was, certainly, uncanny; it was the product of blocked drains, stagnant sewage and mildew along with, possibly, undiscovered corpses. The entire "diplomatic quarter", on the southern side of the Tiergarten Park, was laid waste, and the Tiergarten itself was a desert of tree-stumps, choked waterways and tumbled statues, over which presided the gaunt hulk of the Reichstag, burned-out in 1933 and several times bombed during the war.

The theme of destruction could be pursued endlessly; here only a vignette from the poet and caricaturist, Mervyn Peake. In a letter to his wife he wrote: "Imagine Chelsea in fragments, with not one single house with any more than a few weird-shaped walls where once it stood, and you will get an idea in miniature of what Mannheim and Wiesbaden are like."[14] Beyond the ruins there "is an intense feeling of hatred. Eyes are averted or the stare is insolent. Walking out this evening … nearly every window had a head which stared at the opposite wall when one came abreast". In Aachen, Peake found the only movement among the ruins was the flapping of torn curtains from glassless windows, where houses were mere heaps of rubble. The surviving humans were "ruinous, grey-faced, shabby and usually old". Peake's widow told his biographer that it was "as if he had lost, during that month in Germany, his confidence in life itself".[15]

Peake may have been over-sensitive. There was far less hatred to be found in the Germany of the first post-war years than sheer despair. Averted eyes were an expression of this despair, and a stare which looked insolent was generally no more than a pathetic attempt to keep up appearances. If Peake saw "ruinous" human beings on the streets, there were countless Germans in even worse shape who stayed out of sight altogether. A lasting personal memory is that of an old German couple eking out an utterly miserable existence in a Berlin attic. A small present brought to them was received with pathetic gratitude. The only hospitality they could offer their foreign visitor was to seat him in the tumble-down chair, and ply him with questions. The value of the present was the link which it brought with the world outside and a happier past.[16]

The phrase was coined that post-war Germany became a place in which the men lost all courage – and the women all sense of shame. Such generalizations are never true, but there would have been much excuse for Germans to have reacted in this way. One witness to the misery in which they lived was the British publisher, Victor Gollancz. In the winter of 1946–7 he was in Germany, collecting material for his book, *In Darkest Germany*. He was shattered by what he saw.

He visited living quarters which reminded him of "a vile Daumier cartoon".[17] People in Düsseldorf and other Ruhr towns were living literally "in holes in the ground". The lack of every sort of commodity, soap, food, textiles, household goods, was overwhelmingly obvious, and he was especially disturbed by the lack of shoes – children even went out into the snow barefoot – and of food. In Hamburg he found 100,000 people suffering from hunger oedema, at a time when the British Minister for Germany, Mr John Hynd, was asserting that food rations were being maintained and had "displayed a mixture of complacency and misinformation which is really beyond belief". Victor Gollancz believed that German youth was growing up with no idea of morality, and with a nihilistic contempt of government of every kind. It was, perhaps, ironic that it was a Jew who found himself almost alone in pressing his own British Government to produce more food and more jobs for a German people which had so cruelly persecuted his people, and who was among the first to call for the end of dismantling of German industry and for abandonment of the "Level of Industry Plan" – "What could be madder or more wicked than to throw tens of thousands of men out of work, just in mid-winter and just in the districts suffering most from the food crisis?"[18]

That winter of 1946–7 was devastatingly cold. Willy Brandt, in

Berlin throughout it, described it in graphic terms:

> A new terror gripped the city; an icy cold. In the streets it
> attacked the people like a wild beast, drove them into their
> houses, but there they found no protection either. The
> windows had no panes, they were nailed up with planks and
> plaster-board. The walls and ceilings were full of cracks and
> holes – one covered them with paper and rags. People
> heated their rooms with benches from the public parks ...
> The old and sick froze to death in their beds by the
> hundreds. Within living memory Berlin had not
> experienced such a terrible winter.[19]

It was no better in the Ruhr and other industrial districts,
where food was running desperately short. German ration-scales
were dropping down below the 1,500 calorie mark, and even
then were frequently not honoured. The miniscule meat ration
would be replaced with dried fish. Often there were turnips
instead of potatoes; fats were everlastingly in short supply. In
addition, the Germans did not have enough fuel of one kind or
another to heat their homes. During the day, the old and the very
young often found refuge in so-called "warming rooms",
equipped with one small stove and sustained largely by the
warmth of human bodies in uncomfortably close proximity to
one another. Bread queues often stretched for up to a hundred
yards along the street. Since unemployment was rife, it was the
poor who had no work who suffered most, along with their
elderly dependants and the rest of the old-age pensioners. The
measure of the universal despair in the cities (in the country there
was never any serious food shortage) was that protest did not go
beyond the very occasional, and usually very minor "bread riot"
– generally a most peaceable demonstration.

During these early post-war years the Germans suffered plenty
of other trials. There were more than 150,000 in internment
camps. Some of them were guilty men, others needed to be
investigated. But there were innocent people among them too,
for an organization like the "Waffen SS" (the military arm of the
SS, which was proscribed as a criminal organization at the
Nuremberg Trials) contained young men who had been forcibly
recruited into it. Many of them subsequently only saw service at
the front and had no hand in any sort of war-crime.

Such people, however, joined the long ranks of ex-Nazi Party
members awaiting "denazification". Much has been written
about the absurdities of procedure – under which anyone with

Nazi affiliations had to place himself before a court which could "cleanse", but might condemn him – and about its periodically inevitable injustices. Denazification was intended to be a "purification" process, and was conducted under Allied aegis; critics who maintained that Germans should have had sole control in the matter may have been wrong, for it would have been very difficult to find enough Germans ready to judge those who had exercised unrestricted authority over them for twelve long years. American Military Government, in particular, was imbued with a fanatical sense of duty; in the American Zone alone, twelve million *Fragebogen*, or questionnaires, had to be filled in and 930,000 Germans were sentenced, even if many sentences were suspended or amounted only to a very temporary deprivation of citizens' rights. The Americans tried 169,000 people on relatively serious charges, whereas the figures in the British, French and Soviet Zones were only 22,000, 17,000 and 18,000 respectively.[20]

In a different category were the trials, in 1945–6, of the "major" war-criminals at Nuremberg. Of the 21 who stood trial, ten were executed, seven given prison sentences and three acquitted, while ex-Field Marshal Goering managed to commit suicide. The most conventional German attitude towards these trials was to try, as far as possible, to ignore them; they amounted to the liquidation of the surviving leaders of the Nazi regime, and a considerable majority of Germans simply wanted them out of the way. The question of war-crime was intimately interwoven with that of a wider German responsibility, both for the war and for the brutalities of the Nazi leadership and their minions. Here was a grievous moral problem which most Germans, again, wanted to avoid during the early post-war years. Their usual tendency was to plead both ignorance and helplessness.

This tendency brought a further chain-reaction. It became convenient to remain ignorant of the past; any knowledge of it encouraged an acutely uncomfortable sense of personal failure. Almost equally embarrassing was the revelation that the German Resistance movement had not only nearly succeeded in killing Hitler on several occasions, but had come very close to overthrowing the whole Nazi system in 1944. If a comparatively few brave men had been ready to risk their lives in fighting against tyranny, why had more Germans not come forward to help? The first President of the Federal Republic, Professor Theodor Heuss, was to coin a phrase that "Germans need not

feel a sense of collective guilt, but a sense of collective shame".
That certainly sounded all right, but plenty of Germans either
did feel a sense of guilt, or furiously rejected the thought while
subconsciously dreading that it might still be true. Rejection of
the past, or continued feigned ignorance about it, undoubtedly
increased the widening "generation-gap". Young Germans were
bound, as time went on, not only to ask their fathers why they
had lost the war, but why they had done nothing to save their
country from Nazi tyranny. Coming to terms with the Nazi past
was to remain a deeply worrying psychological problem for the
decades ahead, but in the first post-war years it was particularly
haunting.

Two years after the end of the war, Germans were poor,
hungry and subject to total foreign control in a country
becoming irrevocably divided. Their currency was almost
worthless, their industries were still being dismantled, and one
man in every five of working age was unemployed. Allied
administrators were still talking of an Occupation which might
have to last up to twenty years. The Germans were in complete
isolation, the sole pariahs of Europe; even the Austrians had
managed to create an impression that they had been dragooned
into Hitler's "Greater Reich" against their will. On the face of it,
the situation could hardly have been bleaker; yet signs of hope
were already beginning to appear, and the transformation of the
next two years was only just over the horizon.

First, the Western Allies were beginning to understand the
need to build the new Germany on a sound economic basis. In
March 1947 the former US President, Herbert Hoover, called for
the rebuilding of the West German economy. The US Deputy
Secretary of State, Dean Acheson, went even further two months
later; he said that Germany must become Europe's principal
workshop. To give practical effect to such thoughts, the US and
British Military Governments established a Bizonal Economic
Council in Frankfurt, which became fully operational at the
beginning of 1948. Then in June 1947 the US Secretary of State,
George Marshall, announced his plan for large-scale economic
aid to Europe, including Germany. The Paris Conference,
attended by sixteen nations, confirmed in September that the
three western zones of Germany would participate – the Soviet
Union having boycotted both the Plan and the Conference.

Other practical steps were already being taken. The British
Military Governor, General Sir Brian (later Lord) Robertson, with
the backing of his Government, decided to refuse the Soviet

demand for reparations, from zones other than their own, out of current production. The United States followed Britain's example in June. In 1947, too, General Robertson established the German Zonal Trade Union Federation in Essen. This was the forerunner of the "Deutscher Gewerkschaftsbund" (DGB), the future Trade Union Congress. British and German trade unionists were working out details of its organization into sixteen Unions (in Britain, even in 1979, there were still nearly 400). This streamlining would effectively banish demarcation disputes and promote the quick settlement of Union claims and the cause of industrial peace.

In three other fields there was practical progress. The first was education, and the British example is instructive. British educationalists, headed by Sir Robert Birley, weeded out Nazi teachers and text-books, and helped to find the anti-Nazi and non-Nazi teachers to replace the 16,000 who had to be barred from their profession in the British Zone alone. The hardest task was to find German teachers who would accept responsibility, and not abuse it. In addition, Britain organized exchanges of students and teachers which averaged 2,000 Germans coming to Britain each year and over 1,000 Britons going to Germany.

The British example was equally instructive in the field of the media. After the Nazi experience, it was crucially important for the Germans to establish a free Press. By 1947 the British had established *Die Welt*, West Germany's best newspaper – and had licensed nearly 50 more – DPD, West Germany's best news-service, and the *North-West German Radio*, probably its best radio and television network. British, American and French administrators worked along parallel lines in cooperating with the Germans in what were initially joint ventures. One German writer believes that "Directly after the war, no other people in the world examined themselves with less bias than we did",[21] and another considered that "the new Germany learnt, imitated, and slowly began to think for itself".[22] A free Press was the most operative aid for this new readiness to think and find self-expression.

The third field of successful endeavour was the political. The State of Prussia, which had dominated the German Reich for three-quarters of a century, was formally wound up by order of the Allied Control Council in February 1947. This paved the way for the political reorganization of West Germany on a federal basis, into *Laender* which took permanent shape – save for the later merging of Baden and Wurtemberg, when the American and French Zones later ceased to maintain separate existence from each other. But in the meantime, a crucially important election took place in Berlin, for seats in the Berlin City Parliament, at the same time as purely local elections in the British and Soviet Zones. The Berlin city election was important because the Russians made an all-out attempt to capture Berlin for Communism, by ostensibly democratic methods. A step back in history is needed, to explain how they set about this.

In June 1945, the Communist Party (KPD) was re-founded in Berlin, under Soviet sponsorship. Its titular head was the veteran Wilhelm Pieck, but it was effectively under the control of Walter Ulbricht, a Saxon and Moscow-trained Communist, and his Marxist-Leninist followers. The Soviet leadership quickly came to the conclusion that the KPD could not hope to become the majority party in Germany, or even in the Soviet Zone; nor was it feasible to organize a German–Bolshevik revolution, without incurring the violent opposition of the other Occupying Powers. So, in April 1946, the fusion of the KPD and the Social Democratic Party (SPD) of the Soviet Zone was engineered by the Soviet Military Government. The instrument for this fusion, in the SPD, was Otto Grotewohl, weak, vain but ambitious, fancying himself as the future leader of a working class front – a German Léon Blum. The bait offered to Grotewohl and the Social Democratic voters was the slogan, "The Elbe and the Oder are no frontiers for the Unity Party",[23] and the amalgamated party was named the Socialist Unity Party (SED). The Elbe was, roughly, the dividing line between East and West Germany; the Oder represented the provisional border with Poland. The SED was, then, supposedly committed to German unity and the revision of the eastern frontier. In fact, it was interested in neither: Ulbricht was under Moscow's orders to create a Communist Soviet Zone and a future East German satellite state, and to accept the Oder–Neisse Line frontier with Poland.

The SPD had already been re-formed in West Germany, under the leadership of Kurt Schumacher, with his headquarters in Hanover. He quickly established close relations with the British Military Government and, through it, with the British Labour Government in London. His closest advisers were men who had spent their exile in Britain during the Nazi era, but he himself had been arrested soon after the Nazis came to power and had spent over eight years in all in concentration camps. An East German, from Kulm on the Vistula, Schumacher was a patriot who believed in a strong and undivided Germany, and a social reformer who was absolutely convinced that only a socialist government could restore democracy and give political hope and fulfilment to his people. A British Minister who knew him well wrote of his "moral passion and integrity".[24] He was a convinced anti-Communist, knowing that the Russia of Lenin and Stalin had abandoned the true Marxist ethic and had imposed a tyranny upon the Russian people only less hideous in degree than that of Hitler's Reich.

Schumacher nailed his political colours to the mast in a speech made to SPD members in Hanover on 6 May 1945.[25] He attacked with equal fervour the non-Nazi *Mitläufer* (time-servers), who had gone along with Nazism and who were now asking all over again to be looked after, and the decorous, outwardly "decent" capitalists who had worked so well for Hitler. He claimed that the only sort of democracy which could endure must be founded on a solid and progressive working class, and he expected the Allies to ensure this and to restore the framework of pre-1933 law and government – subject, of course, to some temporary Allied regulations. Reading between the lines, it is easy to see that Schumacher expected complete Allied backing in Western Germany and the fairly early establishment of an SPD Government. One sentence of the speech summed this up: "The Social Democratic Party will be the decisive factor in Germany, or out of Germany will come nothing, and Europe will be the seat of trouble and decay."

Schumacher's hopes were dashed by a series of events, which he came to regard as betrayals. The first was the splitting of his party when the Soviet Military Government entrusted the leadership of the SPD in Eastern Germany to Otto Grotewohl in October 1945. Schumacher must have expected a *démarche* by the three other Occupying Powers, demanding that the unity of the SPD should be maintained. Nothing of the kind happened. He himself had to confirm the split in February 1946 when called to the meeting in Berlin of the party's Soviet-steered central committee. There, necessarily, he refused to take part in the merger of the eastern SPD and KPD into the Socialist Unity Party. An SPD referendum in Berlin gave him overwhelming support, but he had lost the potential support of SPD voters in their former strongholds of Saxony and Thuringia.

The Berlin city election of 20 October 1946 did admittedly give Schumacher a tremendous boost. In East Berlin, containing over one-third of the population of Berlin, the Soviet Military Government did everything in its power to ensure an SED victory. The Soviet-controlled press and radio proclaimed it in advance. All opposition party meetings, and especially those of the SPD, were banned or sabotaged by the closing of halls and the use of strong-arm squads. The SED were given the means to indulge in free hand-outs of food and school-books. Considerable funds were put at their disposal. None of these actions availed: even in the Soviet Sector the SED gained only 21 per cent of the vote, and only 26 seats in the City Parliament. The SPD won 63 seats, and the other two democratic parties 41 between them. The Communist cause suffered a signal, even sensational defeat. It may well be that, because of it, the Soviet leadership never again seriously considered the reunification of Germany.

The election result was a triumph for Schumacher and his courageous lieutenants in Berlin, chief among them Franz Neumann. But he was a man who was not easily satisfied, and his thoughts were embittered by other acts which he regarded as betrayal. The rival, but apparently oddly-assorted and heterogenous Christian Democratic Party (CDU) in Western Germany had already refused his offer of a programme of joint political action. Schumacher had made this dependent on acceptance of SPD leadership, and he was frankly bewildered when the newly-elected Chairman of the CDU, Konrad Adenauer, turned it down. From then on, he treated Adenauer as an enemy – although hardly, as yet, as a serious rival for future political leadership in Germany.

A third "betrayal" came when the local elections in the British Zone gave the CDU unexpected success in the Rhineland, including the working class districts of the industrialized Ruhr. The CDU scored heavily, too, in the subsequent local elections in the US and French Zones. The German people, evidently, were deserting socialism. Worse was to come. Schumacher had set his heart on the nationalization of all heavy industry – he believed that the pre–1933 bosses of German industry had played a key role in helping Hitler into power. He counted on the support of Britain, and even of a section of the CDU, which was toying with the so-called "Ahlen Programme" of modified "socialization" of key industries. But the British Labour Government informed him that nationalization could not be carried out until there were elections on a national basis, and actually countermanded the action of the first SPD *Land* Government in Schleswig-Holstein which had decreed the nationalization of basic industries. Meanwhile, the CDU, under Adenauer's direction, dropped its "Ahlen Programme".

Here was another reason for hatred of Konrad Adenauer, and a word is needed here to explain this man – who had refused to hearken to Schumacher's clarion call for the creation of a new Germany, and who was patiently reassembling the remnants of the old, into which he had been born as long before as 1876.

Adenauer was born in Cologne. His father was an official in the municipal administration and his mother the daughter of a Cologne bank employee. They were relatively poor and Adenauer was brought up in an atmosphere in which industry, piety, family solidarity and a strong "local patriotism" predominated, enlivened by the wit and laughter of which the people of Cologne are so fond. He seems to have been a very ordinary young boy and young man, a trifle shy, industrious without being a model pupil, essentially sober but enjoying the occasional joke and the occasional glass of wine. He made his way by slow stages, but steadily – into the Public Prosecutor's office after passing his law exams, then to a solicitor's office, and then into the Cologne municipal administration, where he became a city councillor at the age of 30. He had already married, very happily, in 1904, Emma Weyer, and his wife's cousin, Max Wallraf, became Mayor of Cologne five years later.

This was to be useful to him. He became special assistant, or "Deputy", to the Mayor in 1909. Max Wallraf was often called away to Berlin on other business, and Adenauer took over charge of the Finance and Personnel Departments of the municipality. He worked immensely hard, and was paid a fair salary. By 1912 he had three children, and when war broke out in 1914 was really prosperous. Difficult years lay ahead; his wife died in 1916 and his mother had to take over the children. His own health was uncertain, and a blood clot in one leg may have been a contributory reason why he was not called up for military service. He was badly injured in the summer of 1917, when the chauffeur of his official car fell asleep at the wheel and the car collided with a tram. Adenauer's nose and cheekbones were broken, his lower jaw dislocated, several teeth knocked out, and his eyesight temporarily impaired. Yet he walked, covered in blood, to a nearby hospital – while the miscreant chauffeur, who only suffered bruising and shock, was carried there on a stretcher.

Adenauer became Lord Mayor of Cologne on 18 October 1917, one of the key dates of his life. He served as Mayor for the next 16 years. It was a coveted post, and it carried power as well as prestige. His Mayoralty was studded with achievements: he saw the people of Cologne through the dark and difficult days of British occupation, hunger and all kinds of shortages; he built the University, laid out the City Park and created a "green belt" round the western side of the city; he was instrumental in the building of a new bridge across the Rhine and the city's own electric power plant. He married again. He was utterly devoted to Cologne, and toyed only twice, briefly, with the thought of making a full-time career in the field of national politics. In 1921, and again in 1926, he was approached by the leaders of the Catholic Centre Party to which he belonged, with a view to standing as a candidate for the post of Reich Chancellor. He insisted on being guaranteed a stable majority in the Reichstag, but such a guarantee could not be given, for the Weimar Republic was already the prey of a multitude of parties, great and small, which made the creation of a stable coalition next to impossible. Had he been able to form a Government in 1926, it would have been the thirteenth in the seven years of the Republic's existence. And there were seven more years of it to come.

A second key date of his life arrived on 13 March 1933. He had already shown his active dislike of the Nazis, and must have known that his post, and even his life, would be in danger when Hitler dissolved the Reichstag in January 1933 and fixed the date of 5 March for new elections. Yet when Hitler arrived in the course of his electioneering campaign in Cologne on 17 February, Adenauer refused to meet him, and on 19 February refused to allow two Nazi swastika flags to be flown on the principal Cologne–Deutz bridge in his honour. Nazi storm-troopers were quartered in his home early in March, and he learnt through private sources that his arrest was imminent. He took the only possible action, and left Cologne.

Twelve years followed, during which he lived for a time in "exile" in Berlin and for a time in hiding in the Monastery of Maria Laach, in the Eifel mountains. There was never, as far as is known, a price on his head; but he was twice arrested, and was lucky to survive both in 1934, when Hitler took the opportunity of "liquidating" opponents in the wake of the so-called "Roehm Blood-bath", and in 1944, after the conspiracy to assassinate Hitler had miscarried. For much of the time, he was allowed to live in Rhoendorf, near Bonn, where he managed to build the family a new home. There were children from his second happy marriage, just after the end of the First World War; now there were seven children in all. For these empty years he lived in enforced seclusion, aware that all he could achieve was to survive.

The Americans arrived in March 1945 and invited him to resume his duties as Mayor of Cologne. He lasted only just over six months in office. In June the British Army took over from the Americans in Cologne. Adenauer had been working more than fifteen hours a day, had built up excellent relations with the Americans, and may have begun with some justice to regard himself as indispensable. After the First World War, he had been in occasional difficulties with the British occupation authorities. But he had made friends with some of them, had in any case regarded their occupation as being of a temporary nature, and had managed when necessary to swallow his pride. In 1945, the situation was different. Germany, and Germans were being treated far more rigorously than before; the occupation was of unlimited duration, and Adenauer was, in any case, not the British nominee for the Mayor's post. There was likely to be trouble.

He was at once offended by the British tapping his private telephone connection in Rhoendorf, and doing it so ham-fistedly that he was informed by the German postal authorities. Then he learnt that a Social Democratic opponent in the City Council, Robert Goerlinger, had sent a memorandum to the British authorities, accusing Adenauer of bringing back ex-Nazis into official posts, of carrying on "underground" political activity himself, and of working to retain denominational schools. The British, for their part, did not like his peremptory requests for more coal and building materials for Cologne, and they were infuriated when he refused to cut down trees in the City Park for use as firewood – Adenauer maintained that the people of Cologne could get through one cold winter, but that it would take at least fifteen years to grow good trees. And he was immensely proud of the fact that, as he said to a relative, "the churches have gone, but my Green Belt is still here".[26]

On 6 October, yet another key date in his life, he was sacked by a British Brigadier, acting ostensibly on behalf of General Gerald Templer, then Director of Military Government. According to his own account, Adenauer was marched into the Brigadier's office like a miscreant, and kept standing while being told of his dismissal. He never forgave the British, but instead made a caustic joke out of the affair. For, although he was temporarily banned from all manner of political activity, the ban was lifted two months later and he plunged at once into a political field in which the embryonic Christian Democratic Party was beginning to take shape. The joke was that, while depriving him of the chance to go on working for his beloved city of Cologne, the British gave him a political career which he had not even dreamt about. His successor as Mayor believed that he might indeed have been fractious (*boeckig*) but that he had right on his side.[27]

The stages in that career are easily delineated. On 19 January 1946, he took the chair without invitation and merely because the convenor of the meeting was late, at the inaugural session of the CDU executive at Herford. On 26 February the CDU Zonal Council confirmed him in the post of Chairman. He travelled far and wide in Western Germany, establishing especially good relations with the CDU groups in Hesse, Wurtemberg and the Rhine-Palatinate, and on 5 and 6 February 1947, presided at a meeting of CDU members from all four zones and ensured that the party headquarters would be in Western Germany, and not in Berlin. The CDU would formally become a unified party throughout Western Germany only in October 1950, but there was little doubt that Adenauer was generally accepted as its leader three years before that. He was to be its automatic choice as President of the Parliamentary Council, formed in the summer of 1948 to draw up a Federal Constitution and prepare the way for the first Federal elections, in 1949.

This is moving a little ahead of the story of what was happening to Germany as a whole. For the first half of 1948 brought two developments which have left a lasting impression on German history. These two events, the reform of the West German currency and the Berlin Blockade, were closely interrelated – improbable though this may sound. For the decision of the three Western Occupying Powers to go ahead with the economic development of their zones and to give them, first a real economic future, and secondly political democracy in a unified state, meant that the Soviet leaders abandoned all real hope of extending Russian influence over the whole of Germany. Periodically, thereafter, they would return to the subject of German reunification – but always with the primary purpose of sabotaging or at least postponing Western plans for greater European unity and cohesion. Confronted in 1948 by the Western plans for Germany, the Russians decided that this was their chance to "bite off" Berlin. The Blockade was their answer to the Western Powers' tacit admission that Four Power cooperation was no longer feasible, and that they must look after their part of Germany as best they could.

More will be written in a later chapter about the effects of Currency Reform. As a procedural step, it is easily explained. It was plainly forecast by the breakdown of the London Conference of Foreign Ministers in November–December 1947. The US Secretary of State, George Marshall, confirmed at this conference that no more reparations would be paid out of German current production. Reparations, to the Soviet Union, out of West German current production had been suspended for five months past. This step was designed to stop the siphoning-off, by the Soviet Union, of Allied aid in goods and finance – something which the Russians had been achieving by printing gigantic quantities of German money. On 6 March 1948, the Six Power London Conference (the three Benelux states of Holland, Belgium and Luxembourg took part) established that there would be full economic and political cooperation in Germany between Britain, France and the United States, that a federal system of government would be established in Western Germany, and that there should be German participation in the International Ruhr Authority.

On 19 March the Soviet representative, Marshal Vassili Sokolovsky, stormed out of the Allied Control Council in Berlin, and on the next day confirmed that he had left for good. Quite certainly, the Soviet plans to blockade Berlin had already been agreed upon by then. There had been one "dummy run" already: on 24 January the Berlin–Bielefeld train, carrying British officials as well as German passengers, had been held up in the Soviet Zone – through which, of course, it had to pass – for eleven hours. On 30 March the Russians demanded the right to control all personnel and their papers on all Allied trains to West Germany. In April, four Allied trains were turned back when Allied officers in charge of them refused to allow them to be searched. On the same day, the three Western Powers stated that they would go ahead with Currency Reform. The implementary steps were, in fact, only taken in June, when the old Reichsmark currency was called in and new "Deutschmarks" issued (one new for twelve old).

The new currency, in conjunction with Allied promises to move ahead with unifying economic and political measures in Western Germany, brought an instant response. Goods began to flow into the shops, working morale was immediately raised, black market activity waned. It is no dramatization to say that a spirit of hope and a sense of purpose were born, within weeks, which have persisted ever since. But there was a Russian response too: the day after the new Deutschmarks were introduced in West Berlin (on 23 June, five days after they were launched in Western Germany), the Russians severed all land and water routes between Berlin and the West.

To some extent, at least, the Western Powers were fore-warned. Soviet intentions had been plain ever since January. The Russians had demanded that Allied "aid posts" on the Berlin–Helmstedt autobahn should be withdrawn. They were. The Russians announced that the Elbe Bridge would be closed for repairs (there was nothing the matter with it). The Western Powers meekly accepted the situation, and tried to make do with a more or less disused and ridiculously inadequate ferry a couple of miles downstream from the bridge. One track was removed from the double-track railway line to the West, and the Russians began building a "ring-railway" round East and West Berlin for the use of Soviet Zone trains. German vehicles were continually being held up on the Helmstedt autobahn, even before it was closed.

British and American officers meanwhile were working out detailed plans for an "Air-Lift" operation, which could keep a fully blockaded Berlin supplied – if only for a few weeks. The first initiative came from a British officer, Air Commodore Rex Waite.[28] When he produced his logistical calculations, the US Military Governor, General Lucius Clay, declared bluntly, "Absolutely impossible".[29] Clay was to change his mind, and become the main driving-force in the operation. The Mayor of Berlin, Ernst Reuter, learnt of the proposed Air-Lift only ten days before it began to operate. One of his aides recalled that he pushed his spectacles up over his head and said: "I just don't believe it, but we've made our decision already – to stick it out".[30] It seemed inconceivable that 2·3 million West Berliners could be supplied solely by air over any length of time.

In fact, the Air-Lift was to last for just under one year and would bring in over two million tons of goods in a quarter of a million flights. Food had to be tightly rationed, and much of it consisted of unappetizing dried foodstuffs like dehydrated potatoes. Fuel was in even shorter supply; electricity was rationed, and Berliners took it in turns to get up or go to bed in the dark. They showed great courage, humour and endurance, and were well-led; Mayor Reuter coined the phrase, "It's cold in Berlin, but colder in Siberia".[31]

As a defensive measure, the Air-Lift succeeded. One historian claimed that it "achieved a demonstration of the defender's will

– but also of his power – to resist aggression ... it was the most successful campaign the West has fought in the Cold War". This may be an overstatement. One could argue that the Blockade should never have taken place at all, that Western diplomatic weakness and hesitation emboldened the Russians, and that even a minimal show of force would have deterred them. One could argue that the autobahn aid-stations should never have been abandoned, and the Elbe Bridge should have been quietly occupied by Allied troops and given a cosmetic face-lift. The Russians failed to starve Berlin out, but they learnt that threats may not be resolutely countered.

The Air-Lift was to have a deep political significance: it convinced Germans that the Western Powers were prepared to defend them, and the courage and commonsense of the Berliners suggested to the Western world that Germans might again become friends and even allies. Paradoxically, it took the Russians' actions in this first phase of the Cold War to drive the Germans and the Western Powers into each other's arms.

It was altogether natural, then, that the latter should have pressed on with their plans to create a West German State which would be both politically stable and economically viable. First, they had to divest themselves of some of their powers. In December 1948 they reached agreement over the duties of the International Ruhr Authority, in which the three Military Governors would have seats but would not exercise control. In January 1949 they created an Allied Military Security Board, which would hold a watching brief on German demilitarization, rather than continue direct supervision. In April military government came to an end, and the Military Governors became High Commissioners. The Allies retained certain reserved rights under an "Occupation Statute". Dismantling of industrial plant was further curtailed; it had been reduced, successively, from 1,600 plants, to 900, to 750. Now, another 159 plants were removed from the dismantling list, and the permitted steel capacity for Western Germany was raised to 13·3 million tons.

At the same time, the Western Powers declared that their "highest purpose" was to secure the integration of a democratic federal German State within the framework of a European community.[32] The Germans were already playing their part in this; the Parliamentary Council began work in Bonn in September 1948 and completed it on 8 May 1949, when the Basic Law of the Federal German Constitution was approved by 53 votes to 12, and nation-wide Federal Elections were ordered for

14 August. Adenauer, who had steered the Council to success, won a final, convincing victory in it: he secured a vote in favour of Bonn as the Federal capital and seat of Parliament and Government.

This was perhaps more significant than it may sound. For the future of a federal democratic German State would hinge on Konrad Adenauer. He was over 72, but he had never been more conscious that he was needed, nor more determined to fulfil his ambitions. Having the capital in Bonn was essential to his plans. His own home was only a mile or two away, on the opposite bank of the Rhine. He was among his own people of the Rhineland, and his old power centre of Cologne was a mere half hour's drive down the motorway. He needed to conserve his energies and he wanted to work where he felt at ease and "belonged". The arguments advanced for Bonn, as against the earlier much more favoured Frankfurt, were ingenious: it would cost less, it was nearer the industrial heart of Western Germany – the Ruhr – and, above all, it was so very obviously "provisional" and could be readily abandoned when Berlin once again became the capital of a united Germany.

On the eve of the first Federal elections, it would have been wildly premature to have assumed that all was set fair in Germany, or even for the Federal German Republic which was about to be proclaimed. Germany was divided, apparently for good. Economically, Eastern Germany continued to be bled white by the Russians. Politically, it was under the heel of the Soviet occupiers and a servile Socialist Unity Party which claimed to have a million and a half members in a zone with only 18 million inhabitants; other political parties were the merest puppets. Eastern Germany was a police state in the making, with concentration camps only less horrible in degree than those of the Nazis, lacking all human freedoms. Refugees from it were pouring into Western Germany. The Soviet purpose was to ensure that Eastern and Western Germany should grow apart.

Western Germany was not yet to be by any means sovereign. Under the Occupation Statute, the Allies retained control of foreign policy and much besides. The West German State was to be totally disarmed. Its industrial potential was still under constraint – one instance was the 13·3 million ton steel-producing capacity, another the ban on building ships other than coastal craft. Moreover, economic recovery was only in its first stage. Cities still lay in ruins. Unemployment was running around the 10 per cent level. Schools were terribly overcrowded, and the road network was still in a mess. Nor was it yet clear whether a balanced economy could be created in a truncated German State west-of-the-Elbe; the eastern provinces which had been areas of food surplus were lost, so were the coal-mines of Silesia and the open-cast brown coal-fields of Saxony, and the optics, electronics and precision-tool industries of Saxony and Thuringia.

Who was to rule the infant Federal Republic? Most of the Parliamentary candidates would, necessarily, be middle-aged or old – for one had to step back across twelve years of Nazi rule and four years of Allied occupation to find them. It was a commentary on this problem that the two outstanding politicians who had already emerged were Adenauer, aged 72, and Schumacher, admittedly more than ten years his junior but lacking one leg and reasonable health. Again, the 1919-33 Weimar Republic had died partly as a result of the plethora of political parties and the difficulty of organizing stable coalition governments. All too many parties were lining up for these first Federal elections. The SPD and CDU were nation-wide parties, but even the CDU had a semi-independent "Christian Social" branch in Bavaria. The Free Democrats (FDP) contained conservative-liberals in the Rhineland and Northern Germany, and old-fashioned liberals calling themselves the "Democratic People's Party" south of the river Main. The Bavarian Party was strictly parochial; so, too, to a large extent was the "German Party", centred on Hanover, and the residual "Centre Party" in the Rhineland. The Communists were in the field, and full of high hopes; there were more than half a dozen other groups campaigning. It was all disturbingly reminiscent of Weimar days.

And then there were the suspicions of the outside world with which to contend. It was only a small minority, of statesmen, educationalists, and the like, in the Western world, who were beginning to believe in a truly "new" Germany. Old slogans die hard; "the leopard cannot change his spots" was one of the milder ones applied to Germans. "The only good German is a dead German" had become commonplace during the war, while Winston Churchill had coined "The German is always at your throat, or your feet", and General Slim the even more unappetizing "Bloodthirsty sheep". Even liberal-minded men found it hard to stop distrusting Germans; it was, after all, only two years before that the British Military Government had finally discarded the weird idea of marooning 16,000 ex-Nazi school-teachers (and their families!) on an island in the North Sea.

One man, at least, stood poised to take advantage of the first genuinely free vote in Germany for nearly two decades. Konrad Adenauer had emerged as the most sagacious politician in post-war Germany, even though his Social Democratic opponents were heavily tipped to win the elections. It was too soon for the much younger men to emerge yet. But four other future Federal Chancellors were making their way, if less outstandingly. Ludwig Erhard had proved himself an economist of real prescience, had underwritten Currency Reform and advised on its consequences, had advocated the ending of price controls and enunciated his theory of a "Social Market Economy". He only joined the CDU in June 1949, for he had always thought of himself as a liberal, and he was standing for Parliament (the Bundestag) in Ulm-Heidenheim, on the Bavarian–Wurtemberg border. Another Bundestag candidate, also in Wurtemberg, was Kurt Georg Kiesinger, who had already proved an orator with a silver tongue and a poetic turn of phrase, a son of Swabia, which has produced so many clever, capable and industrious citizens.

In Berlin, Willy Brandt was understudying the Governing Mayor Ernst Reuter, having returned to Germany only in November 1946. His decision to reclaim German nationality came soon after that, at a time when there seemed so little hope for Germany as a whole, and least of all for a divided, isolated former capital city. He took a brave decision when he doffed the uniform of a Norwegian press attaché, and sacrificed a career as a Norwegian citizen which could have taken him to the top in the country of his adoption. Finally, Helmut Schmidt, only 30 years old, had become Chairman of the Socialist Student League, after joining the SPD in 1946. Little else was known of him, save that he had served through the war and risen to the rank of lieutenant and battery-commander.

There was talent enough in the Germany of 1949, if it could be given time to mature. The Germans had come a long way since the total defeat and despair of 1945, and the talk of a twenty-year Allied military occupation. But the Federal German Republic was no more than an experiment. There were plenty of well informed observers who expected it to fail.

1. Paul Schallueck. *German Cultural Developments since 1945*. Edited by Paul Schallueck. Munich, 1971.
2. Walter Henry Nelson. *Germany Rearmed*. New York, 1972.

3. Aidan Crawley. *The Rise of Western Germany*. London, 1973.
4. Terence Prittie. *Germany Divided*. Boston, 1960.
5. Aidan Crawley, op. cit.
6. Robert Haeger. *This is Germany*. Edited by Art Settel. New York, 1950.
7. Ibid.
8. Aidan Crawley, op. cit.
9. Robert Haeger, op. cit.
10. J. Gimbel. *The American Occupation of Germany*. London, 1973.
11. Paul Weymar. *Konrad Adenauer*. London, 1957.
12. Terence Prittie. *Konrad Adenauer*. London, 1972.
13. Willy Brandt. *My Road to Berlin*. London, 1960.
14. Tom Pocock. The London *Times*, 5 August 1978.
15. Ibid.
16. Personal experience of the author, in Berlin, winter of 1946/47.
17. Victor Gollancz. *In Darkest Germany*. London, 1947.
18. Ibid.
19. Willy Brandt, op. cit.
20. Eugene Davidson. *The Death and Life of Germany*. New York, 1954.
21. Heinz Schwitzke. *German Cultural Developments*.
22. Paul Schallueck, op. cit.
23. David Childs. *From Schumacher to Brandt. The Story of German Socialism*. London, 1966.
24. Lord Pakenham (later the Earl of Longford). *Born to Believe*. London, 1953.
25. Kurt Schumacher. *Der Auftrag des demokratischen Sozialismus*. London, 1966.
26. Paul Weymar, op. cit.
27. Dr Hermann Puender, in conversation with the author, December 1970.
28. Richard Collier. *Bridge across the Sky*. London, 1978.
29. Ibid.
30. Willy Brandt, in conversation with the author, March 1973.
31. Terence Prittie. *Willy Brandt*. London, 1974.
32. John Mander. *Berlin. Hostage of the West*. London, 1962.
33. Communiqué of the Washington Agreement, 10 April 1949.

CHAPTER THREE

The Step into the Unknown

The results of the August 1949 elections to the first Federal Parliament came as a surprise to much of the outside world and a terrible shock to Dr Schumacher and the Social Democrats. This was, of course, one of the most "open" elections in history, for the people of the Federal Republic were voting, in freedom, for the first time for well over twelve years. Yet, although the overall results might have been unpredictable, informed opinion was virtually unanimous on one point – the Social Democrats would emerge as the strongest party and would, presumably, seek to form the first Federal Government in Bonn. Instead, the Christian Democrats collected 7,360,000 votes, 400,000 more than their chief rivals, and won 139 seats in Parliament against the SPD's 131. To Schumacher this must have seemed like the final betrayal of his party, this time by the electorate.

Against this salient fact the rest of the election results faded into relative insignificance. The Free Democrats (FDP), canvassing especially among refugees from the East and middle class voters, won 52 seats; the German Party (DP), based on Hanover, and the Bavarian Party, came next with 17 each. The only other party of more than passing interest, the Communists (KPD), collected only 15 seats; the Cold War, the Berlin Blockade and Russian rapacity put paid to their electoral chances. The remaining 31 seats were divided among small parties which were mainly right-wing in character.

The general supposition had been that Schumacher would,

with 150 or more seats in his pocket, have approached the Christian Democrats (CDU) as his most obvious coalition partners in order to form a strong left-centre government. There was speculation as to whether this would mean the immediate disappearance of the strongly anti-socialist Adenauer from the scene; a more acceptable CDU Vice-Chancellor would have been Jakob Kaiser, the former leader of the CDU in the Soviet Zone and a fervent believer in steps to restore the unity of Germany. All such ideas were swept away by the CDU victory.

Least surprised by the election results was Konrad Adenauer. A week earlier he had declared: "We must win power now. And we must remain in power for at least eight years. If we can do that, we shall have placed Germany firmly on a road along which she can move in safety."[1] Adenauer had believed in the possibility of a CDU victory, but he had a valuable card in reserve. Short of truly sweeping success, the SPD would be unable to find coalition partners and thus unable to form a government. The Communist KPD was steered from Moscow and was opposed to the very existence of the Federal Republic. The FDP had already shown its hand in opposing socialization of industry. Perhaps the only feasible allies for the SPD were the twelve followers of Alfred Loritz in his oddly assorted and incoherent party of "social reconstruction" and the ten members of the Rhineland remnant of the once great Roman Catholic Centre Party (Zentrum).

A Government of the centre and the right had, in fact, always been on the cards, and this is what Adenauer proceeded to form, with singular ease and dispatch. Remembering one of the chief lessons of the failure of the Weimar Republic, he took in as few coalition partners as possible – with the FDP and DP, he would command 208 votes in a Federal Parliament of 402. The smaller parties, he calculated, would in some cases wither away; they were to be helped into extinction by subsequent modifications of the electoral law, which laid down that only parties with 5 per cent of the total vote, or winning at least two seats by direct election, could qualify for "reserve list" seats. The Basic Law of the Federal Constitution had established that half of the seats in the Federal Parliament should go to directly elected candidates, and half to nominees of the parties on the reserve lists – allocated on the basis of proportional representation.

At a meeting of CDU leaders on 21 August at his home in Rhoendorf, just across the Rhine from Bonn, Adenauer accepted the proposal that he should be the party's candidate for the

Chancellorship, remarking that his personal physician, Dr Paul Martini, had stated that his health was good enough to undertake this task.[2] He would be able, at the age of 73, "to carry on for two years"; in reality, he was to remain Chancellor for more than fourteen. Equally casually, he produced his own candidate for the Federal Presidency, Professor Theodor Heuss of the FDP, and fended off a question about the latter's cool attitude towards organized religion with: "His wife is a good Christian, and that's enough".[3] Wit, generally dry or caustic, was to be one of Adenauer's most effective weapons in office. It came into play when, on 15 September, he was elected Chancellor by the narrowest possible margin, 202 votes out of 402. His comment was: "When I was later asked whether I had voted for myself, I replied – 'Naturally, anything else would have been hypocrisy' ".[4] But this narrow margin was a reminder of the precarious nature of the first Federal Parliament. It was underlined by three resolutions which the SPD, fuming over what they considered to be a political "restoration" of Germans who had done little or nothing to combat Nazism, put forward immediately after Adenauer's election. They were that the Western Powers should be asked to slow down the dismantling of German industry, that West Berlin should become an integral part of the Federal Republic (this would have made the SPD, at one blow, the strongest single party in Bonn), and that the capital should be moved from Catholic Bonn to traditionally socialist Frankfurt. It was clear that Adenauer was going to be under heavy pressure from the outset.

Adenauer outlined his future policies in an interview with a British newspaper[5] a week before his election as Chancellor. A CDU-led Government would request the scaling-down of dismantling, shared ownership of heavy industry based on "a balance between private capital and public control", and the removal of Allied restrictions on the rights of the German citizen and the freedom of the German economy. Other aims were German diplomatic representation abroad and a peace agreement with the Western Allies – "If we must wait for a peace treaty with the Soviet Union, our wait is liable to be a very long one." His first Government statement, on 20 September, was as concise and unemotional as the hundreds of speeches he would subsequently make to Parliament. His aims, in outline, were: to win political and economic concessions from the Western Allies, to become their loyal partners, to be good friends with all neighbours, to make economic progress, and to end anti-semitism and modify denazification in the course of welding a civilized and unified community. Only one reference in the speech caused concern in the outside world, to the unacceptability of the "Oder–Neisse Line" as Germany's permanent eastern frontier. The London *Times* commented: "Whatever may be thought of the justice or injustice of the [Oder–Neisse] line ... it does not follow that Europe accepts and supports all Germany's claims for frontier revision."[6] Otherwise, Adenauer's statement was given a cautious welcome in the press of the free world.

Simple in essence, this first statement gave a good idea of the way in which Adenauer's mind worked. Patient, precise, guardedly sceptical but utterly logical, Adenauer sought to found his policies on an understanding of the past and an exact appreciation of current problems. His long-serving personal secretary quoted him as having told her: "One cannot conduct foreign policy without a knowledge of the past. One needs knowledge, and experience. As in a man's life, one stone has to go upon another. One must ... understand the developments in one's own country and in others ... if one wants to evolve a successful policy."[7] What held good for foreign policy, held good for domestic affairs too.

One of Adenauer's cardinal virtues was his ability to reduce problems to simple terms – this, and his logic were his "Roman virtues". One view is that he was animated by five factors in Germany's post-war situation.[8] These were the decline of Europe and the rise of two super-powers in the USA and Soviet Union; Soviet expansion, especially into Central Europe; the Cold War between East and West; the structural weaknesses of the western world; and Germany's disastrous history up to 1945. The tremendous power of the Soviet Union was a fact, not a habit of mind passed on by Josef Goebbels. Its immense inroads into Europe, the huge annexations of territory, the creation of a forward bastion of satellite states, and the partial occupation of Germany and Austria, were facts too. (Today, an Adenauer would note that Soviet expansion has become global, into the Horn of Africa, Southern Africa, Cuba, Afghanistan and the Persian Gulf.) The structural weaknesses of the western world were self-evident too. As for past German history, Adenauer was totally convinced that the "new" Germany had to recover prestige and respectability by making moral as well as practical restitution for the crimes of the Nazis.

Adenauer's principal aims derived from his reading of

Germany's and Europe's situation. The first aim, of course, was to restore German sovereignty. Then, the Federal German Republic would, inevitably, become the spokesman and representative of the German people – it never occurred to Adenauer that an East German regime could be other than a puppet of the Soviet Union, and this has indeed proved the case during the last thirty years. Adenauer wanted the maximum cooperation within the free world, and this general aim would be canalized into cooperation between Europe and the United States and cooperation among the free countries of Europe itself. Behind these immediate objectives was the imponderable problem of German reunification; whether Adenauer ever intended to do more than simply keep it in mind may never become entirely clear.

The clue to European cooperation, Adenauer knew, lay in France. He was himself a "Carolingian", believing in the heritage of Charlemagne's Empire, whose two main pillars were the Teutons and the Franks. As a Rhinelander, he found the peoples adjacent to Germany's western borders more understandable than the East Germans – one of his own phrases was "You can smell Prussia when you cross the Elbe". But it was more relevant that France could accept Germany's return into the European fold, and other European nations would follow France's lead; though France could, by herself, block that return. General Charles de Gaulle was right when he wrote of Adenauer: "This patriot was aware of the barriers of hatred and distrust which the frenzied ambition of Hitler, passionately obeyed by the German masses and their élite, had raised between this country and all its neighbours, and which France alone, he knew, could succeed in breaking down, by offering the hand of friendship to the hereditary enemy."[9]

The first Federal Government, at all events, had to get on initially with the more immediate tasks of political organization, economic retrenchment and developing a sense of respect for the rule of law. Behind the strategic aims which built up into a "Grand Design" for the German people was the more fundamental, more mundane but crucially important need to normalize German life, to instill moderation and commonsense, to discard dreams and slogans and impossible missionary visions. No man was better suited for this task than Adenauer, who as Mayor of Cologne had dealt essentially with practical problems and had contrived to solve the lot.

His talents were badly needed. That first Federal Parliament was a strange, even alarming assembly. In the first place, it was incredibly noisy; after twelve years of Nazi dictatorship and four years of Military Government, the reaction of many members was that of children just let out of school. Interruptions were incessant and insults were exchanged, very often across the Chamber, between left and right-wingers. Many of the speeches were incomprehensible, especially when they came from the small but extremely active Communist group; other speeches were nonsensical – it never became clear, for instance, what the Loritz party stood for. The Speaker (his title was President of the Bundestag) had a hard time indeed; his bell was for ever ringing, and his voice raised in expostulation or reprimand.

The Government, moreover, looked like a contrived and improvised coalition and it included ex-Nazis in its ranks. The CDU had still not taken cohesive shape, and the FDP seemed to be only vaguely "liberal" – one of its founders, Dr Friedrich Middelhauve, was often at pains to explain that liberalism no longer had a role in Germany. The DP consisted of worthy but unreconstructed Hanoverian conservatives. With its slender overall majority, the Government coalition had one consolation: its opponents were absolutely unable to unite on any issue at all. But this, too, was unhealthy; a good Government is all the better for a good Opposition. Schumacher's leadership of the SPD in Parliament left much to be desired – although his courage in reorganizing it and his resolute rejection of Communism should never be forgotten. The KPD were intent on breaking up Parliamentary sessions and bringing the Bundestag into ridicule. There was nobody else on the Opposition benches who mattered.

It was over this Government and Parliament that Konrad Adenauer asserted his authority, a blend of paternalism, school-masterly discipline and shrewd commonsense. He achieved this with an altogether masterly lack of evident effort. He dealt with interruptions with an easy irony. His speeches were kept short and were always to the point. Almost invariably, he kept his temper, but even his anger was strangely compelling. He could be tetchy – one cannot translate the French word *mèchant*, and this is what Adenauer was on these occasions – or vitriolic, when what the writer George Orwell described as a "false note, a yellow note" crept into his voice. He had the gift of venting his anger while remaining calm. He was the exact antithesis of the demagogue, and he set an example which this first post-Nazi Parliament badly needed.

He presided equally effectively over his Cabinet. He banned smoking at its meetings, but in other respects was by no means as autocratic as has often been suggested; he let Ministers have their say and only cut them short when they were obviously long-winded. He was correct and courteous, but made it plain that he expected results by the end of the weekly four-hour session. He had to make Ministers out of men who had never served in that capacity before, and except for perhaps four of its members, this first Cabinet was undistinguished. As Minister for All-German Affairs, Jakob Kaiser was much concerned with Berlin and with monitoring events in the Soviet Zone and in East Berlin. Gustav Heinemann was Minister of the Interior, and was to resign from that post and from the CDU when the issue of German rearmament arose. Fritz Schaeffer was the peppery and persistent Minister of Finance, the only Minister who was ready to argue with the Chancellor about subjects which were not his personal concern. Finally, Ludwig Erhard was an automatic choice as Minister of Economics, a field in which he had already been so successful and about which Adenauer cared very little and knew even less. All the more understandable, therefore, that he gave Erhard *carte blanche* in this important initial phase of government.

The erratic and often wild Bundestag debates were the outward expression of the uncertainties of mind of the pioneer democratic legislators. One British observer described a Bundestag debate as a "desk-slamming, feet-thumping, brawling brouhaha".[10] A future British Ambassador to Bonn thought the quality of its members to be "abysmal", most of them "freaks or dullards".[11] The second man to hold the job of British High Commissioner, Sir Ivone Kirkpatrick, used a dry phrase: "The antics of the German Parliamentarians brought home to me the demoralizing effects of a long occupation."[12] Speeches were almost always read and seldom dealt with points raised by other speakers; they gave the impression of being mere declamations, and speakers of not listening to what anyone else said. But behind the scenes excellent work was going on: expert committees were formed, Ministries were efficiently staffed, and a tremendous amount of effective legislation was carried through. There was so much to be done, as the Federal Republic was confronted with problems which did not exist in other European countries. Much of it had to do with the consequences of a disastrous and lost war.

In the first place, there were the refugees, at least eight million

of them by 1949 and more arriving daily from the Soviet Zone.
They had to be found homes and jobs – generally it was the other
way round, for there was a desperate shortage of housing, even
though nearly half a million homes were built in the first year of
the Federal Republic's existence. But homes and jobs were not
enough; it was inequitable that Germans should have suffered
almost total loss of their possessions, simply because they had
lived in East Prussia, Silesia or the Sudetenland. The
"Lastenausgleich", or "equalization of burdens", law spread
these losses over the whole population. Immediate financial aid
to the refugees totalled 6,000 million marks up to 1952; the
programme resulted in the payment of a further 47,000 million
marks in the following ten years.

Later would come the "Bundesentschaedigungsgesetz", or
"Federal Law of Restitution", under which millions of marks
were paid to victims of Nazism. Its framing was complex and
took a long time, and its implementation was sometimes slow,
being dependent on the attitude of the normal courts of law, but
it offered a striking example of German thoroughness and
German goodwill to the outside world. It was supplemented by a
special agreement with the infant State of Israel, which was
concluded in 1952 and under which 3,450 million marks worth
of goods were shipped to Israel as a contribution towards the
massive resettlement in that country of refugees who had
survived Hitler's atrocious persecution of the Jews.

Of lasting importance, too, was the securing of
"Mitbestimmung", or co-partnership, for workers in heavy
industries. This was not so much a German obligation as
enlightened and opportunistic pioneering in the field of labour
relations. The old pattern of German heavy industry was broken
by Allied measures designed to "decartelize" and split up the
huge combines in the steel, coal and chemical industries. The
1951 co-partnership law provided for Trade Union
representation on supervisory and managerial boards. It had the
complete approval of the "Deutscher Gewerkschaftsbund"
(DGB), the German Trade Union Congress, under Hans Boeckler.
Ever since, workers' participation in industrial management has
been a factor in maintaining a record of remarkable industrial
peace and keeping the Federal Republic relatively free of strikes
compared with its principal European partners and competitors.

These three pieces of early legislation have been selected
because of their uniquely German connotations. In eliminating
the consequences of war, Adenauer's main activity was

diplomatic, and it was here that his very special talents could be put to the best possible use. For as long as the Federal Republic was not a fully sovereign state, Adenauer was in effect his own Foreign Minister. He had, it was true, to deal with only three foreign countries, Britain, the United States and France. But his dealings with them were complicated, continuous and of crucial importance to his country; they amounted, very essentially, to "foreign relations".

In seeking to establish sovereignty for the Federal Republic, Adenauer was keenly aware of Allied reservations and of the degree of residual distrust of Germany and all things German. This was not so marked in the United States, where there was always readiness to look at new ideas and revise old ones. French foreign policy operates strictly on a basis of *raison d'état*, or French self-interest. The Quai d'Orsai and its representatives conduct diplomacy with cold and calculated elegance; for them, it is an exact science. Even before the Berlin Blockade began, the United States had decided that the Germans might become allies in the not too distant future – hence the Stuttgart speech of the US Secretary of State, James Byrnes, in September 1946, when he spoke of the need to restore a politically responsible and economically viable Germany. Hence, too, the readiness with which Marshall Plan aid was made available to West Germany. Adenauer could expect approaches from the United States; with the French, he had to make the running, but with the utmost tact, and wait patiently for a favourable reaction. It came with the proposal in May 1950 of the French Foreign Minister, Robert Schuman, to create a European Coal and Steel Community. From then on, a worthwhile Franco-German dialogue was always feasible, and was often under way.

Adenauer wanted alignment with the USA and reconciliation with France; with Britain, he was dubious. Perhaps with reason, he was acutely mistrustful of the British Labour Party and post-1945 Government which, he believed, introduced ideology into its conduct of foreign relations. In his September 1949 interview with the *Manchester Guardian*,[13] he pulled no punches:

> I must add here that the British Government has openly supported the German Social Democrats in their Zone of Occupation. Its representatives have influenced the North-West German Radio, the news agencies and the military-governed paper *Die Welt*, which has been given special advantages and which pursues a definitely Socialist policy. As a member of the CDU I must oppose this policy energetically.

Adenauer may have mistaken for partisanship the automatic assumption by British Military Government, that the SPD was the only immediately acceptable representative of a new German democracy, and that the SPD would have to produce the first West German Government. This assumption did seem justifiable. But Adenauer was unassailably right in his second "complaint", made in this same interview. He said: "I would be glad if the British Government and British public opinion would accept the facts that England is a European power, that her history is bound up with that of Western Europe, and that she is bound in duty to play her part in European development." Britain had "accepted" nothing of the kind, in 1949. This is understandable. What is truly frightening is that the British Labour Party had still not accepted a British role in Europe, honestly and realistically, 30 years later.

Adenauer's doubts about Britain's readiness to join with Europe, help Europe and belong to Europe, were justified. Labour leaders like Clement Attlee and Ernest Bevin never rid themselves of their deep suspicion of "the" Germans. Admittedly, there were some British statesmen – Winston Churchill and Anthony Eden, for instance – who were ready to revise their views and judge the government and people of the Federal Republic on their track record. Churchill took the lead in proposing the entry of the Federal Republic into the Council of Europe in August 1949, and in March 1950 called for German rearmament within a European or North Atlantic framework. But in his views about the Germans he was well ahead of the great majority of the British people – slow to take offence, but slower still to forgive or forget. Bismarck has been quoted as saying, sadly, about the British: "These people do not want to be loved by us."[14] What appears to be a kind of racial frigidity is, in fact, the product of a British insularity which to this day has not been broken down.

Good diplomatic relations with all three Western Occupying Powers were a necessity if progress was to be made towards achieving full German sovereignty. Adenauer established excellent personal relations with General Sir Brian (later Lord) Robertson, the British Military Governor, with Sir Ivone Kirkpatrick, Britain's High Commissioner, and thereafter with a series of British Ambassadors. But he did not seek real friendship with Britain in the way that he did with the United States and France. Plainly, Adenauer was aware of the mistake made by Bismarck's successors in failing to find firm friends. Equally plainly, he realized that the Federal Republic could not pursue independent policies, let alone aspire to being a Great Power. He moved with circumspection, apart from his premature proposal in March 1950 of a Franco-German "union". This was out of keeping with his usual method, of setting himself limited but attainable objectives and never losing sight of them.

Negotiations with the three Allied High Commissioners absorbed a great deal of Adenauer's time during his first three years in office. One of them, Kirkpatrick, paid an outstanding tribute to his pertinacity and finesse:

> In negotiation I found him a redoubtable but charming adversary. He certainly enjoyed the clash of wits at the conference table. He relished his brushes with the High Commission and he told me more than once that he had enjoyed our long and often dreary sessions over the Bonn treaties.
>
> He was always quick to detect any weakness in the opponent's armour and to drive his weapon through the chink. On the other hand, he was equally quick generously to recognise the strength in the opponent's case.
>
> He is always the rational man. The argument is conducted on the plane of reason with courtesy, humour and understanding. The tall figure sits stiff as a ramrod at the table. In carefully articulated German the sentences fall from his lips – impassive, authoritative sentences with a flavour of Chinese detachment. But from time to time events seemed to provoke him to anger. I once told him that he must never allow himself to get angry because excitement was bad for his health. "On the contrary," he replied with an impish grin, "that is what keeps me young".[15]

Kirkpatrick recalled one early incident. It had been his duty to introduce Britain's Field Marshal Lord Montgomery to Adenauer, and Montgomery, holding Kirkpatrick's coat lapel, remarked jokingly: "Does this chap give you much trouble?" To which Adenauer answered, with a twinkle in his eye: "Not half as much as I intend giving him."[16] He meant it, and he was as good as his word.

A bond between Adenauer and Kirkpatrick was their Catholicism. Between Adenauer and the American High Commissioner, John McCloy, there was a different bond – McCloy's wife was a distant relation of Adenauer's second wife,

Gussi, who died in 1948. McCloy was not aware of this before coming to Germany,[17] but it probably helped towards a firm friendship between the two men. McCloy at first found Adenauer "reserved and austere, and not above striking a pose or two for political effect".[18] But he was impressed by his wisdom, shrewdness and courage; while Adenauer was quickly won over by McCloy's warm-hearted interest in Germany. Even so, the streak of mischievousness in Adenauer's character came out on occasion – as when McCloy told him ingenuously that he "felt at home" in the High Commission offices on the Petersberg opposite Bonn, and Adenauer, pausing at the front door, answered: "In *that* case, Mr McCloy, after *you*!"

The first milestone in the progress of the Federal Republic towards sovereignty was the statement of aims of the Foreign Ministers of the three Western Powers on 10 November 1949, in Paris. These aims included the future extension of German rights in self-government and the incorporation of the Federal Republic in the European community. On the same day, the Allied High Commission empowered the Federal Government to sign trade agreements with other countries. Ten days later, the Federal Republic joined the International Authority for the Ruhr, which the Social Democratic Opposition sought to portray as a partial take-over by foreign powers of Germany's greatest industrial centre but which was, in fact, the first step along the road to European economic integration.

More important was the Petersberg Agreement, reached on 22 November. Seventeen major industrial plants were struck off the dismantling list, three others were to be almost totally spared, and dismantling ended in West Berlin, from which vast quantities of industrial equipment had in the past been removed to the Soviet Union. The Federal Republic, under the Agreement, could again build ocean-going ships for its own use and for export, although some restrictions on size and speed remained – until then only coastal ships could be built. The level of steel production was now to be held down to 11 million tons a year, adequate for German needs at the time, but in fact less than the figure previously agreed. Of immense psychological importance was the fact that the Federal Republic had been able to negotiate the Petersberg Agreement freely – no time-limit was set to the talks, and the High Commissioners estimated correctly that the Federal Government would wish to reach agreement as quickly as possible.

Yet Adenauer was violently assailed in the Bundestag. The

Communists claimed that he had signed away both the Ruhr and the chance of Germany being treated as a single economic unit. More serious was the Social Democratic attack; it culminated in Schumacher calling Adenauer "the Chancellor of the Allies" and being suspended for twenty days from Bundestag sittings. Schumacher was particularly incensed by the Trade Union leadership stating in Düsseldorf that the Petersberg Agreement represented a "serious effort" by the High Commissioners to meet German needs, and that the Ruhr Statute was acceptable. Schumacher, it must be remembered, was by now virtually a dying man; to the loss of his right arm in the First World War had been added the loss of his left leg, amputated in the previous year. Only a man of Schumacher's exceptional courage and dedication could have carried on in political life.

One SPD spokesman, Professor Carlo Schmid, called the Ruhr Statute "the hand at the throat of Germany" and claimed that "its fruits will be the nationalism of a dog on a chain".[19] This was purple prose, but one can understand SPD concern. Part of Germany's birthright was apparently being signed away, and the SPD contention was that what was needed was the internationalization of Europe, not of the Ruhr. In fact, this apparent German sacrifice was what was needed for progress towards European cooperation. It is probable that Adenauer was given a very clear hint to this effect.

Certainly he was told that other Allied concessions were on the way. On 15 December, McCloy signed an agreement with the Federal Government under which Marshall Plan aid would cease to be channelled through the occupation authorities but would be put at the direct disposal of Federal Ministries. In January 1950, Adenauer was empowered to send Consul-Generals to Washington, Paris and London. In March, the Federal Republic was accepted into the European Payments Union and was invited to send representatives to the Council of Europe, becoming a full member of that body in August.

On 9 May the French Foreign Minister, Robert Schuman, announced his plan for a European Coal and Steel Community. Rightly, he has been given great credit for this dramatic step, which was to lead eventually to the creation of the European Economic Community. The idea, however, was not new; a strikingly similar proposal had been made two years earlier by Karl Arnold, the Prime Minister of North Rhine – Westphalia, one of the ten *Laender* which made up the Federal Republic.[20] Schuman's initiative, however, was decisive; talks between the six countries concerned, France, the Federal Republic, Italy and the three Benelux states, began in June and were concluded in April 1951. The Federal Republic became a fully entitled and equal partner in the Community. It made, potentially, the biggest contribution to it, but at the same time secured the winding-up of the now superfluous International Authority for the Ruhr. Characteristically, Schumacher and the SPD refused to accept the Schuman Plan. Schumacher called it "a second capitulation" which would bring "the perpetuation of the Occupation Statute for fifty years".[21] "I warn you," Schumacher said in the Bundestag, "not to misuse the word 'European' in connection with a plan which embraces only this south-western corner of Europe." In one of his evocative flights of rhetoric he claimed that this south-west corner was "the home of capitalism, clericalism and cartels".

German agreement to join in the Schuman Plan talks brought a further Allied statement of aims, on 15 May 1950. The Federal Republic was to be accepted into "the community of free European nations", and when this decision had been fully implemented, all forms of control would be abolished. The Western Powers undertook to form a commission to study ways in which to divest themselves of the rights reserved to them under the "Occupation Statute", and they pledged themselves to work for the peaceful reunification of the whole of Germany.

Of course, the Federal Republic did not receive all these assurances and concessions for nothing. Two things were asked of the Federal Republic in return. The first was agreement to French plans to detach the Saar, apparently permanently, from the rest of Germany. The second demand, which was slower in coming, was German participation in the defence of Western Europe. SPD opposition was not to Allied concessions on their own – although Schumacher always maintained that too little was being given, too late – but to what was regarded as an unacceptable "package".

First, the Saar. This area, with a million inhabitants, the biggest coalfields in Western Germany outside the Ruhr and a thriving steel industry, had been detached once before, from 1919 to 1935, when 90 per cent of its voters opted in a referendum for the end of League of Nations trusteeship and return to Germany. In 1946 France brought the Saar into a customs-union with herself, sequestrated its coal-mines and increased the original area by over 30 per cent. Rigged elections in 1947 resulted in 48 out of 50 members of its *Land* Parliament belonging to parties favouring union with France. The other two members were Communists and no pro-German political party was allowed to take part in the elections. The French franc became the legal currency and in 1948 the Saar was proclaimed "an autonomous state, organized on a democratic and socialist basis, and economically united with France".

In June 1948, its railways were put under French management; in July, Saar "nationality" was invented; in December the teaching of French became compulsory in all schools. In the French Chamber of Deputies, Jacques Bardoux declared: "The Saar is not yet a free state; she must become one without delay. In fact, she must become a second Luxembourg."[22] The steelworks came under French control, and with them, the process of economic annexation was virtually completed. The population of the Saar was utterly cowed, and attempts to organize political opposition were scotched by the puppet government of Johannes Hoffmann. In March 1950 what appeared to be a final step was taken, when Schuman and Hoffmann signed twelve economic conventions, which provided for the autonomy of the Saar and the leasing of its coal-mines to France for a period of fifty years. The Saar, totally German in speech and customs, seemed to have been torn from the body of Germany for ever.

The Federal Government remained mute, up to March 1950. So did the Allied High Commission, in spite of its responsibility for all parts of Western Germany. Only the United States Government protested, in October 1948, declaring that the Saar remained legally part of Germany.[23] Moreover the French had evidently secured the complaisance of Adenauer. Later, he maintained that he was influenced by a meeting with Schuman, in October 1948:

> Schuman intimated that France regarded the return of the Saar to Germany as possible. France's main concern was the securing of her economic interests. Robert Schuman's views on this nerve-point of Franco-German relations had put my mind at rest. After our conversation I observed the greatest reticence on the Saar in my speeches and was under constant attack for it by Dr Schumacher.[24]

Adenauer was writing twenty years after the event and was trying to justify his Saar policy, but his explanation was flabby. A "possible" return of the Saar was not reassuring, and he quoted nothing from the conversation which merited his mind being

"put at rest". The announcement of the twelve economic
conventions, at all events, spurred the reticent Chancellor into
action; a protest was sent to the Allied High Commission. All
that came back was an "opinion", that the conventions had a
temporary character only (50 years seems rather more than
that!), and would have to be confirmed in a German Peace
Treaty.

At this late stage, Adenauer called for "democratic rights" for
the Saarlanders; they had been deprived of them for five years.
After much badgering, he managed to obtain a letter from
Schuman which said:

> The French Government declares that it acts in the name of
> the Saar, on the basis of its present status, but that it does
> not regard the signing of the [Schuman Plan] Agreement by
> the Federal Government as a recognition of the status of the
> Saar ... It does not consider that the Agreement anticipates
> the final status of the Saar, which is to be settled by a Peace
> Treaty or by an agreement concluded in place of a Peace
> Treaty.

Adenauer's comment was that "in the treatment of the Saar
Question what mattered most was to keep one's nerves steady".[25]
At least the Schuman letter helped to secure the Bundestag's
approval of the European Coal and Steel Community Plan. But it
offered little comfort to the Saarlanders; no pro-German
political activity was allowed, no pro-German newspaper could
be printed, only 80,000 German newspapers, or one to every 300
of the population, could be imported, over 2,000 Saarlanders had
been expelled from their homes in five years, and students were
debarred from studying at German Universities. The Saar police,
under the instructions of the Minister of the Interior, a
Frenchman, M Edgar Hector, harassed everyone suspected of
pro-German sympathies.

In 1952 there were, once again, rigged elections, with all
genuinely pro-German parties banned save the Communists.
Sixty per cent voted for the pro-French parties, and more than
25 per cent deliberately spoilt their ballot-papers. The official
line now was that the area would be "Europeanized", and even
that grimy, unprepossessing Saarbruecken should become the
European capital. In 1953 and 1954 the issue of the Saar
slumbered until in October of that year Adenauer met with the
French Prime Minister, Pierre Mendès-France, and agreed that
the Saarlanders should vote in a referendum on a Saar Statute

which would link the Europeanized area with France. Free elections would be held three months after the referendum.

In his *Memoirs*, Adenauer claimed that he knew the Saarlanders would vote as "good Germans" in the referendum, which was fixed for 22 October 1955.[26] In his view, "The Saar was in no way sold. The population of the Saar was given the opportunity of freely developing politically and economically, and implementing their chosen decision at a peace treaty."[27] This was not true; the Saarlanders had been kept under heavy pressure, their political institutions and their economy had been placed under strict French control, and their morale undermined by ten years of bullying. A Europeanized Saar would never return to Germany. Adenauer did well to get agreement to free elections after the referendum, but he had to pay an additional price for that – agreement to canalize the Moselle river, giving French Lorraine cheap water-transport for the Ruhr coking coal which it needed and for the iron-ore and steel products which could be shipped to Rotterdam and beyond. Moreover, acting on the bad advice of his Foreign Ministry, Adenauer told the Saarlanders to vote for the Statute in a speech which he made in the Ruhr town of Bochum only a few days before the referendum. Foreign Ministry experts believed that 70 to 80 per cent would vote for the Statute and Europeanization.[28]

Nothing of the kind happened. Sixty-three per cent rejected the Statute, and although the pro-German parties had only a short time in which to organize, 65 per cent voted for them on 18 December 1955. On 31 January 1956, the new Saar Government declared the area to be part of Germany and formal reunion took place on 1 January 1957. Opinions differed sharply over Adenauer's own role in the Saar Question. One of his closest personal advisers, Dr Hans Globke, believed that he did the best that he could, by securing a free vote for the Saarlanders, and that he could not break the spirit of his agreement with Mendès-France – so his Bochum speech was proof of his honest intentions towards France.[29] The Federal Minister of the Interior at the time, Dr Gerhard Schroeder, agrees with this view; Adenauer had to "marry" his obligations to France and to the people of the Saar, while giving a chance for a "European" solution.[30] Adenauer remained discreetly silent in his *Memoirs*, but years later, when visiting the Saar and looking down from the hillside at the great bend of the river at Mettlach, was heard to say: "Thank God that it has been possible to reunite this land with Germany."[31] The truth was probably that Adenauer was prepared to sacrifice the Saar, while playing for higher stakes – the full acceptance of a sovereign Federal Republic as a member of the European community. Certainly, he miscalculated the mood of the Saarlanders; at the very least he risked their future unnecessarily. Luck, rather than his usual good judgement, saved him and saved the situation. It is a sombre reflection that, had the Saar been Europeanized against the underlying wishes of its inhabitants, and had come under French tutelage, bitter feelings would have been stirred up which could have put an end to Adenauer's own dream of lasting Franco-German friendship.

The second sacrifice – if sacrifice it really was – that Adenauer had to make in order to restore German sovereignty was participation in the defence of Europe. The demilitarization of Germany had been a prime Allied aim. By the time that war ended, for that matter, the great majority of the German people desperately desired peace and were, thereafter, bound to be in favour of disarmament. Adenauer had his own, considered views on the matter. Somewhat ingenuously, he wrote in his *Memoirs* that "in November, 1949, the foreign press suddenly began to discuss the question of the rearmament of Germany".[32] In fact, it was Adenauer himself who opened the discussion on 3 December, in an interview which he gave to John P. Leacacos, a correspondent of the *Cleveland Plain Dealer* of America. In it, he said that he would be prepared to consider the provision of a German contingent in the armed forces of a European Federation – he did not want to see an independent German Army re-created, or even German mercenaries serving under foreign colours. Adenauer said much the same thing in a press conference on 5 December, and again, to the *Frankfurter Allgemeine Zeitung*, on 7 December. It was his habit to "fly a kite" by giving the occasional newspaper interview, and talking strictly about what was on his mind. On this occasion he was determined that discussion should continue; on 8 December he told a CDU meeting in Düsseldorf that a German contribution to the defence of Europe would not diminish the opposition of the German people to war. On 9 December he told the press that the para-military "People's Police" which had been recruited in the Soviet Zone amounted to "a regular army".[33] On 10 December he asked the *Neue Zuercher Zeitung* if the Soviet threat to the western world were not a greater threat than a German contingent brigaded with the armed forces of other nations.[34]

Finally, he told the Bundestag on 16 December: "Even in the event of the Allies demanding in a categorical form a German contribution to European security, there can be no question whatever of the establishment of a German Army. The utmost that we would be prepared to consider would be a German contingent within the framework of a European Army." The formulation was brilliant: Adenauer, in front of the Bundestag, appeared to be opposing movement towards creating an independent German Army, and suggesting a compromise. Yet it was he who had raised the subject in the first place! In his *Memoirs* he made his underlying purpose perfectly plain: "Rearmament might be the way to gaining full sovereignty for the Federal Republic. This made it the essential question of our political future."[35]

Events were to play into his hands. The Western Powers were still suffering from the near-panic caused by the Berlin Blockade. The Soviet Union was manifestly not disarming, and the creation of the East German "People's Police" was highly provocative. The Soviet Union was blocking all attempts to secure an equitable solution of the "German Question", and would continue to do so. Winston Churchill's proposal for the rearmament of the Federal Republic came on 16 March 1950 in the House of Commons. Adenauer kept the pot boiling by appealing for a security guarantee for the Federal Republic on 2 April; this included a reminder of the vulnerability of the long and rambling interzonal frontier and of the presence of over thirty Red Army divisions on the other side of it, some of them only 60 to 70 miles from the Rhine. Ironically, Allied military experts continued to work on legislation to prevent German rearmament, and this actually went into effect on 1 June 1950.

Three weeks later the Korean War broke out. Once again, Churchill took the initiative; on 11 August, in the Council of Europe in Strasbourg, he proposed the creation of a European Army, with West German participation. Adenauer added his own gloss eight days later; he proposed West German "defence units" as a counterpoise to the East German "People's Police". Some commentators surmised that this suggested that Adenauer had changed his mind about a European Army. It was more likely that he saw these "volunteer units with a total strength of 150,000 men"[36] as a half-way stage to the creation of regular military formations. It was, at least, an immediate step which could counter the menace of the "People's Police".

Adenauer was now determined to force the pace. On 29 August he compiled a memorandum, urging a German contribution to a European Army, and adding the demand that the Allied High Commissioners should become Ambassadors and the Federal Republic should enter into normal diplomatic relations with its Western partners. The memorandum was rushed to the Frankfurt offices of the US High Commissioner, John McCloy, for France's High Commissioner, André François-Poncet, would become "Chairman of the month" on 1 September, and Adenauer was pretty sure that he would hold the memorandum up. It arrived in time; McCloy, who was on his way to a Western Foreign Ministers Conference in New York, took the document with him. On 5 September, McCloy told the press in Washington that he had personally recommended a German military contribution to the defence of Europe to the US President.

There were other repercussions. On 11 September the Minister of the Interior, Gustav Heinemann, resigned. He was a declared pacifist and he believed that nothing should be done which jeopardized the chances of reunifying Germany, through agreement with the Soviet Union. He left the CDU, formed his own neutralist political party, and later took his few followers with him into the SPD. The reason that he gave for resigning was the simpler and indeed operative one that Adenauer had failed to consult his Cabinet before taking his momentous step. On 19 September the Western Foreign Ministers issued a communiqué forecasting revision of the Occupation Statute, the creation of a Federal German Foreign Ministry, and the pooling of German defence equipment for the common cause of European security. So far, so good, from Adenauer's point of view; there was better to come. On 26 October France's Prime Minister, Réné Pleven, proposed the creation of a European Army, with German participation, and the National Assembly endorsed his plan by a vote of 343 to 225. So did the NATO Council a few days later, with certain reservations; the prevailing NATO view was that the European Army should come within an Atlantic framework, and that the supreme commander should be America's own General Dwight Eisenhower. To cap everything, the Foreign Ministers of the three Western Occupying Powers met in Brussels and on 19 December confirmed the decisions to replace the Occupation Statute by a system of treaties, and to go ahead with a German military contribution to Europe.

Adenauer's 29 August memorandum had succeeded beyond his most optimistic expectations, but there was much to do before his proposals could be implemented. In the first place, the Pleven Plan was utterly impractical. Divisions made up of mixed nationalities could not have worked – the language problem alone would have ensured that. There would have been additional problems of manning, equipment and command. Then, neither the Americans nor the British could make their minds up on what should supercede the Pleven Plan. There was a prolonged period of shilly-shallying, during which Adenauer repeatedly explained that opposition to rearmament in Germany would vanish, if full sovereignty were restored and a position of equality achieved in Europe. Once again he got his way; on 6 March 1951, the Allied High Commission revised the Occupation Statute and gave the Federal Republic control over its foreign relations. Adenauer took over the post of Foreign Minister, in addition to the Chancellorship, on 15 March.

The Federal Republic was promised membership of the International Monetary Fund and the World Bank, and on 2 May became a full member of the Council of Europe. More important, a new round of talks with the High Commissioners began on the Petersberg on 10 May. They dragged on until the summer holidays, were resumed in September, and continued into 1952. Much was happening in the meantime: the Western Powers officially ended a state of war with the Federal Republic, UNESCO opened its doors, Adenauer was invited to London, and, at long last, agreement was reached in May 1952 on ending the Allied Occupation of Western Germany. In Bonn, the so-called "Deutschlandvertrag", or "German Treaty", gave the Federal Republic sovereignty on 26 May. On the next day the Paris Agreement on creating a European Defence Community was initialled; the EDC was to include France, the Federal Republic, Italy and the three Benelux countries, while Britain added an undertaking to come to its help if any member state were attacked.

Before the year was out, Adenauer would open, as its President, the inaugural meeting of the Council of Ministers of the "Schuman Plan" European Coal and Steel Community, in Luxembourg. At this very first meeting, it was decided to begin work on a treaty which would create a European Political Community – one of Adenauer's own dearest wishes. In two respects, then, 1952 closed in triumph for the Federal Chancellor. He had won back for the German people an equal place in the European comity of nations, and he had restored German sovereignty. There were, admittedly, two clouds on the horizon. The first was the absence of Britain from the two European institutions which really mattered – the Coal and Steel

Community and the EDC. The second was the continuing
uncertainty as to when France would ratify the Bonn and Paris
Agreements – other countries concerned were ready to do so.

When Adenauer met Churchill in London in December 1951,
there had been some friendly badinage. Churchill asked him if
he was a Prussian. When Adenauer denied it, Churchill declared
that Prussians were "villains" (a wild generalization for a man
who was so well-read in European history!). Adenauer slyly
remarked that his chief German opponent, Schumacher, was
indeed a Prussian (this was correct: Schumacher was born at
Kulm, on the Vistula).[37] Churchill was friendly, but in another
talk with Adenauer he made a drawing on a menu card of
"western civilization". He drew three concentric circles –
representing the USA, a united Europe, and Britain with her
Commonwealth. Adenauer noted cryptically that Britain's
attitude had not changed;[38] what he meant was that Britain still
did not feel she belonged in Europe.

The French position was obscure. The Socialists, led by Eduard
Herriot, opposed German rearmament. There were others,
especially on the Right, who disliked any surrender of French
military independence. France was going through an extremely
difficult period of her history. Prime Ministers came and went,
there was a sad lack of coherence in her political life and of self-
confidence among her people, and it was clear that France had
not yet recovered from the shock of defeat in 1940 and the shame
of four years of German occupation. Yet it was assumed that
France would ratify the EDC agreement, sooner or later. It
seemed inconceivable that progress towards European military,
as well as economic and political integration, would be held up
by a single state and essentially out of a feeling of weakness.

There was one other, less obvious fly in the ointment: no
progress whatever towards German reunification was in sight.
When the idea of a European Defence Community was first
mooted, the Soviet Union lost no time in proposing a Four
Power Conference on Germany. The Conference, which
convened intermittently from March to June 1951, achieved
nothing – in fact, agreement was never reached even on an
agenda. No immediate Soviet interest was shown in a fourteen-
point plan for all-German elections put forward by the Federal
Government in September 1951; but in 1952 Western and Soviet
notes on the subject were exchanged over a period of six
months. Once again, there was no progress. In press conferences
and interviews Adenauer made it plain that he was deeply

sceptical about Soviet intentions, for the Russians were continuing to arm the East Germans, suppress civic liberties and human rights, and seize every opportunity of trying to undermine the credibility of the Federal Republic. Adenauer insisted therefore on a militarily strong and alert Western Alliance – although probably less because of fear of a possible Soviet invasion than because of the political pressure which the Russians would apply, if they felt that the West was not prepared to defend itself.[39]

The end of 1952, then, brought the virtual completion of the first phase of the Federal Republic's existence, that of the gradual loosening of the bonds of foreign occupation and the eventual regaining of German sovereignty and independence. It was an astonishingly full and productive phase of German history. A democratic form of government had been set up and consolidated. A free German state had, once again, a free press, a judiciary which did not have to operate under duress, free and independent trade unions, educational and communal institutions which had been rid of their Nazi ideas and associations. Tremendous economic progress had taken place, under Ludwig Erhard's psychologically perceptive direction (see Chapter 6).

This was a crucial phase in what can only be described as the "normalization" of German life. True, there were awkward problems which had still not been wholly solved, like coming to terms with the past and eliminating the lingering influence of Nazi ideas and unteachable Nazi personalities. But a great majority of Germans had shown every readiness to cast aside wild dreams and inflated ambitions. An overdone obeisance to the State was being replaced by a welcome readiness of the average citizen to evolve his own ideas, and stand up for them. In the three and a bit years of Federal government, the people of West Germany had moved a very long way from the fatalistic and obsequious mentality implicit in the 99 per cent "Yes votes" of the Nazi era. The older German virtues were being rediscovered; it may be that commonsense was being added to them.

In all of this Konrad Adenauer played an absolutely outstanding part. Urbane, calm and clear-headed, he led his people with greater wisdom and vision than shown by any other European statesmen of the twentieth century. His brand of paternalism was exactly what was needed in these early years. So was his austerity, dedication and sense of self-discipline. Ahead, in 1953, lay Federal elections, and a host of problems still to be solved. He was 77 years old, and as fresh as a daisy – a tribute to his regular and sober habits, his moderation in eating and drinking, and his love of exercise and fresh air. He faced the future with the utmost confidence.

1. Terence Prittie. *Germany Divided*. Boston, 1960.
2. Paul Weymar. *Konrad Adenauer*. London, 1957.
3. Ibid.
4. Ibid.
5. *Manchester Guardian*, 9 September 1949.
6. The London *Times*, 21 September 1949.
7. Anneliese Poppinga. *Meine Erinnerungen an Konrad Adenauer*. Stuttgart, 1970.
8. Hans Peter Schwarz. *Konrad Adenauer. Seine Deutschland und Aussen-politik 1945/63*. Mainz, 1971.
9. Charles de Gaulle. *Memoirs of Hope*. London, 1971.
10. Brian Connell. *Watcher on the Rhine*. London, 1957.
11. Sir Christopher Steel, in conversation with author, May 1969.
12. Sir Ivone Kirkpatrick. *The Inner Circle*. London, 1959.
13. *Manchester Guardian*, 9 September 1949.
14. Grand Admiral Alfred von Tirpitz. *My Memoirs*. London, 1919.
15. Sir Ivone Kirkpatrick, op. cit.
16. Ibid.
17. John McCloy, in letter to the author, December 1969.
18. Ibid.
19. Terence Prittie. *This is Germany*. Edited by Art Settel. New York, 1950.
20. Karl Arnold, in conversation with the author, December 1948.
21. Kurt Schumacher, in interview with the *Manchester Guardian*, 10 April 1951.
22. Terence Prittie. *The Listener*, March 1952.
23. Konrad Adenauer. *Memoirs*, Vol 1. London, 1966.
24. Ibid.
25. Ibid.
26. Konrad Adenauer. *Memoirs*, Vol 2. Stuttgart, 1966.
27. Ibid.
28. F. Ray Willis. *France, Germany and the new Europe*. Stanford, 1965.
29. Dr Hans Globke, in conversation with the author, March 1971.
30. Dr Gerhard Schroeder, in letter to the author, April 1970.
31. Will McBride and Hans Werner Graf von Finckenstein. *Adenauer. Ein Portraet*. Starnberg, 1965.
32. Konrad Adenauer. *Memoirs*, Vol 1.
33. Paul Weymar, op. cit.
34. *Neue Zuercher Zeitung*, 11 December 1949.
35. Konrad Adenauer. *Memoirs*, Vol 1.
36. Ibid.
37. Ibid.
38. Ibid.
39. Hans Peter Schwarz, op. cit.

CHAPTER FOUR

Germany into Europe

Adenauer's mind was very much concentrated in 1953 on the further steps needed to bring the Federal Republic into Europe. What, immediately, was needed was ratification by all of their signatories of the Bonn and Paris Agreements. The Bundestag itself ratified them only on 19 March 1953, and this delay was probably based on a desire not to hurry the French over their all-important decision. The French, at all events, showed absolutely no intention of being hurried; throughout the whole of 1953 they dickered, and their hesitations had an effect on Italy and the three Benelux countries. They, too, failed to ratify the Paris Agreement on the EDC. For Adenauer these delays were deeply frustrating; his sole consolation was his belief that the Paris Agreement would, eventually, be ratified and that another, great stride towards European union would be taken.

Meanwhile, he had to content himself with minor gains. The European Coal and Steel Community began work in February, and decided that all restrictions on West German steel production would end from 1 May. A Cultural Agreement with the USA was signed in April and came into force, along with trade and friendship agreements, two months later. The Bundestag approved the German–Israeli Debts Agreement, concluded in Luxembourg on 10 September 1952. The Agreement was a simple and necessary act of reparation, but Adenauer did not have it all his own way in the Bundestag. Only three small parties opposed the bill – the Communists, mainly because not one cent of compensation was being paid out to victims of Nazism in Soviet-controlled East Germany, let alone to the State of Israel. But the bulk of the FDP abstained, although it was a partner in the Government coalition. The outcome, 288 votes to 34, looked good on paper, but there were 86 abstentions. The Government, and the West German press, hastily glossed over the somewhat disturbing thought that nearly half as many members of the Bundestag, as had voted for the bill, were unable to support it. One must recall the phrase of the Federal President, Theodor Heuss, that the German people did not need to feel guilt for the misdeeds of the Nazis, but must feel shame. Shame, surely, should have ensured an almost unanimous vote in favour of making due reparation to the small country which had accepted, and was in the process of resettling, the survivors among Hitler's Jewish victims.

Hitler's appalling persecution of the Jews was one painful legacy from the past; another was the awkward fact that there were millions of ex-Nazis living in the Federal Republic, who would only die out slowly – even in 1979 there are inevitably plenty still left. Small, "neo-Nazi" parties had appeared on the political stage from 1948 onwards, and a few completely unrepentant ex-Nazis continued to sit in the Bundestag. Ex-Nazis had found their way back into the judiciary and government service. Adenauer's view was that only ex-Nazis who had committed criminal acts, and remained unrepentant, should not be entrusted with positions of responsibility and influence.[1] He employed as one of his closest confidants Dr Hans Globke, who had helped draft the "commentary" to Hitler's infamous Nuremberg "Racial Decrees" – knowing that Globke had subsequently tried to help individual Jews and was utterly committed to helping establish a democratic Federal state. The Chancellor was bitterly criticized, but remained impervious. His attitude was defended in, perhaps, the most understandable terms, by the US High Commissioner, John McCloy.[2] He compared Adenauer's attitude to that of Abraham Lincoln towards "Southerners", after the end of the American Civil War. Both men wanted national reconciliation.

In 1951 came the first serious neo-Nazi challenge. Ex-General Otto Remer, who had arrested the conspirators of the 20 July 1944 plot against Hitler, formed a "Socialist Reichs Party" in *Land* Lower Saxony, and in May obtained 400,000 votes in the *Land* elections. This was 11 per cent of the poll, and other extremist parties collected another 27 per cent. Lower Saxony was a partly backwoodsy and politically reactionary area, although its capital of Hanover was an SPD stronghold. But a few months later, the SRP did almost as well in Bremen, supposedly as progressive as any *Land* of the Federal Republic. The Federal Government felt obliged to act: Remer was sent to prison for slandering the men of the German Resistance to Hitler, and the SRP was banned. Its lineal successor, the "German Reich Party", failed to attract anything like the same support.

Now, in 1953, a more disturbing challenge to democratic authority took shape. A small group of ex-Nazis, led by Josef Goebbels' former deputy in the Nazi Ministry of Propaganda, Dr Werner Naumann, evolved a plan for infiltrating at least three political parties, with the FDP the most important among them. Naumann hoped in this way to create a body of 40 to 50 Bundestag members who, after the 1953 elections, would hold the balance in the Bundestag and might even dictate the course of German history. Later, a single Nationalist Party could be formed. A man of suave and sinister charm, Naumann was a far more formidable adversary than Remer and his bully-boys.

The Western Powers still possessed reserved rights, and one was that of taking action if German democracy were threatened. The British High Commissioner, Sir Ivone Kirkpatrick, ordered the arrest of Naumann and other leaders of the conspiracy on 14 January 1953. He called them "a pirate gang, which intends to seize the ship by gaining control of the bridge, then board other ships and collect a nice little navy".[3] Adenauer displayed a certain ambivalence; he was probably glad that dirty work had been done on his behalf, but he could not ignore the popular reaction against Allied "interference". He was also maddened by the simultaneous publication by the US High Commission of a public opinion poll showing that 44 per cent of those asked thought there was more good than bad in Nazism, and only 34 per cent thought Nazism was thoroughly bad. Ironically these results were published by mistake! Adenauer told the press that he had been consulted by the British High Commissioner and that Naumann and his cronies should not be allowed to return to political life. But in a radio interview he said that "A real threat to the security of the Federal Republic does not exist in any way … A few ex-Nazis don't add up to National Socialism. We have a viable, a watchful democracy."[4] Adenauer was never above using Macchiavellian tactics, in the national interest. Kirkpatrick's action was all to his advantage in the long run. Naumann and his friends vanished from the political scene, and there has been no dangerous threat to German democracy since.

1953 was to produce another, more serious event in German history. On 17 June a popular rising began in East Germany against the crypto-Communist, so-called "Socialist Unity" regime installed there by the Russians. The rising had nothing to do with East–West differences in the political field, or with Western "propaganda". It was entirely spontaneous and was triggered by the raising of "work-norms" on which workers' wages were based. Stalin had died in March; the expectation was that the people of the satellite East German state would be given easier living conditions as a result. Some restrictions were, in fact, eased, but not the work-norms; the Soviet leadership was determined to raise output in this, their most industrious satellite state. The rising was preluded by a peaceful demonstration in East Berlin on 16 June. On the next day it spread to every town of over 50,000 inhabitants, save Plauen in Saxony, and the demands voiced everywhere were for free elections and a secret ballot, as well as better working conditions. The rising was repressed by the Red Army with the utmost brutality; hundreds of unarmed workers were shot down – 30 in the streets of Leipzig alone were killed and over 100 wounded – about 50 death sentences took place after the rising ended, there were 20,000 arrests and 7,000 East German citizens simply "vanished". Some died in the concentration camps which the Russians had taken over from the Nazis; others were deported to Siberia and the Urals.

The Western Allies did nothing. It could be argued that there was nothing that they could do. But Berlin was still, theoretically, under Four Power jurisdiction, and the Allies had every right to make their presence felt in East Berlin and at least demand the end of military action in its streets. The Federal Government in Bonn was helpless; all that it could do was to protest and call for immediate steps to bring about the peaceful reunification of Germany. Willy Brandt, now a leading member of the SPD and the understudy in Berlin of its Governing Mayor, Ernst Reuter, had this to say about the rising:[5]

> This could have been a key moment. We know rather more now than we did then; there was real crisis in the Soviet leadership and the German Question really was in the forefront of the Russians' minds; the Russians might have agreed to German reunification, with the Communist (Socialist Unity) Party in the minority. But what then

happened – the East German rising – actually set things back. There was still a chance for the Western Powers to demand negotiations over the *whole* of Berlin. As it happened, the sector boundaries were closed during the rising. Nothing could be, maybe nothing in fact *was* done about it. In a way, this episode was a forerunner to the much later building of the Berlin Wall.

The results of the rising were mainly negative. The Russians brought the Red Army in East Germany up to a strength of 400,000 men, with 7,500 tanks, 8,000 artillery weapons and 800 combat planes, while the East German armed forces were given a standing strength of 190,000, with their own reserve of 120,000 and other para-military units totalling 80,000 men. The Russians had a ready-made excuse for this 30 per cent increase of armed strength; it was to safeguard East Germany from internal and external "subversion". In the second place, the rising did indeed doom future efforts to reunify Germany. The Russians could not fail to be aware of their unpopularity even in their own zone of occupation; there was no chance of using it as a spring-board to gain control over the whole of Germany. Future East–West exchanges of views about reunification, including those at the Four Power Berlin Conference in January 1954, were without real meaning or purpose.

Finally, the impotence and irresolution of the Western Powers confirmed Adenauer in what can best be described as a "play safe" policy over reunification. The Western Powers did not lift a finger to help the people of East Berlin, let alone the seventeen million inhabitants of the Soviet Zone beyond its gates. What, then, could the Federal Government in Bonn do? Adenauer argued that Western Europe must continue to unite and consolidate its forces, and that the Federal Republic should cooperate to the full with its western neighbours. The West should set out to negotiate from a position of strength – although it is not clear how or why Adenauer believed that the East–West balance of strength would move in favour of his own side. The East German rising was to be of considerable value to him and the CDU in the Federal elections, held on 6 September 1953. Like him, the people of Western Germany wanted to "play safe", after the tragic failure and waste of the East German rising.

The elections hinged on the personality and record of Adenauer. In 1949, Ludwig Erhard had played an almost equally prominent part, as the man who had restored economic normality. By 1953 West Germans were taking prosperity very much for granted. In 1949, too, Kurt Schumacher had been a powerful adversary. But Schumacher died in August 1952. Adenauer paid him a suitable tribute – "Despite many differences which divided us in our political concepts, we were yet united in our common goal to do everything possible for the benefit and well-being of our people."[6] Schumacher's political impact had been reduced by chronic ill-health and a desperate impatience to achieve results while time was running out for him. But his courage, personal integrity and probity, and fearless denunciation of the injustices perpetrated by the Russians, had won him admiration and popular esteem. His successor, Erich Ollenhauer, comfortably rotund, innately decent and averagely competent, was not the man to lead the SPD to victory. Nor did he: the SPD did achieve a modest gain, from 131 to 150 seats in the Bundestag, but the CDU vote went up from 31 to 45 per cent and its seats from 139 to 244. This gave the party an absolute majority of the 487 seats in the Bundestag.

The ghost of Weimar was banished. Only six parties were represented in the new Bundestag, and one of them – the residual Centre Party – held only three seats and would soon merge with the CDU. The ghost of Hitler was banished, too; not a single member of a right-wing radical party was elected, although there was a distinctive ex-Nazi element in the newly-created BHE Refugee Party. The Communist vote dropped to a miserable 2·2 per cent, and it failed to secure a single seat. Three years later it was banned, on the grounds that its members were working to undermine and destroy German democracy. This had always been their aim, although it might have been wiser to let them go on working in the open.

The Parliamentary system had been fully vindicated, and Adenauer had won a tremendous personal triumph. He had been at the top of his form, speaking all over the country, never retiring for the night before 2 a.m. and preserving the utmost good humour – during the campaign he told his Press Chief, Felix von Eckardt: "Do me a favour, and don't sit in the front row at my meetings. When I see your bored face, I can't think of a thing to say".[7] He had been helped by a thoroughly successful visit to the United States, just before election campaigning began. Everywhere he had been greeted with admiration and respect, and had enjoyed himself. The only bad moment on the trip came when his plane several times overshot the runway at Denver in a snowstorm. While his companions either remained deathly still, or muttered in terror, Adenauer sat placidly reading a book about botany.[8] For a man approaching 80, his nerve was as remarkable as his energy; not for nothing had he called himself "70 per cent of the Cabinet".[9]

There were Cabinet changes; three new Ministers require special mention. Gerhard Schroeder, a 43 year-old ex-barrister, became Minister of the Interior. His appointment was criticized in some quarters because he had been a member of the Nazi Party. It was perhaps more relevant that he had married a girl in 1940 who had one Jewish parent, and that he left the Party before the end of the war – both acts of courage. He was supremely reserved – his family came from Friesland, whose people are the least demonstrative of all Germans and most akin to their erstwhile "cousins" across the water, in East Anglia. Cool and efficient, he was a fervent admirer of Adenauer – he talked of a "father-and-son relationship"[10] – and a special asset to the CDU, as a pillar of the Evangelical Churches.[11]

Heinrich von Brentano, who was to become Foreign Minister, had none of Schroeder's drive and dynamism. Outwardly, he was a little flabby, even ineffectual and colourless. Adenauer found him an appropriate butt for his sometimes mordant wit. When Brentano came puffing up the 53 steps which led through the garden of the Chancellor's home to his front door, Adenauer remarked "And this is the new German youth I'm always hearing about!"[12] In Paris, on one occasion, Brentano and Adenauer got into a lift together; they wanted to go two storeys higher, but headed for the basement when Brentano pressed the button – "The only time," as some wag remarked, "that the Chancellor ever let Brentano take the initiative."[13] Brentano's strength lay in his selfless devotion to the cause of European unity and his sincere belief in the efficacy of Adenauer's foreign policy. One of his phrases was, "We cannot be assured of the reunification of Germany, if we begin by surrendering the security of the Federal Republic".[14] He became Foreign Minister only in 1955, but was already being groomed for the post while leading the CDU on the floor of the Bundestag.

The third new appointment of importance was that of Franz-Josef Strauss, an ebullient and immensely energetic Bavarian, a brilliant orator who could be mistaken for a tub-thumper if one failed to note the clarity and sense of what he was saying. His rhetoric had infuriated Schumacher, who referred to him as "a thundering nullity".[15] Immensely ambitious, he turned down

Adenauer's proposal that he should become Minister for Family Affairs, grudgingly accepted a Ministry without Portfolio, and worked his way into, first the Ministry for Atomic Affairs and then the Ministry of Defence. Strauss would later become Chairman of the Bavarian "Christian Social Union" branch of the CDU, and Bavaria's "favourite son". Under his leadership, the CSU would move towards semi-independence, as a "fourth force" in West German politics. He himself quickly became the most controversial figure in the whole political arena, feared in some quarters, admired in others, and compared by friends and foes to a Roman gladiator, a tank and even a brick oven![16]

In his second Government, Adenauer maintained all the control that he had exercised in the first. He continued to look after foreign affairs until Brentano's appointment in 1955. He kept a close watch over defence matters – the Ministry of Defence was only created in 1956, and for the time being defence planning was carried out by the "Amt Blank", an embryonic department headed by the pliable and mediocre Christian Trade Unionist, Theodor Blank. In the Ministry of the Interior, Schroeder would do his bidding. Finance and economics were subjects about which he knew next to nothing and was ready to leave to experts. But it was clear that he was doing more than the average head of government, and there were already mutterings about his brand of "Chancellor-democracy", in which personal policies played a bigger part than the role of Parliament or the will of the people.

Adenauer, possibly as a result of his long experience as Mayor of Cologne, never hesitated to go to friends and confidants for advice which might later be translated into operative political decisions. If he wanted a view on finance and economics he consulted Robert Pferdemenges, the Cologne banker who was an old family friend. His "moral tutor" was Cardinal Frings of Cologne, and his publicity expert was Ernst Bach, a burly ex-member of the "Free Corps" which continued to do battle on the Polish border after the First World War. But Adenauer went beyond merely taking outside advice periodically; he formed his personal "bodyguard" of regular advisers and their influence began to rival that of his Cabinet Ministers.

There is nothing unusual about "kitchen Cabinets". Mrs Golda Meir governed through her own in Israel, while President John Kennedy surrounded himself with a notorious band of "whizz-kids". Britain, for the last hundred years, has been governed increasingly by the Civil Service (and with what increasingly deplorable results!). Adenauer may have taken matters further than a Mrs Meir or a President Kennedy, for one of his salient characteristics was a highly developed sense of responsibility. One Government servant who worked for years in the Federal Chancellery considered that "he regarded the Germans as a sick people".[17] Certainly, he believed implicitly in his own judgement, given the advice in private which made what his critics called his public "lonely decisions" possible.

Otto Lenz was Adenauer's "personal expert" on information policy. He was unpunctual, gregarious and indiscreet.[18] He dabbled in secret service work as well, interfered with the Federal Press Office, and finally lost the Chancellor's confidence when he proposed the creation of a "Super-Ministry of Information" which, in some respects, bore an unfortunate resemblance to the Nazi Ministry of Propaganda. Where foreign policies were concerned, Adenauer relied on Herbert Blankenhorn and Professor Walter Hallstein. Blankenhorn was an apostle of *Erfüllungspolitik*, the policy of fulfilment of the terms imposed by victor on vanquished, and never tired of explaining that dignified initial acquiescence and subsequent negotiation could have saved the Weimar Republic.[19] Blankenhorn's wonderful memory and sound political instinct must have been invaluable in helping Adenauer to deal with the Allied authorities. Hallstein's usefulness lay, rather, in the field of European relations; he was a total believer in European political and economic unity. Something of a theorist, he evolved the "Hallstein Doctrine", under which the Federal Republic would reject diplomatic relations with countries recognizing the East German "Democratic" Republic, created by Soviet decree on 25 March 1954. Adenauer needed to have a butt, even in his small "political family". Hallstein was what one of Adenauer's daughters called a "willing victim" (*dankbares Opfer*).[20] He never resented the Chancellor's jests; nor were they ill-intended.

The key adviser in the Chancellery, however, was Dr Hans Globke, perhaps the most controversial appointment in the history of the Federal Republic. Adenauer offered him the post of State Secretary in the Chancellery in 1949; Globke turned it down, on account of his political past as a servant of the Nazi regime. He accepted in 1953 and became the hub of Adenauer's personal office, with the efficiency of a computer and the discretion of a mole. He informed Adenauer on the work of the different Ministries, briefed Ministers on Adenauer's own decisions, looked after personnel policy and supervised the

Chancellery archives. (He kept his own, extensive archives equally meticulously. Showing them to the author, he discovered that one document had been mislaid; his comment was "einfach unglaublich" (frankly unbelievable)).[21] Globke was both Chief of Staff and major-domo to Adenauer. He was dedicated to his job, and without ambition – several times he asked to be allowed to resign, on the grounds of poor health.[22] Adenauer always refused his request. He regarded Globke as indispensable, and on occasions when the Chancellor was ill, as in 1955, the State Secretary was the only official who consulted at his bedside.

Arnulf Baring[23] has painted a somewhat negative picture of the Chancellery office at work in Bonn's Palais Schaumburg; the Chancellor, he felt, was prone to making favourites, playing his personal advisers off against each other, and encouraging intrigue and envy. He compared Adenauer with the worst kind of schoolmaster. Certainly, Adenauer enjoyed "atmosphere" and had a genius for picking on human failings, but the Chancellery on the whole functioned well and smoothly. Indeed, the complaint which might have been made was that it was in one sense too efficient: it removed decision-making from Ministries by getting on with the job itself with speed and precision. Hallstein's view, for instance, was:

> Adenauer loathed wasting time. He made his decisions quickly – in my case, for instance, he talked to me about the Schuman Plan and three days later asked me to lead the German delegation. When he gave you work to do, he expected you to get on with it. He would not have had the time to play us off against each other. He was much too interested in the job to be done, much too busy. Of course, he liked teasing people sometimes. Who cared? He didn't mind being teased himself.[24]

Adenauer's advisers would at all events have had one consolation, the benefit of Adenauer's ever-present wit. There were very many examples of it, and only one or two can be given here.

Of journalists, he said in 1960, "One should be careful with small children and journalists. They will always take a shy at you with a stone afterwards."[25] Of a government spokesman, he remarked that he suffered "from having his tongue too near his brain".[26] And, when an importunate journalist went on asking for an interview: "Tell the chap I was buried yesterday, and nobody knows yet. Then he's got his scoop."[27] Repartee came equally easily. His gardener proposed planting poplars at his Rhoendorf home, but added – with obvious meaning – that they took fifteen years to grow. Adenauer, aged 83, commented – "Well, what about it?"[28]

Wit is a saving human grace, and Adenauer needed it in the daunting tasks which lay ahead. He had re-created a genuinely sovereign German state (the DDR has remained a puppet-state of the Soviet Union to this day). He had opened the way into Europe for the Federal Republic; but this road had turns and twists on it. His own belief was that a German military contribution to Europe was the ultimate guarantee of German good faith. Rearmament, then, was the most important problem to be tackled.

Adenauer's own view that German rearmament would be necessary went very far back indeed. Even 18 months before the Korean War began one of the Chancellery staff, Ernst Wirmer, recalled him saying that within four years there would be Germans in uniform again.[29] He never wavered in face of the SPD anti-rearmament, *Ohne mich* (without me) campaign. Now he wanted to go ahead. In February 1954 the Bundestag approved the codicil to the Basic Law of the Constitution, enabling rearmament to take place. All necessary advance planning had been undertaken by the "Amt Blank", with the help of military experts like ex-Generals Adolf Heusinger and Hans Speidel. There was only one obstacle, one over which Adenauer had no direct control. This was French approval of the EDC Agreement. The three Benelux countries had already approved. Italy's ratification was regarded as certain, once the French Government and National Assembly made up their minds.

Typically, the Soviet Union sought to intervene. In June the Foreign Affairs Committee of the French National Assembly rejected the EDC Agreement by 24 votes to 18; the Government led by Joseph Laniel fell a few days later and was replaced by one led by Pierre Mendès-France. As Adenauer said: "The European idea faded, because it was put on the shelf."[30] On 24 July 1954 the Soviet Union proposed new Four Power talks on the future of Germany, hinting once again that German reunification would be possible if German rearmament were shelved. The proposal was, doubtless, insincere, and was directed at France. Mendès-France evidently felt that it strengthened his hand, in safeguarding France's interests within the western alliance. He now submitted a new list of conditions for ratifying the EDC Agreement: it was to be valid for twenty and not fifty years, the only "integrated" armed forces would be those on German soil, EDC headquarters would be in Paris, and EDC decisions would have to be unanimous – thus enabling a French veto.

Adenauer was sure that Mendès-France, a man whom he personally distrusted, was trying to sabotage the EDC, but was afraid of doing so openly.[31] He met Mendès-France and other European leaders in Brussels from 19 to 22 August. There, in a personal talk, Mendès-France played a confidence trick on him; he offered to put the issue of the EDC fairly and squarely before the French National Assembly. Adenauer assented cautiously – what else could he do? But Mendès-France gave no support whatever to the EDC Agreement in the Assembly, which voted by 319 to 264 against resuming talks on it. The French Government and Assembly did not even give an honest vote against the Agreement; they merely swept it under the table.

According to one biographer, Adenauer was so furious that he did not speak for two days.[32] Another authority had it that he considered resignation.[33] Certainly, he was disappointed and angry. He convened the Cabinet in special session and secured its support for a demand for full and independent German sovereignty, a demand which he repeated in an interview with the London *Times*.[34] He claimed that France had wrecked the "European idea", that the French Communist Party had destroyed France's "destiny", and that the German people were being driven into adopting an outworn nationalistic attitude and into seeking accommodation with the Soviet Union. This was fierce talk indeed, but it was understandable. The French had taken well over two years to reach a negative decision, and the European cause had indeed suffered a grave setback. Adenauer was probably right in supposing that a Military Community would have led to a Political as well as an Economic Community, and European unity would have been assured. Now, everything was back in the melting-pot.

For once in her post-war history, Britain stepped into the breach and took the initiative. A nine-power conference was convened in London in September, and recommended the entry of the Federal Republic into an enlarged Brussels Pact (this had been signed in 1948 by Britain, France and the three Benelux states), and later into NATO. The same nine states met again in Paris in October, and confirmed this decision. Yet another Soviet effort to intervene failed; a Soviet note to France proposing a European Security Conference was discussed by the three previous Occupation Powers and rejected. The Soviet riposte was to declare early in December that the rearmament of the Federal Republic made German reunification impossible, and that an East German Army would now come into being. This was no way in which to influence the French, for they, among all Europeans, were probably least interested in reunifying Germany. On 27 and 29 December the French National Assembly approved the entry of the Federal Republic into both NATO and the enlarged Brussels Pact.

Eden should be given much of the credit for success snatched out of the jaws of defeat. In order to secure support for the first nine-power conference, he undertook a lightning tour of European capitals in September. He offered to keep four British divisions and a tactical air force in Germany for 50 years, an unprecedented step for any British Government to take. And he caught a shame-faced French Government and Assembly on the rebound. The essence of his success was the speed with which he acted.

Although the Soviet Union made one further effort – in January 1955, it proposed the reunification of Germany on a basis of free elections, if the Federal Republic's agreements with the West were scrapped – Adenauer was now free to go ahead with rearmament. The Bundestag ratified the agreements to join NATO and the Brussels Pact. The Bonn *Deutschlandvertrag* entered into force and the last remnants of the occupation regime were abolished. The Federal Republic became the fifteenth member of NATO on 9 May 1955, and the DDR (East German State) became, almost simultaneously, a member of the Warsaw Pact (the military alliance of Soviet Bloc powers). Germany was, perhaps, even more irrevocably divided than ever, but Adenauer believed that the security within the framework of NATO obtained by the Federal Republic was more than adequate compensation. His sadness over the failure to create a European Defence Community lingered; membership of NATO was second-best, and his own sporadic efforts thereafter to give NATO a "political content" were half-hearted and doomed to failure.

The build up of the West German armed forces which now began is a fascinating study in itself. Here, only an outline of a complex and sometimes frustrating procedure:

In November 1955, ex-Generals Heusinger and Speidel, with 99 others, were accepted as the first members of the Federal German armed forces, or "Bundeswehr". In March 1956, the Bundestag approved the *Soldatengesetz*, which established regulations for what was intended to be a "citizen army".

Soldiers would become ordinary citizens when off duty, would retain full civic rights, and could belong to a trade union, while military prisons were abolished and conscientious objection was permitted. In July, the conscription law was passed in the Bundestag by a handsome majority. In spite of the brutal Soviet attack on Hungary in October, the SPD continued to oppose rearmament doggedly, and it took time to win public opinion round to acceptance – at the end of 1956 a public opinion survey showed 45 per cent against rearmament and only 40 per cent for.[35] One German captain remarked that "I have to explain to almost everyone I meet why I'm in the forces".[36] But by the end of 1956 there were 67,000 in the Bundeswehr and recruiting was going smoothly. To begin with, almost all of those applying for long-service commissions, in fact for "regular" service, were ex-veterans of the Nazi era Wehrmacht (the name which Hitler gave to his armed forces). They included "reformed" ex-members of the proscribed Waffen SS, but screening was ultra-careful. It was found that returning Wehrmacht officers were fully in touch with civilian life, where they had spent a whole decade in jobs of every kind.[37] Old-type officers and NCOs, imposing an "iron" Prussian discipline, had died out. A completely new, democratic army was coming into being.

The Bundeswehr received its most formidable "recruit" in October 1956, when Franz-Josef Strauss became Minister of Defence. He was at once engaged in a major controversy over planning. NATO had originally, at the 1952 Lisbon Conference, aimed at being able to field 96 divisions within thirty days of the order for full mobilization. This number was revised downwards to 70–75, in 1954. But NATO continued to plan for 30 divisions to be aligned for battle, in fact on German soil. The Bundeswehr was committed to having 240,000 men under arms by the end of 1957, and 500,000 by the end of 1958. Before taking on his new post, Strauss pointed out that these figures were unrealistic – it had taken Hitler five years to build up the 100,000 Reichswehr into the 600,000 Wehrmacht.[38] Strauss pointed out, too, that soldiers were being called up when neither uniforms nor barracks were available, and were having to live at home.[39] He secured, with NATO acquiescence, a target figure of 350,000, by 1961. Adenauer, still inclined to regard the Bundeswehr as a political pawn, was unhappy and upbraided Strauss for the forthright exposé which he gave to NATO partners. But he agreed to the revised figure. Early in 1957 the first conscripts were called up, without incident.

The SPD had one more shot in its locker, the last in fact fired in its campaign against rearmament. This was an all-out attack against the stationing of nuclear weapons on German soil. The Federal Republic had undertaken to make no use itself of the so-called ABC weapons (atomic, biological, chemical). But the United States reserved the right to station tactical nuclear weapons in Germany, and Strauss and the Federal Government upheld this right. Strauss argued strongly in favour of United States nuclear potential being fully available for the defence of Europe – anything less than this would make the defence of the Federal Republic and the rest of Europe impossible.[40] Unwisely, for he was out of his depth, Adenauer entered the lists; at a press conference on 4 April 1957, he said that tactical nuclear weapons were "basically nothing but an improved form of artillery", and that "we cannot deny our own troops the newest types, and prevent them from sharing in these latest developments".

This brought a hornet's nest about his ears. He was assailed by part of the West German press. Then, on 12 April, eighteen leading West German scientists sent him a telegram of protest, urging the renunciation of all kinds of nuclear weapons. Adenauer invited them to Bonn to meet Generals Heusinger and Speidel, and informed them himself that they were interfering in political matters which they did not understand. At the end of April, the philanthropist, Albert Schweitzer, declared in distant Lambarène in West Africa that nuclear bombs were a danger to the health of the human race. The SPD were so delighted that they put up a huge poster of Schweitzer at their Bonn headquarters and kept it there until 1959. They coupled his statement with the motto *Lieber rot als tot* ("Better red than dead") and turned their anti-rearmament campaign into a "War against atomic death". Adenauer was intensely irritated; his comment was "What Albert Schweitzer said was regarded by a great part of the German people as a sort of gospel."[41]

While West German rearmament was proceeding apace, relations between Germany and the Soviet Union took an all-important turn. The issue of German rearmament cannot, indeed, be divorced from Russo-German relations or from East–West relations in general. For the Soviet leadership never ceased insisting that German rearmament made a satisfactory solution of the German Question as a whole impossible. The Soviet arguments were historical. German armies had conquered huge areas of Russia in the First World War, and in 1917 had sought to impose a cruelly unjust peace on Russia in the Treaty of Brest-Litovsk. In the Second World War, Hitler attacked the Soviet Union without provocation, and his armies reached the gates of Moscow, Leningrad and Stalingrad. The Soviet Union, so the argument ran, had every reason to dread an alliance between American technology and wealth and German military efficiency (the Russians have never forgotten that, in actual combat, their own losses were of between five and six men for every dead German). Soviet armed strength had, of course, developed sensationally since 1945. But the Soviet argument, even if specious, sounded convincing, especially when used in conjunction with the facts of appalling Soviet wartime losses.

Adenauer's belief that the Soviet Union used proposals for German reunification only in order to delay the integration of the Federal Republic with Western Europe was almost certainly well-founded. Every move in that direction brought a Soviet reaction, and the most significant of all followed the entry of the Federal Republic into NATO. Just under one month later, on 7 June 1955, the Soviet Government invited Adenauer to Moscow, to discuss the establishment of cultural, economic and diplomatic relations between their two countries. With some misgivings, Adenauer accepted; he asked that German reunification and the fate of the many thousands of German prisoners-of-war still in Russian hands should be on the agenda.

The Soviet intention in inviting him to Moscow was clear. In their foreign policy the Soviet leaders have always believed in opportunism and in keeping options open. German reunification could have been acceptable to them only if a unified Germany could have been brought into the Soviet orbit, or at the very least completely neutralized between East and West. Soviet plans for reunification provided, therefore, for equal representation between the puppet East German "People's Chamber" and the democratically elected Bundestag in Bonn. The Russians reckoned that they could keep full control over their East Germans, and that a reasonably strong West German Communist Party would assist their "side" to an overall majority in an all-German Assembly. The miserable showing of the West German Communist Party really doomed such obscure hopes, while a clear majority of the people of the Federal Republic decided against neutralization. This did not mean that Soviet proposals for reunification needed to be totally abandoned; they could still be used as a delaying action, as long as the Federal Republic was still not fully sovereign and had not been fully accepted into the European community.

The second, and from 1949 onwards, more promising option for the Soviet Union was to keep Germany divided and consolidate its hold on the "forward bastion" of East Germany. It was neither as big nor potentially as rich as the Federal Republic but, as compensation, it would be that much easier to control. The acceptance of the Federal Republic into NATO left only this second option open. Since Germany was to remain divided, therefore, the Soviet Union stood to gain by opening direct relations with Bonn; it could certainly benefit economically by doing this, and possibly politically too.

Adenauer's doubts about going to Moscow were understandable. The last thing that he wanted to do was to conjure up visions of a "second Rapallo" – the 1922 Treaty signed there had entailed *de jure* recognition of the Soviet Union, and the Weimar Republic had been the first major power to accord it. He was also worrying at the time about Britain. Eden had been airing the idea of a "zone of limited and equalized armaments" in Germany. This foresaw the withdrawal of armed forces on both sides of the German interzonal frontier, and the creation of a zone perhaps 50 to 60 miles wide, in which relatively small and roughly equal forces would be stationed. There was an obvious advantage in this plan: the Russians and East Germans would lose their main military training areas and points of military concentration, and would be pushed back east of Berlin into an inadequate strip of territory. But Adenauer was advised that the Western Alliance would have been left with a disturbingly small area of manoeuvre in Germany, and a large part of the American forces would have to retire to the United States – whereas the Russians would only go back to the Polish frontier.[42] Adenauer, again, was in close contact with the US Secretary of State, John Foster Dulles, who was thinking – and sometimes talking aloud – about a "roll-back" of Soviet occupation in Europe, as an adjunct to the previous policy of "containment". Finally, the Eden Plan looked too defensive and lacked political content.[43]

Adenauer's reasons for going to Moscow were not very convincing. One view was that he wanted a greater voice for the Federal Republic in the affairs of the Western Alliance, and might even have been afraid of NATO becoming "an American officers' club".[44] He may have had some vague hope that the Soviet Union was more inclined to look for an accommodation over the German Question, owing to domestic problems and the beginning of trouble with Communist China – Adenauer was the first European statesman to forecast continuing and increasingly serious tension between the two Communist giants. The Chancellor may also have hoped for ameliorations in West Berlin's situation; in 1956 control over traffic between West Berlin and Western Germany would be handed over by the Russians to the DDR, a system of tolls introduced, and interference with traffic stepped up, with no effective Allied response. Even before the Moscow visit, the Russians were threatening steps of this kind.

There was, at any rate, one concrete problem to discuss, that of the German prisoners-of-war. More than ten years after the end of war, there were still 1,150,000 German soldiers posted as missing. Of 750,000 who had been deported into the Soviet Union, at least half a million were known to have died, and the German Red Cross had by means of careful questioning established that at least 130,000 should still be alive, "somewhere in Russia". The Russians insisted that there were only 9,628 German prisoners in their hands, and that they were all war criminals.

The Moscow visit took place from 8 to 14 September. It was a daunting affair. Adenauer had to deal for much of the time with Nikita Khruschev, with his rumbustious peasant coarseness and brutally direct and aggressive style of negotiating. This had the effect of actually making Adenauer's Foreign Minister, Brentano, feel physically sick. One British statesman thought that the Moscow visit had been a salutary experience for Adenauer – "At least it will stop the Germans rebuking us for our weakness towards the Russians."[45] This was Mr Harold Macmillan; ironically, he was to share Brentano's experience four years later when he himself went to Moscow. Khruschev employed all of his debating devices against Adenauer: he shouted frequently, swore, and shook his fists.[46] The Russians first refused to discuss the prisoners-of-war at all, then plainly stated that diplomatic relations must be established first. Adenauer's Press Chief, von Eckardt, was instructed to send for the Chancellor's special plane, which would fly from Frankfurt. Von Eckardt ordered the plane by an "open" telephone call, which was at once reported to the Kremlin.[47] The next day Marshal Nikolai Bulganin, Khruschev's team-mate, took Adenauer aside and told him the prisoners would be sent back to Germany, if he would write an appropriate letter. A few minutes earlier, Bulganin had been maintaining that virtually every German prisoner had "been buried long ago".[48]

Adenauer went down with pneumonia when he got back to Bonn. He had given two undertakings before leaving for Moscow. The first was that he would not trade the fate of the prisoners-of-war for the re-establishment of Russo-German diplomatic relations. That was precisely what, in the event, he did. The second undertaking was that diplomatic relations would only be established if there were progress towards German reunification. There was no such progress. If his political gamble did not come off, at least he showed all his moral fibre. He out-stared Molotov, the Soviet Union's long-serving Foreign Minister, remarking what an uncomfortable experience it must have been to reach agreement with Hitler. He never flinched when Khruschev was at his most violent, and told him that friends should indeed speak openly, but that rebuke was inevitable if openness of speech went beyond the bounds of civilized intercourse.[49]

In a negative sense, the establishment of diplomatic relations may have resulted in a temporary relaxation of Soviet political pressure in the German Question, and have given West Berlin temporary respite. 1956 was a quiet year in both respects, and early in 1957 the Bundestag solemnly confirmed the status of Berlin as the capital of Germany, and the Federal Republic followed this up with a joint declaration on German unity signed by the three Western Powers with special responsibilities in the country. By then, Adenauer was involved in the run up to the 1957 Federal elections; before they took place, on 15 September, he was given a political shot-in-the-arm: on 25 March, the Treaty of Rome was signed, setting up the European Economic Community.

The Treaty laid down the aims and nature of the Community (EEC) which was to become a fully functioning customs-union within three to four years. A fully integrated Common Market was to come into being at the end of fifteen years at the most; its members would have a common external tariff. Special concessions were made to the Federal Republic; the other members of the EEC Six (France, Italy and the three Benelux states) would re-examine the Treaty in the event of German reunification, and would regulate their trade with the DDR in deference to existing interzonal trade between the DDR and the Federal Republic. The Bundestag resoundingly approved the Treaty early in July.

Adenauer saw European economic integration as a step towards political integration and the creation of a truly united

Europe. No economist, he was not much concerned with the
technical details of the proposed EEC. He still bitterly regretted
the demise of the EDC, a body which would have played a bigger
role in his Grand Design. But he was delighted with the ease and
unanimity with which the Treaty of Rome had been signed and
approved, and he went straight from the Bundestag debate into
election campaigning with the utmost confidence.

His coalition had lost two of its component parts, but had
gained in solidarity. The FDP (Free Democrats) had split in 1956,
over proposals for electoral reform which Adenauer initiated,
and which never came to anything. Breakaway members formed
a separate party, and then merged with the CDU; the rump of
the FDP went into opposition. The BHE Refugee Party split too,
with two Ministers staying in the Government and the bulk of
the party, again, leaving the coalition. It might have been
thought that Adenauer planned these moves, collecting voters
and useful personalities at the same time. This seems unlikely;
Erich Mende, later the leader of the FDP, believed that Adenauer
wanted a fair deal with the FDP and did not try to "kill with
kindness", in order to emasculate smaller parties which were
allied to his CDU.[50] But the fact remains that the CDU was the
"centre party"; it was difficult for parties other than the SPD to
maintain an identity which mattered. In alliance with the CDU,
they tended to be smothered; in opposition, they were in limbo.

The 1957 elections were bound to produce a CDU victory; only
the extent of it remained in doubt. Adenauer's electioneering
was based on the sort of administrative record which no
European Government, twenty years later, could claim.
Unemployment was ended and the German labour force was up
by six million since 1949. Consumption had rocketed, and the
standard of living was now as high as that of any country in
Europe. All sorts of extra benefits were passed out in the weeks
before the elections. They included ordinary pensions, turnover
tax, tax-free allowances for wives, and disability pensions. These
were hand-outs, according to Adenauer's critics. Well and good;
but they were hand-outs which an efficient government could
afford. This was, maybe, a "stomach election",[51] but it was
solidly based on results. Adenauer and the CDU were in the truly
remarkable position of needing only to state facts; the German
voters were receptive. They had suffered, very much, in the past,
and they were doing very well at the present. Adenauer's first big
election campaign speech was in Essen, the coal-and-steel heart
of the industrial Ruhr. A crowd of 20,000 braved a high wind,

rain, thunder and lightning to come to listen. Blue and white CDU banners proclaimed "Tot up your facts" and "At peace, our daily bread". The meeting set a pattern of success for Adenauer and his party.

Even so, the results of the 1957 elections were remarkable. The SPD, struggling along without a real programme, still managed to increase its vote and representation in the Bundestag, from 151 to 169. The reason was that the electoral law had again been revised: it was now necessary to win three seats by direct election as well as 5 per cent of the overall vote, in order to secure a "proportional" number of seats on the reserve list. Smaller parties were bound to suffer; apart from the two main parties, only the FDP and the DP (still in coalition with the CDU) survived. The FDP, somewhat chastened, obtained 41 seats, the DP 17. But the CDU, with just over 50 per cent of the votes, held 270 seats. They needed no partners, but would take the DP into the next government. They were rid of FDP allies, who had become increasingly troublesome – but, as it happened, they had lost them very nearly for good. The FDP would not trust Adenauer ever again.

In purely statistical terms, this was the most resounding victory for a single party in German Parliamentary history. In that sense, it marked the climax of Adenauer's career. Everything seemed to be going his way. The Treaty of Rome opened the road to real cooperation with a reluctant France. His personal friendship with Dulles ensured a close working relationship with the USA. The return of the Saar to Germany settled the last problem which could have caused havoc in inter-European relations. German rearmament was under way, not in too much of a hurry and with the approval of the Federal Republic's friends, and, more grudgingly, of the German people.

Adenauer was already over 81 years old. He had no intention of giving up. His favourite story at the time was about Pope Leo XIII receiving the *corps diplomatique* on his ninetieth birthday. The senior diplomat congratulated him, and expressed the hope that he would be as strong and healthy when he reached one hundred. The Pope answered: "But, why, gentlemen, should you set so low a limit on the compassion of God?" To Adenauer, continued service to his country, until he was ready to drop, was axiomatic. He was no megalomaniac, but he honestly believed that he was indispensable.

1. Terence Prittie. *Konrad Adenauer.* London, 1972.
2. John McCloy, in letter to the author, December 1969.
3. Terence Prittie. *Germany Divided.* Boston, 1960.
4. In interview with Ernst Friedlaender, broadcast nation-wide, 30 January 1953.
5. Willy Brandt, in conversation with the author, June 1973.
6. Paul Weymar. *Konrad Adenauer.* London, 1957.
7. Felix von Eckardt. *Ein unordentliches Leben.* Düsseldorf, 1967.
8. Ibid.
9. Brian Connell. *Watcher on the Rhine.* London, 1957.
10. Gerhard Schroeder, in conversation with the author, May 1971.
11. Walter Henkels. *Bonner Koepfe.* Düsseldorf, 1968.
12. Charles Thayer. *The Unquiet Germans.* London, 1958.
13. Dr Ernst Wickert, in conversation with the author. December 1970.
14. Heinrich von Brentano, in Bundestag, March 1958.
15. Walter Henkels, op. cit.
16. Thomas Dalberg. *Franz Josef Strauss.* Gütersloh, 1968.
17. Horst Osterheld. *Konrad Adenauer, 1876/1976.* Edited Alois Rummel. Bonn, 1975.
18. Arnulf Baring. *Aussenpolitik in Adenauer's Kanzler-Demokratie.* Munich, 1969.
19. Herbert Blankenhorn, in conversation with the author, May 1971.
20. Frau Libeth Werhahn, in conversation with the author, March 1971.
21. Terence Prittie. *Konrad Adenauer.*
22. Felix von Eckardt, op. cit.
23. Arnulf Baring, op. cit.
24. Professor Walter Hallstein, in conversation with the author, May 1971.
25. Walter Henkels. *Gar nicht so pingelig.* Düsseldorf, 1965.
26. Ibid.
27. Ibid.
28. Ibid.
29. Walter Henry Nelson. *Germany Rearmed.* New York, 1972.
30. Konrad Adenauer. *Memoirs,* Vol 2. Stuttgart, 1966.
31. Ibid.
32. Charles Wighton. *Adenauer. Democratic Dictator.* London, 1963.
33. Arnulf Baring, op. cit.
34. The London *Times,* 4 September 1954.
35. Walter Henry Nelson, op. cit.
36. Ibid.
37. Walter Henry Nelson, op. cit.
38. Thomas Dalberg, op. cit.
39. Ibid.
40. Hans Gert Poltering. *Adenauer's Sicherheitspolitik 1955/63.* Düsseldorf 1975.
41. Konrad Adenauer. *Memoirs,* Vol 3. Stuttgart, 1966.
42. Dr Hans Globke, in conversation with the author, March 1971.
43. Klaus Gotto. *Konrad Adenauer. Seine Deutschland und Aussenpolitik 1945/1963.* Mainz, 1971.
44. Ibid.
45. Harold Macmillan. *Tides of Fortune.* London, 1969.
46. Konrad Adenauer. *Memoirs,* Vol. 2.
47. Felix von Eckardt, op. cit.
48. Konrad Adenauer. *Memoirs,* Vol. 2.

49. Dr Hans Globke, in conversation with the author, March 1971.
50. Dr Erich Mende, in conversation with the author, May 1971.
51. Terence Prittie. *Konrad Adenauer.*
52. Ibid.

CHAPTER FIVE

Running out of Steam

In spite of his years, in spite of a slightly increasing, if still only occasional testiness and a growing vulnerability to bronchial colds, Konrad Adenauer entered into his third term of office with great confidence. Few would have guessed that his Government would begin to run out of steam and that the decline of his personal reputation would begin in two years' time. The Parliamentary situation suited him perfectly. The BHE Refugee Party had now dropped out of the Bundestag; there was practically nothing that it could do for refugees who were now almost completely integrated in the life of the Federal Republic and who were painfully aware that pursuit of their claims to the return of the lost eastern territories was purposeless, as long as the Red Army sat on the banks of the Elbe. The Bavarian Party and the "Zentrum" had lost their seats in the Bundestag even earlier, and the Communist Party was banned. The German Party (DP) existed only on sufferance, by virtue of an electoral "arrangement" with the CDU in its sole stronghold of Lower Saxony. In 1960 it, too, would disappear.

The FDP was a fading force, and the Federal Republic seemed to be on the way to a two party system, which presaged rule by the CDU for an indefinite period. For what had the SPD to offer? Its leader, Ollenhauer, was in the nature of a gift to Adenauer; he had opposed so many popular and constructive actions by the Government and had produced only negative initiatives. Marxist doctrines were suspect, and middle-of-the-road votes were

magnetically drawn to the CDU. The SPD needed strong
and charismatic leadership, and it needed new ideas even
more.

These new ideas were, in fact, on the way. During 1958 and
1959 the SPD leadership debated its future policies long and
earnestly. The outcome was the Bad Godesberg party conference
in November 1959. Its main purpose, as one historian put it
resentfully, was not to find a new ideological *raison d'être*, but to
bring the SPD into line with the political philosophy of post-war
Germany, and rid itself of an unpopular Marxist image.[1]
Ollenhauer presided over the conference; he was always an
excellent chairman. But out of it emerged a formidable
triumvirate, whose members were becoming the real forces in
the party. Herbert Wehner, a former Communist, had by now
been accepted as the real organizational manager of the SPD.
Fritz Erler was its foremost spokesman on defence, and often on
foreign affairs too. Willy Brandt, who had been elected
Governing Mayor of Berlin at the end of 1957, would become
SPD candidate for the Chancellorship at the SPD party
conference in Hanover at the end of 1960. According to one
authority,[2] Wehner was in fact the "king-maker", and Brandt
was dependent on him for his sudden elevation. But Brandt had
already made his own way in the political field and he had the
advantage of youth on his side – he was not yet 46 when the Bad
Godesberg Conference took place. The SPD were right to invest
in youth; they had put up elder statesmen against Adenauer in
the past, and had failed.

At Bad Godesberg the SPD ceased to be exclusively the party of
the "cloth-capped" workers: "The Social Democratic Party is a
community of men holding different ideas and beliefs. Their
agreement is based on the moral principles and political aims
they have in common."[3] The party ceased to be anti-clerical, or
even anti-capitalist. It dropped the slogans of revolution, the
insistence on the symbolism of the red flag, and the raised fist of
the embattled worker; it dropped Marxist arrogance and
omniscience.[4] It even shelved the idea of a Utopian society, and
set out to plan social betterment realistically, by adjustment and
compromise. At Bad Godesberg, the SPD jettisoned class
warfare, state planning of all key sectors of the economy, the
nationalization of heavy industries, and opposition to
rearmament within the framework of NATO. It sought to
become a middle-of-the-road party and challenge the CDU for
the floating vote. This was the only possible road to political

power, but it would take another ten years for the SPD challenge to become menacingly clear.

Meanwhile, Adenauer – for so long the total master of his own fate – had taken an irrevocable step in linking his personal policies and his country's fortunes with those of France. He had seen French troops march into the Rhineland at the end of the First World War. He had watched the French encouraging Rhineland separatism and occupying the Ruhr by unilateral action in the 1920s. He had nearly forfeited the Saar to France, and had found the French his toughest adversaries in negotiating the return of German sovereignty. But at heart he was always a Francophile, captivated by the elegance, finesse and reason of the French, convinced that French and Germans should unite to fashion a new Europe, in the spirit of the Europe of Charlemagne. The advent of Charles de Gaulle to power in Paris, in May 1958, gave him a chance to realize his dreams.

De Gaulle might well have not, at first sight, looked a promising prospect for Franco-German partnership. He made no secret of his contempt for the United States, on which Europe's security depended. He had called the European Defence Agreement "half-baked" – with some reason, for unlike Adenauer, he had seen service in two World Wars. He had made sundry, opaque references to *rapprochement* with the Soviet Union – and had conducted a war-time flirtation with Stalin.[5] Worst of all, he had promised to repeal and effectively wreck the Treaty of Rome. He could well have been taken for a chauvinist, in evocation of French *gloire* and *patrie*.

His thoughts about running Europe and the whole Western Alliance through a triumvirate, consisting of the United States, France and Britain, had deeply worried Adenauer. De Gaulle himself maintained that "As soon as he [Adenauer] realized that my return was something more than an interlude, the Chancellor asked to see me".[6] In fact, the advances came from de Gaulle himself. First he sent Maurice Picard, the Prefect of the Department of the Yonne, to tell Adenauer that he should "propose" a visit to Paris. This was in July; without waiting for an answer, de Gaulle dispatched his Foreign Minister, Maurice Couve de Murville, to suggest a meeting when the Chancellor was on his way back from his holiday resort of Cadennabia, in Northern Italy. Early in August, de Gaulle talked with the Federal German Ambassador in Paris, Baron Vollrath von Maltzan; he held out a more attractive bait, a visit to his home in Colombey-les-deux-églises, rather than to the Elysée Palace in

Paris. He was well-advised: Germans regard an invitation to "the home" as a special honour. Adenauer accepted. Apart from the way in which he had been flattered, Colombey was much handier than Paris. From Baden-Baden, where Adenauer intended to spend the night on his way home, Colombey was a mere two hours' drive – at the break-neck speed which the Chancellor enjoyed.

He made the journey on 14 September 1958. One can imagine his thoughts as he crossed the Rhine, the river which he loved and which had so signally divided the two countries in the past; sped up the gentle slopes of the Vosges and through the Saverne Gap, scene of much fighting in countless Franco-German wars; then on, across the Moselle to the banks of the Marne. He was travelling through the heartland of Charlemagne's Empire, across almost the whole breadth of the "Middle Kingdom" of Lothar which was one of that Empire's three successors. European history had so often gone rotten, at this core: European history was there, to be made afresh, at de Gaulle's home of Le Boisserie.

Adenauer's own account of the meeting was a rosy one.[7] De Gaulle and his wife were friendly and informal. The General was alert and debonair – Adenauer used the word *frisch* to describe him – and the Chancellor was charmed by the sort of urbane and elegant welcome which he himself loved to give his guests. The two men found much common ground. They shared a scepticism about Britain, and Adenauer remarked (presciently) that "England is like a rich man, who has lost all his property, but does not realize it".[8] De Gaulle stressed his interest in a united Europe, but added, significantly, that it must cease "to be the tool of America". He gave Adenauer a solemn assurance: "In Germany they said, when I was in political life, that my policy towards Germany was one of might and vengeance. I can prove the contrary to *you*."[9] There was a heavy emphasis on the pronoun.

Did Adenauer know of de Gaulle's question to Couve de Murville when appointing him Foreign Minister – "How much remains of my policy for dismembering Germany"?[10] Couve's answer had been "Nothing". The Chancellor was at pains to be tactful, and did not find this difficult. Whereas he generally adopted a resentful attitude towards the British, as people who had botched things in Europe, he had a genuine sympathy for French sufferings at the hands of the Germans in the Franco-Prussian War and two World Wars. He agreed with everything that de Gaulle had to say, praised his grasp for the "big" problems, and was enchanted when de Gaulle told him he was the younger man of the two "in spirit".[11] His delicate riposte was that the General would regain youth in office "as has been the case with myself".

François Seydoux, French Ambassador to Germany, said that this first meeting produced "a magical moment", and "Whatever they had expected in their heart of hearts was transcended by their immediate impression of one another".[12] One of de Gaulle's biographers agrees – "Adenauer was captivated by de Gaulle's charm and even found Colombey congenial."[13] According to Dr Hans Globke, Adenauer at once found de Gaulle's "personal aura" congenial – he was "so clearly upright, correct, moral".[14] One of Adenauer's daughters, Frau Ria Reiners, put it a little differently: the Colombey meeting had been a "pleasant surprise", for her father had looked forward to it with apprehension – he had remarked that de Gaulle thought that he was "a second Joan of Arc".[15]

Other views differed fundamentally. One of Adenauer's biographers wrote that he found de Gaulle "very strange", with his military aura, his mystical sense of mission, his esoteric diction and his pompous gestures.[16] A member of the Chancellor's "kitchen Cabinet" found Adenauer uneasy and dubious on his return to Bonn, in spite of de Gaulle's courtesy – the Chancellor had been particularly pleased at being greeted with a few well-chosen sentences in German.[17] The British Ambassador in Bonn at the time, Sir Christopher Steel, confirmed this view; Adenauer talked to him, if somewhat obliquely, about the "militaristic" and even the "fascist" tendencies of the General.[18]

Adenauer may well have been sounding the British Ambassador; this was a technique of his. What is sure is that the second meeting between Adenauer and de Gaulle, at Bad Kreuznach, on 26 November, was a resounding success. The place was chosen for the return visit because it was almost equidistant between the two men's homes, at Rhoendorf and Colombey. At the Kurhaus, which had once been the military headquarters of Kaiser Wilhelm II and Field Marshal von Hindenburg, the two men got on famously. Adenauer repaid de Gaulle's compliment to him by greeting the General in French (which according to his official interpreter, Herr Weber, was execrable). The main result of the meeting was agreement on continuing close contact, although one observer believed that de

Gaulle enlisted Adenauer's support in opposing the "Maudling Plan" for a European Free Trade Zone, and sowed seeds of distrust in Adenauer's mind over Britain's Berlin policy.[19] The appearance of the two men before the news-starved press at the end of the conference was dramatic – De Gaulle called his host "a great man, a great statesman, a great European and a great German".[20] His follow-up gesture was to turn to Adenauer, clasping him by both shoulders, leaving him for once at a slight loss, but looking absurdly pleased and somehow like a favourite pupil who has been commended by his revered teacher.[21]

The Bad Kreuznach meeting was the starting point for the creation of a Bonn–Paris "axis". There were fifteen further meetings between the two men during the next two years, and 40 letters were exchanged between them. In an ocular sense, the "Entente" which eventually led up to the signing of the Franco-German Pact of Friendship in January 1963, brought cordial cooperation. Adenauer was invited to Rambouillet and Marly-le-Roi as de Gaulle's guest, and much later, in 1962, de Gaulle made a triumphal tour of the Federal Republic. But the Entente was a somewhat one-sided affair; on the one hand, Adenauer confided readily in de Gaulle; on the other, the General went his own way whenever it suited him to do so.

Thus, in February 1959, de Gaulle withdrew the French Mediterranean Fleet from NATO. In June, he refused to allow the USA to stockpile nuclear weapons on French soil. In November, he told the Centre for Advanced Military Studies in Paris that European military integration was dead. No protest came from Adenauer; yet de Gaulle's words and actions were running directly counter to the Chancellor's oft-repeated precept that the West must unite and must negotiate with the East from a position of strength.

De Gaulle siphoned-off French troops for service in Algeria, and meanwhile failed to reinforce absurdly under-strength French contingents in Germany. He proposed that NATO forces in Europe should be commanded by a Frenchman, rather than an American, and indicated that this could be a necessary condition for France to remain in NATO. In March 1960, he received Khruschev in Paris with every mark of cordiality, and Adenauer's suspicions must have been aroused when Antoine Pinay arrived in Bonn, with the news that de Gaulle had sacked him and expressing the view that the General was obsessed with his own importance and pride.[22] In October, de Gaulle announced France's complete nuclear independence of the

Western Alliance, following the successful exploding of an atom bomb in the Sahara. To cap all, France's Prime Minister, Michel Debré, arrived in Bonn with a blueprint for European reorganization: NATO should be directed by the triumvirate of the USA, France and Britain, France should be able to veto use of the nuclear deterrent in Europe, and the Gaullist plan for a *Europe des patries* should be substituted for the supra-national European Community envisaged under the Treaty of Rome.

For once, with de Gaulle, Adenauer's patience cracked. He told Debré that the Western Alliance must be kept intact, and he rejected the French blueprint; nothing more was heard of it. In November he repeated his views about the Alliance to the foreign press in Bonn, adding that American military leadership of NATO was as necessary as ever. François Seydoux believes that Adenauer had made a conscious decision to go all the way with de Gaulle during his Rambouillet visit in July, in fact while praying in his "favourite" cathedral, Chartres.[23] Certainly Adenauer could hardly fail to be moved by that awe-inspiring interior and those magnificent stained-glass windows; and there is something grandiloquently evocative about praying in other people's cathedrals. But Seydoux's view that Adenauer knew that Europe could not be led by a German, and so it had to be de Gaulle "with his more limited horizons",[24] is strangely jejune for an experienced diplomat. Adenauer, momentarily, gave some attention to de Gaulle's plan for a "Confederation" of the Six, with consultative bodies at all levels. But he did not abandon his own concepts; in the event, de Gaulle's plans were quietly shelved.

There had been, at least, a Franco-German honeymoon; it was over, and what was left was rather more a *marriage de convenance*. The exchanged official visits in 1962 – Adenauer was in Paris in July, and de Gaulle in Bonn in September – reawakened interest and activity. The final step towards the consummation of Adenauer's dream of Franco-German friendship was, however, unhappily interlocked with a matter of European interest, which should have been kept apart from it. In October, negotiations began – almost simultaneously – on the Franco-German Treaty of Friendship and on Britain's request to join the European Economic Community. A fatal symbiosis was born.

De Gaulle had repeatedly told Adenauer that Britain was neither needed nor wanted in the EEC. He had brushed off proposals made by the British Prime Minister, Mr Harold Macmillan, in Paris in June, and subsequently told Adenauer that Macmillan asked for too many concessions on behalf of the Commonwealth.[25] France, of course, wished to continue to lead the Six; Britain could have challenged her leadership. Adenauer, according to his own account,[26] made no attempt to explain Britain's case – he even stated that Macmillan had proposed economic union with the USA and had been turned down by President Kennedy. In addition, Adenauer told de Gaulle that British sterling was shaky, and that Britain should only be accepted into the EEC if entry brought economic benefit to all member states.

Adenauer – and again this is his own account – piled argument onto argument.[27] He said that the EEC was not sufficiently consolidated to absorb other countries, that Britain had to make prior concessions, that the British Labour Party was against the EEC and could soon come to power, that even the Macmillan Government might seek to undermine Franco-German understanding, and finally that the British people had not abandoned their "insular concepts". De Gaulle needed no convincing; on 14 January 1963, he dropped his diplomatic atom bomb by announcing that France would veto Britain's entry into the EEC, come what may. The follow-up came eight days later; the Franco-German Treaty of Friendship was signed in Paris, with de Gaulle and Adenauer embracing – there were tears in the latter's eyes, but he was able to proclaim, with global rhetoric, that "the gates of a new Europe" had been opened to "France, Germany, Europe and, in consequence, the whole world". In fact, those same gates had been closed against Britain and all other applicants to join the Six.

François Seydoux has stated that Adenauer, by supporting de Gaulle and blocking Britain's entry into Europe, received his "reward", the Treaty of Friendship.[28] This is a crude explanation of what happened. Adenauer did honestly believe that the British people were not ready to become true Europeans. There was, in any event, a fundamental choice to be made – between expanding the EEC or consolidating what was already there, the Six. Adenauer's instinct – a natural one for a man of 87 – was to play safe. He did not make his decision with an easy mind; there were rumblings of disapproval within his Cabinet and Government coalition. Vice-Chancellor Erhard and Foreign Minister Schroeder were strongly in favour of bringing Britain and other applicants into the EEC; so were the Free Democrats. So, for that matter, was the SPD Opposition and, in all probability, a majority of the German people.

Looking at the matter with the aid of hindsight, there was something to be said for Adenauer's somewhat devious actions – on returning from Paris he claimed to have spoken to de Gaulle "in the same spirit" as had Schroeder, which could not possibly have been true, and suggested with mock innocence that the synchronization of the Franco-German Treaty with the rebuff to Britain was fortuitous. Was there a risk of France walking out of the EEC? If so, such a risk could not be taken. Could a fair bargain be struck with a Britain which was making a great deal out of its Commonwealth obligations and which would have asked for all sorts of concessions for herself? Finally, what sort of partner would Britain make? It is a sad reflection that the British contribution to the EEC, after eventually entering it, has been generally inadequate and often obstructionist. Had he been alive today, Adenauer would consider himself vindicated.

But there are arguments on the other side. Macmillan, like Churchill, thought in European terms, and his chief negotiator, Edward Heath, was the best kind of European. The Conservative Government would have brought Britain into the EEC with a good will and a real determination to make an effective contribution. A decade later, a half-hearted Labour Government first subjected the British people to a referendum and subsequently treated the EEC with contempt, even sending as its chief representative to Brussels a man who had opposed Britain's entry. Britain could have been an asset to Europe, in 1963, and could have been helped into the EEC against her lack of will for Heath was plainly ahead of his time, and the Labour Party, the Trade Unions and a great body of insular thought was opposed to giving up any of Britain's supposed independence. The most sombre reflection is that Britain could only have benefited from earlier exposure to European competitiveness and the more manifest European will to work. A Britain entering Europe in 1963 would scarcely have caught up with the Federal Republic, for instance, by 1979; but she would have been saved from tragic and possibly continuing economic decline.

Two views may be cited, on the question whether Adenauer was right or wrong in January 1963 – a question which will never be convincingly resolved. Gerhard Schroeder, who had fought hard for close and fair consideration of the British application to join the EEC, quoted from Milton: "The desire for fame is the last infirmity of noble minds."[29] He was thinking of Adenauer's "Grand Design", the Franco-German friendship which could transform Europe. General Lord Robertson put it bluntly:

"England did not form part of Europe, as Adenauer saw it."[30] What is certain is that the Franco-German Treaty was not a mirage; nor was it a transformation. One highly-informed view was: "He [Adenauer] was over-sanguine about the Treaty and about the direction that de Gaulle's policies would take. He may have been blinded by the supposed affinity with de Gaulle; old age, too, was a factor."[31] Still, the Treaty was, and is, a useful milestone. It formalized the innate, usually unspoken desire of two peoples to be friends. Milestones are valuable and indicative; they generally survive.

One must return in time and touch on a very different problem. One of the first events of international importance after the 1957 elections was the successful launching of a Soviet earth-satellite, "Sputnik". This was on 4 October, and Adenauer – maybe in euphoric mood after his election victory – welcomed this sinister event. It would, he thought, wake people up. It was, in reality, the signal that the Soviet Union was now becoming the potential equal of the USA in the nuclear arena.

The Sputnik has a close connection with subsequent developments in East–West relations; these inevitably affected Germany. First came the tabling of the "Rapacki Plan" (Adam Rapacki was Poland's Foreign Minister) on 2 October 1957, at the United Nations. It proposed a nuclear-free zone of limited armaments in Central Europe, which would include both German states, Poland and Czechoslovakia, and which could later be expanded. There had been similar, earlier suggestions, by the American diplomat George Kennan and the British Labour Party leader Hugh Gaitskell, but the Rapacki Plan was obviously "official", in that it had to have the blessing of the Soviet Union. It was doubtless linked intimately with the launching of Sputnik, and with the Soviet desire to re-examine the German Question at a summit conference.

Adenauer quickly rejected the plan on the grounds that even a zone 400 miles wide could be straddled by intercontinental rockets, and the plan would only divert attention from the need for general, controlled disarmament.[32] Privately, he admitted his fear that the plan would leave the Western Alliance without a "strategic hinterland".[33] He empowered his Foreign Minister, Brentano, to say that any localized European disarmament plan would mean "a death sentence for Europe", unless Germany were at the same time reunified. Brentano believed that a plan of this kind would encourage isolationist thinking in the United States, would lead to massive reductions of American forces in

Europe and would leave Germany defenceless.[34] The Federal Minister of Defence, Strauss, was totally against the Rapacki Plan and was urging the equipping of the Bundeswehr with "tactical" nuclear weapons; in March 1958, the Bundestag approved this step. A powerful voice was raised in favour of Adenauer's nuclear policy; the American statesman, Dean Acheson, wrote in the magazine *Foreign Affairs* of April 1958: "Disengagement – it is called now; but it is the same futile, and lethal attempt to crawl back into the cocoon of history."[35]

An ex-officer of Hitler's Wehrmacht and a future Federal Chancellor, Helmut Schmidt, supported the Rapacki Plan.[36] By now he ranked as the SPD's most vocal expert on military matters. Another ex-officer and military expert, Erich Mende of the FDP, thought differently. Adenauer's periodic ally, but always a ready critic, Mende believed that the Soviet Union had only offered "formal" chances of real détente, which could have included German reunification, in 1952, 1955, and now once more.[37] All that Adenauer might possibly be blamed for was not testing Soviet intentions more openly. On the whole, this seems a fair judgement. But rejection of the Rapacki Plan was undoubtedly one factor which encouraged the Soviet Union to return to the diplomatic offensive.

During 1958 there was a marked slowing down of physical movement between the DDR and the Federal Republic; thus in July 1958, the East German authorities issued only 78,000 travel permits, against 468,000 in July 1957. The Western Powers had mistakenly scrutinized such developments in isolation. In fact, the Soviet leadership was planning a sensationally new step: on 10 November 1958, Khruschev, speaking in the Leningrad Sports Stadium, demanded the revision of the 1945 Potsdam Agreement and a new Four Power agreement over West Berlin. He followed this up with a note to the three Western Powers on 27 November: all agreements over Berlin were to be regarded as null and void, West Berlin was to be turned into a demilitarized "free city" and the two German states should work out plans to establish a "confederation". Khruschev set a six month time-limit on his proposals.

A flurry of diplomatic activity ensued. The Western Powers replied, asking for the holding of free, all-German elections as a prerequisite to reunification. Khruschev responded in January, rejecting this suggestion, and adding the demilitarization of the Federal Republic to his previous demands. He stuck to this position during the Four Power Foreign Ministers Conference, which met intermittently in Geneva from May to August. A Western four-stage plan, for the reunification of Berlin, the formation of an all-German Committee, all-German elections, and a peace treaty, was not even discussed by the Soviet representatives. All that the Geneva Conference achieved was the withdrawal of Khruschev's six-month deadline – a Pyrrhic victory, indeed, for the deadline had already passed.

Next came the Paris Summit Conference of May 1960, and again nothing was settled – Khruschev exploited the shooting-down of an American U2 "spy-plane" over Soviet territory in order to denounce the West in frantic language, and then left the Conference. He predicted the signing of a separate peace-treaty with the DDR, and the conversion of West Berlin into a free city. His objection to its freedom and existing status was that it was supposedly a centre for spying and subversion. The true reasons were that West Berlin was a centre of free thought, a magnificent shop window for the West, and the obvious destination for four out of five East German refugees, who could cross over from East Berlin with relatively little difficulty. West Berlin had a generally unsettling effect on the DDR, especially on its economy – an ever larger proportion of refugees were skilled workers who could sell their services in the West, and intellectuals who could utilize their qualifications there. Khruschev's bellicosity, according to one observer, did not mean that he wanted war, but only that he felt strong enough to put pressure on the West in order to secure tactical gains in Germany.[38] Berlin was the most neuralgic point for the West: "The beauty of the Berlin situation, from the Communist point of view, is that it enables them to influence events over which they would otherwise have no control".[39]

There was more, even, to it than that. The Soviet Bloc as a whole, and the DDR in particular, suffered from glaring weaknesses. The satellite states lived under regimes imposed upon them by the Soviet Union, and their populations have never come to terms with Communism. Economic muddles, and serious failures, were endemic. There were stirrings of a spirit of resistance among peoples which had not lost their sense of identity – there were even the first stirrings in the Soviet Union itself. The DDR was a particular worry to the Soviet leaders; its economic potential could never be realized as long as thousands upon thousands of its best citizens continued to seek refuge in the West. Nor was it merely a matter of those who left, for those who stayed behind could always feel that they had the option of going too, and as long as they felt this way they would not settle down to building an efficient and successful entity.

These were the considerations which prompted Soviet use of the DDR in 1960–1 as a pressure point on the West. The death of the President, Wilhelm Pieck, enabled Walter Ulbricht – totally true to Moscow and totally ruthless – to take over all administrative authority and political control. From September, all West German citizens had to apply for a permit to enter East Berlin. In January 1961, the Evangelical Churches, regarded in the Communist world as a dangerously diversionary factor, were banned from holding their synod in both parts of Berlin, and the Chairman of the Evangelical Church Council was later expelled from East Berlin. In June, the Vienna meeting between President John Kennedy and Khruschev was fruitless, and Khruschev formed the dangerously misleading impression that Kennedy was a weak man – Kennedy was suffering from back trouble, and Khruschev, with the physique of Apollyon, considered that a man who was physically weak would turn out to be morally weak too. On 15 June, Khruschev announced that there had to be a German settlement in 1961, and Ulbricht followed this up with a press conference in which he said that West Berlin must become a free city and that the refugee reception centres and airfields must be closed down. He let slip a hint: nobody, he said, was thinking of "building a wall". This was exactly what happened – in the night of 12 to 13 August the building of the "Berlin Wall" began.

The Western Powers and the West Berlin authorities were caught completely by surprise; their intelligence services failed them, and refused to pay any attention to reports of unusual movements of traffic into East Berlin. The Western Powers, with rights in the whole of Berlin, took no action whatever. Their representatives argued that the situation was unique, but this was not correct; they had failed to act in a similar situation during the East German rising of 1953. Their armed forces in Berlin could, at the very least, have been used to impede the building of the Wall by passing to and fro across the sector boundaries and even bivouacking there. No Soviet troops took part in the building operations and no DDR troops were allowed, under Four Power regulations, in the city.

No Western protest was made on the spot, to the Soviet Commandant of East Berlin, until 15 August. The Western Powers did not protest in Moscow until 17 August, whereas they could easily have done so by the evening of 13 August. Their diplomatic paralysis was inexcusable; the only explanation, according to the latest book on the incident, was that they had written off East Berlin altogether.[40] Even the United States Government felt that it was wiser to concentrate on defending and maintaining Western rights in West Berlin only.

Adenauer did no better. He was telephoned at his Rhoendorf home at 4.30 a.m. on 13 August. He attended early mass as usual and ignored an appeal to go to Berlin at once. He continued to treat that crucial Sunday, quite literally, as a "day of rest", and on 14 August merely spoke on television, saying there was no cause for alarm. He did nothing at all on 15 August, presumably waiting for some Allied action. On 16 August, he told the Bundestag that the Wall was "a declaration of bankruptcy on the part of the 16-year tyranny [in East Germany]". Not until 22 August did he go to Berlin, where he had a chilling reception. His only excuse was that there was a West German election campaign going on at the time. In the course of it, he told a shocked audience at Hagen, in Westphalia, that Khruschev organized the building of the Wall in order to help the SPD in the election. Willy Brandt, now SPD candidate for the Chancellorship, retorted that "the old gentleman really cannot grasp what's going on any more" and advised him "to seek a peaceful evening to his life".[41]

Willy Brandt's own part will be described later. The consequences of the Wall were far-reaching. It made escape from the DDR next to impossible and it destroyed virtually all contact between members of the same families, close friends, sometimes even between husband and wife and mother and son. The implications in the field of human rights were considerable, but organizations which claim to concern themselves in such matters seem to have taken singularly little interest in the sufferings of the East and the West Germans. Attempted escapes, incidentally, led to at least 64 people being killed, and over 100 wounded, during the next ten years. Hundreds of shooting incidents could not be observed from the western side of the Wall, but over 4,000 escape attempts were reported. All would-be escapers were certain to be punished, rigorously.

The people of the DDR were cowed by the creation of the Wall. In November 1961, an officer of the East German armed forces escaped to the Federal Republic, and his report was published on 13 January 1962. Ex-Major Siegfried Behr stated that the twenty Soviet and seven East German divisions were put on full alert on 12 August and remained ready until 24 August to put down the national uprising which was feared.[42] But the Wall made such an event illusory, particularly when it became plain that the West was taking no real interest. The East Germans had risen in 1953, and the West did nothing for them. The West, again, had been inactive during the Hungarian rising of 1956. After thirty years of Nazi and Communist dictatorship, the East Germans were not ready to risk their necks.

This left them with no alternative but to make the best of things and collaborate with the Ulbricht regime in its unhurried, but ruthless organization of a disciplined communist society. All the weapons of a dictatorship were used to encourage them – propaganda, intimidation, cajolery and occasional material benefits. The West simply washed its hands of these seventeen million East Germans; one commentator wrote: "Many people talk blithely of writing off Eastern Germany and its inhabitants. It may, indeed, be deemed necessary. But ... it will be an act which the conscience of the Western world will hardly be able to forget."[43] But it proved to be yet more shameful; the Western world *has* forgotten.

The Wall made the DDR viable. Its population did not only have to accept a communist society; it had to get down to work. Being German, it worked very hard and efficiently. The DDR has since become the workshop of the Soviet Bloc and has been allowed to raise its living-standards faster than in other satellite states. The East Germans have developed a pride in their own achievements, and even in their own state. The division of Germany has become more absolute – a division which one writer claimed was "the real source of danger in Europe".[44] In Pharaoh's dream the lean kine ate up the fat kine; there are a great many West Germans who are glad that the lean kine of the DDR are being kept in their own pen.

Finally, the Wall had subtly different effects on the thinking of leaders in the Federal Republic. A man like Franz Josef Strauss took the uncomplicated view that it was further proof of the duplicity of the Russians and their East German lackeys. For the West, the logical answer was to organize more efficiently for its own military defence, and firm up its political concepts.[45] But Willy Brandt, and many others, took a more pragmatic view. Thus, Brandt argued that the West had written off East Berlin; this left West Berlin to be looked after and safeguarded.[46] This, in turn, gave a special point to a policy of détente between East and West, which was not to be sought for West Berlin's sake alone but which would treat West Berlin as the central point in any process of reconciliation. Confrontation, as people like Brandt saw it, had been all very well in an era when the West was positively interested in German reunification. But the West's climb-down over the Berlin Wall showed this was no longer the case. Regrettably, Adenauer's policy of negotiating from a position of strength would be superseded by a policy of seeking détente from a position of weakness.

The Berlin Wall was only one of Adenauer's setbacks during his third term in office. In 1959 occurred the "Presidential Crisis", which did more than any other event to damage his reputation, and which marked the watershed between years of achievement and years of decline. The saddest thing about the crisis was that it need never have happened.

Professor Heuss, after two terms in office as President, was due to retire in September 1959. He himself favoured an extension of the term of office from five to seven years, but only after his own retirement. Heuss belonged to the FDP; his candidature, back in 1949, had been very amenable to the CDU, and his calm, authoritative performance had made him acceptable to the SPD. To some extent, he was a compromise candidate originally, but the two big parties, locked in everlasting political battle, did not think in such terms in 1959. The SPD put up the portly, witty man-of-the-world, Professor Carlo Schmid, as their candidate. The CDU had none immediately available. This is where Adenauer came in.

He regarded Carlo Schmid as highly unsuitable; he had opposed the Federal Republic's entry into the Council of Europe and NATO, and had been vociferous in opposing the stockpiling of "tactical" nuclear weapons on German soil. Adenauer must have disapproved strongly of his private life which was, put discreetly, "modern". He regarded it as vital that the CDU should put up a rival candidate, who would become President; and he would have to be a good one, for the CDU did not have a majority in the electoral "Bundesversammlung", or Federal Assembly. He proposed Ludwig Erhard and secured the support of a special CDU "electoral committee".

According to Adenauer, Erhard first said he was "agreeable", and five days later, on 2 March, turned the offer down.[47] Erhard claimed that Adenauer telephoned him on 24 February, that his immediate reaction was to refuse, but out of deference to President Heuss he waited until the next day, and explained his reasons for refusal to Heuss. Erhard said categorically: "I never showed any interest in becoming President. The truth was that Adenauer wanted to kick me upstairs."[48]

It was fairly sure that the CDU wanted Erhard to remain in active politics, as the logical successor to Adenauer. On 2 April Hans Globke informed Adenauer that a number of influential members of the CDU wanted him, the Chancellor, to run for the Presidency. Adenauer was at first amazed, but showed interest when Globke explained that the President's office, as in France under de Gaulle, could carry more political power than hitherto.[49] Some of Adenauer's closest confidants – especially Heinrich Krone – advised him that his transfer into the President's office could give a real "continuity" to CDU rule.[50] With his sense of history combining with his sense of mission, Adenauer took his bearings, consulted all and sundry, and agreed to run for the Presidency on 7 April. Almost comically, he noted that the new job would entail "being fair to the SPD"!

Krone bewitched him, and Krone was acting from the best of motives. He was utterly sympathetic to Adenauer, but aware that his powers were beginning to fade. He was in very close touch with opinion in the CDU, and realized that Erhard was its natural candidate for the Chancellorship – once Adenauer retired from it. Krone really believed in the theory of "continuity", but what he could not have allowed for was Adenauer's reaction to the news brought him in his holiday home in Cadennabia, for which he left on 8 April.

All of it was bad, from the Chancellor's point of view. He believed that the Constitution gave the President the right to nominate the Chancellor. Good: he would be able to block the way to Erhard, in his opinion a "man without character"[51] and incapable of understanding the intricacies of foreign policy. He would nominate Franz Etzel instead, a man whom he could trust and whom he expected to be able to steer. But on 15 April, Robert Pferdemenges arrived in Cadennabia, with a personal message from Erhard. The latter pledged his loyalty to Adenauer but claimed that there could be no objection to his becoming Chancellor. This was bad enough, but Adenauer was incensed to learn that his old friend Pferdemenges agreed!

On 2 May Heinrich Krone and Hans Globke arrived, with the news that a substantial majority of the CDU Members of the Bundestag favoured Erhard's candidature. Then, on Adenauer's way back to Bonn on 4 May – he liked to break the journey at Baden-Baden – the emissary of the Bavarian CSU branch of the party, Hermann Hoecherl, called on him and told him that the CSU, which was increasing its vote in every election and steadily gaining power in its own right in the Bundestag and the party, was solidly behind Erhard. There had been talks between Erhard and the CSU's most forceful personality, Strauss; from now on, Strauss was an "Erhard man" – he knew Erhard's weaknesses and he rightly visualized himself as the strong man in an Erhard Cabinet. Adenauer's reaction was to summon Erhard on 13 May and try to talk him out of running for the Chancellorship. Erhard, so often depicted as a "rubber lion", remained obstinately silent during most of the interview. At the end of it, he told Adenauer that it was his duty to run for the Chancellorship and that, as Chancellor, he would continue to manage the Ministry of Economics "on ten per cent of his time".[52]

Adenauer has been bitterly criticized for his actions during the next weeks. He told the Cabinet that the international situation could force him to revise his decision to stand down as Chancellor; but the spirit of the meeting was unsympathetic. He saw Pferdemenges again; he thought he had talked him round at Cadennabia, but now found that this very special friend had been enlisted all over again on Erhard's side. On 19 May he gave Krone a letter listing his objections to Erhard's candidature, and asked him to make effective use of it; instead, Krone urged him to change his mind about Erhard.

If Adenauer had a failing which he managed to convert into an asset it was his obstinacy. He gave Krone a second letter, which formally stated his reasons for now wishing to remain Chancellor – chief among them was that the CDU, under Erhard, would lose the 1961 elections. He wrote to Erhard too, appealing to him to consider the national interest and not his own. On 25 May John Foster Dulles died, a bitter personal blow to the Chancellor, but – a politician to the fingertips – he used Dulles' death as a pretext for claiming that experienced statesmen should stay at the helm in the Western world. Adenauer's mind was now completely made up; he flew to Dulles' funeral in Washington and on his return to Bonn withdrew his candidature for the Presidency on 4 June. Another letter went off to Krone, deploring that a controversy had been publicly conducted, which was doing "grave damage to our party and our cause" – a shrewd tactical move – and he called a CDU Parliamentary Party meeting for 11 June, to decide on the candidate for the Presidency.

He presided over the meeting with masterly authority. One of the chief "rebels", Eugen Gerstenmaier (the President, or Speaker, of the Bundestag) confronted him at the door of the party conference chamber. Adenauer dismissed him with a crushing phrase – "It's a curious thing that you can tell, just from a man's eyes, the hate in his heart." Gerstenmaier left in a huff, and all opposition collapsed. In the Bundestag the Chancellor used his sardonic humour to fight off a bitter attack by the SPD – he was accused of demeaning the office of President, trampling on his own party and showing a profound contempt for his fellow-beings. Adenauer did not trouble to answer these charges; he told the Bundestag that he was staying on as Chancellor because "I would have missed you all so much", and because "As President I should have been unable to make a single fighting election speech". On 1 July the CDU candidate, Heinrich Luebke, a simple and honest man whose knowledge was confined to the field of agriculture, was elected Federal President.

Ahead lay the run-up to the Federal elections, in September 1961. The economy was in good shape, and there had been no domestic problems of sufficient importance to worry Adenauer who, inevitably, was running for a fourth term in office. The trial in Israel of Adolf Eichmann, captured in Argentina by Israeli agents and one of the worst of the Nazi war-criminals, was causing some embarrassment – it did not culminate, with Eichmann's death sentence, until after the elections. There had been some disturbing evidence in the Federal Republic of anti-semitism, and in January 1961, Adenauer retired to bed with bronchial trouble. At his tea-table, on 19 January, Georg Schroeder, veteran correspondent of *Die Welt*, found his face thinner, with new lines to add to the previous intricate network, and he was forced to speak slowly and softly. But his mind seemed as keen as ever.[53] He campaigned with his usual flair and his hopes were high.

The result of the 1961 elections was a shock to him. The CDU vote dropped by 700,000 and its Bundestag seats from 277 (some members of the DP switched to the CDU in 1960) to 242. It lost its overall majority. The SPD increased its seats from 181 to 190, and the FDP did even better – up from 43 to 67 and now very much a "third force". Adenauer's poor showing during the Berlin Wall crisis told against him; so, to a minor extent, did memories of the "Presidential Crisis". The SPD had, at last, a really good candidate for the Chancellorship in Willy Brandt, while the FDP had gained from a period of independence from Adenauer's smothering patronage.

Adenauer was 85 years old. He was aware of the feeling within his party that the time was ripe to hand over leadership to Erhard. He had to secure the support of the FDP to form a new government, and the FDP leader, Erich Mende, demanded that Erhard should become Chancellor. Surely, this was the time for Adenauer to give up? On the contrary, he showed all his old skill, first putting out feelers to the SPD and then partly cajoling and partly frightening the FDP into coalition. But he had to make concessions. First, he agreed to retire in two years' time, and Adenauer gave Mende one of only two copies of a letter promising this: the letter remained for the time being a secret document.[54] Then Mende insisted that Heinrich von Brentano should cease to be Foreign Minister – this was perfectly fair, for Brentano simply did Adenauer's bidding and was not the right man to hold such a key office under a Chancellor under notice to quit. Adenauer should have been reasonably satisfied, for his overtures to the SPD had been a total bluff.[55] But he was less pleased with the vote of 259 out of 499 members of the Bundestag when he was re-elected Chancellor. It was estimated that 17 members of the CDU–FDP coalition voted against him, and 26 abstained.

In retrospect, Adenauer would have been wise to have bowed out in 1961. At best, his foreshortened two-year term in office was undistinguished; he gained nothing in reputation from it. He carried on because he believed that he was indispensable. The events of these two years in office need be only briefly summarized.

First, there was the failure to bring Britain into the EEC, due to de Gaulle's insistence and the exaggerated value that Adenauer placed on the Franco-German Treaty of Friendship. On the whole this was not in the best interest of the Europe in which Adenauer so fervently believed and which he wanted so dearly to serve. Then there was total failure to make any progress in East–West relations, and towards German reunification. It may be unfair to blame Adenauer for this, and it may be true – as at least one of his advisers maintained – that he was beginning to give his mind to East–West problems and might have produced an initiative, given time.[56] These matters have already been dealt with, as has Adenauer's failure – admittedly, second to that of the Western Powers – to show due interest in the building of the Berlin Wall.

The domestic scene was a clouded one, too. In this, the Defence Minister played a flamboyant part. Nobody could doubt the energy, imagination and industry of Franz Josef Strauss. In spite of a habitual unpunctuality, he discharged a formidable work load.[57] The Bundeswehr was bound to have teething troubles, and Strauss was not necessarily to blame for them. A number of recruits were drowned on an exercise on the Iller river; two West German pilots flew, by mistake, over East Germany and landed in West Berlin; the F104 Starfighter plane bought from the United States turned out to be much more expensive than expected, and difficulties in flying it exacted a heavy toll in casualties; then came the FIBAG (Finanzbau Aktiengesellschaft) affair in 1961, in which Strauss was unjustly accused of having a financial interest in the building of 5,000 quarters for US Army families. But the Bundeswehr was brought up to a strength of 400,000 in 1962; by now it was well armed and efficient. The Federal Republic was well-launched along the road towards providing the best contingent in NATO's European command.

In October 1962, Strauss ran into real trouble. A *Spiegel* (*Der Spiegel* is Germany's liveliest political weekly) correspondent, Conrad Ahlers, wrote an article on the "Fallex '62" NATO manoeuvres in West Germany. The article claimed that the manoeuvres showed how Western nuclear counter attack would fail to prevent the enemy occupation of a large part of the Federal Republic. This disproved Strauss's contention that a single nuclear bomb was worth a whole armoured brigade, and indicated that the size of the Bundeswehr should be increased – to ensure a "forward strategy" on the Elbe – and that it should be equipped with medium-range rockets. This information was obviously leaked – it was later suggested that Ahlers' informant was a Colonel Alfred Martin of the Bundeswehr's headquarters staff. The *Spiegel* editorial staff had helped to establish contact between Ahlers and Martin, and there was nothing sinister about this. But the paper was a fearless critic of the Government, and especially of Strauss (it had been responsible for "blowing" the FIBAG story).

Strauss, with Adenauer's connivance, instigated action which was plainly out of step with the rule of law. The Hamburg and Bonn offices of the *Spiegel* were raided by the police, members of the paper's staff were arrested and their homes searched, and Strauss engineered the arrest of Ahlers in Malaga, where he was on holiday. Worse was to follow: the Minister of the Interior, Hermann Hoecherl, first denied knowledge of the affair and was later forced to admit that he had known all the time, while it was revealed that the Minister of Justice, Dr Wolfgang Stammberger, had been kept in the dark – when all this was within his province. Strauss issued various denials of complicity until 30 November, when he resigned, while Adenauer, rather typically, mounted a counter-offensive; in the Bundestag he attacked the publisher of *Der Spiegel*, Rudolf Augstein, for "systematically betraying the state in order to make money".[58] In addition he produced any red herring he could think of; thus "There had even been talk of Tangier, and just how would one collect a German citizen in Tangier?"[59]

Adenauer would probably have had to stand down in 1963 anyway; the "*Spiegel* Affair" ensured that he did. The FDP Ministers resigned, and he began, for the very first time, to lose control of his own party. In 1963 the CDU was in a state of sad disarray. The last struggle with Erhard was beginning; Adenauer's foremost paladin of the past, Schroeder, was at odds with him over the exclusion of Britain and other applicants from the EEC; the trusty von Brentano had been thrown to the wolves, and there was no reconciliation with Gerstenmaier. (Yet something of the Chancellor's ingrained mischievousness lingered; the short, dumpy Gerstenmaier had a block of wood which he pushed into position when mounting the Speaker's rostrum, and Adenauer, just within reach, took to kicking it round the corner, out of Gerstenmaier's sight.) Kiesinger would have been a valuable man for Adenauer to have at his elbow at such a juncture, but he had left the Bonn arena in 1958 to become Prime Minister of *Land* Baden-Wurtemberg.

Adenauer made his final effort to bar Erhard from the succession in April 1963. He gathered what remained of his once serried ranks of followers – the ever-faithful Krone, and the obscure Ministers of Posts, Labour and *Laender* Affairs. One is reminded of Napoleon throwing in the last loyal remnants of his once Grand Army at Waterloo. Adenauer called on them to help; Krone was to "discipline" the CDU Executive, Blank was to raise the Christian Trade Unions, and Niederalt the Bavarians (the last-named was reported to have replied, "Don't make me laugh!")[60] They refused, and the game was up. Ahead lay an extended summer holiday, meetings in Bonn with Presidents de Gaulle and Kennedy, a farewell visit to de Gaulle at Rambouillet. Only routine work otherwise at the Chancellery, until the final good-byes, in Berlin and in the Bundestag. There, Gerstenmaier congratulated him on being the first German Chancellor in a hundred years to withdraw of his own free will. Nothing could have been further from the truth, but withdraw he did, and with elegance and grace. A whole era of German history came to an end.

Adenauer was the greatest, probably the only great German statesman since Bismarck. There has, inevitably, been a tendency to compare the achievements of the two men. Thus Golo Mann[61] saw in Adenauer the citizen who thought in social terms, compared with Bismarck, the aristocrat, intent on building up German influence and power; Adenauer, the ultra-careful chess-player in the diplomatic field, Bismarck, showy and a brilliant gambler. Bismarck left the Germany which he had helped to unite dominating Central Europe, while Adenauer integrated the truncated Federal Republic with a Western Alliance led by the United States. Such comparison would seem to favour the "Blood and Iron" Chancellor, who did not hesitate to instigate three wars in order to get what he wanted for Germany. Adenauer, in contrast, was essentially a man of peace. But one should not forget the situations which the two men inherited. Bismarck led a Prussia with a great military tradition behind it and a claim to lead the whole German nation contested only by a decaying Austrian Empire. Adenauer inherited next to nothing; he had to rebuild a remnant of Germany which might regain freedom and independence, and to restore German honour and credibility. Bismarck made alliances; Adenauer made real friends. Bismarck consolidated an oligarchy of Kaiser, aristocracy, industrialists and army; Adenauer presided over a new and successful experiment in functioning democracy. Of the two achievements, Adenauer's has the chance of lasting very much the longer. For the foundation of the democracy of the Federal Republic has been an organic process, unlike the Weimar democracy of a failed revolution.

It is, indeed, beside the point whether Adenauer was as "great" as Bismarck. It is of far more significance that he led his people in the right direction, towards toleration, human dignity and understanding, and a healthy and sane Europeanism, and that he helped to shift Germany's centre of gravity back to old centres of learning and light – Cologne, Frankfurt, Munich, Stuttgart and even the much derided "federal village" of Bonn. The "Adenauer era" has been criticized for a measure of spiritual frustration, for the growth of materialism, a spirit of rejection among the youth, signs of anarchy and violence. Much the same has been happening in other European countries, bearing no such burden of the past as the Germans, but beginning to lose sense of purpose, self-confidence and faith. These were trends which Adenauer strove to combat; nobody could accuse him of apathy or indifference. Prosaic he may sometimes have been, in his pursuit of "die kleine Habe" – the decent competence for the average citizen – and of moderation and commonsense. But he helped to banish the cults of hysteria and hate, of wild dreams and global ambitions.

One of his chief political opponents, Willy Brandt, was equally prosaic in this tribute: "He made the free part of Germany an ally of the West, lent powerful impulses to West European unity ... devoted himself to Franco-German reconciliation ... Even his political opponents of yesterday are conscious that Germany is poorer for the loss of a man who set standards."[62] He did much more than this: he conquered the despair of Hitler's criminal war, and after the old Germany ceased to exist, he was the principal architect of the new. His was a mighty achievement.

1. Theo Pirker. *Die SPD nach Hitler*. Munich, 1965.
2. Abraham Ashkenazi. *Reformpartei und Aussenpolitik*. Cologne, 1968.
3. Helga Grebing. *The History of the German Labour Movement*. London, 1969.
4. Terence Prittie. *Willy Brandt*. New York, 1974.
5. Aidan Crawley. *The Rise of Western Germany*. London, 1973.
6. Charles de Gaulle. *Memoirs of Hope*. London, 1971.
7. Konrad Adenauer. *Memoirs*, Vol 3. Stuttgart, 1966.
8. Ibid.
9. Ibid.
10. Aidan Crawley, op. cit.
11. Konrad Adenauer. *Memoirs*, Vol 3.
12. François Seydoux. *Konrad Adenauer 1876/1976*. Edited by Dr Alois Rummel, Bonn, 1975.
13. Aidan Crawley. *De Gaulle*. London, 1969.
14. Dr Hans Globke, in conversation with the author, March 1971.
15. Frau Ria Reiners, in conversation with the author, May 1971.
16. Burghard Freudenfeld. *Adenauer und die Folgen*. Edited by Hans-Joachim Netzer. Munich, 1965.
17. Felix von Eckardt, in conversation with the author, May 1971.
18. Sir Christopher Steel, in conversation with the author, February 1971.
19. Ibid.
20. *Manchester Guardian*, 27 November 1958.
21. Terence Prittie. *Konrad Adenauer*. London, 1972.
22. Aidan Crawley. *The Rise of Western Germany*.
23. François Seydoux, op. cit.
24. Konrad Adenauer. *Memoirs*, Vol 4. Stuttgart, 1966.
25. Ibid.
26. Ibid.
27. Ibid.
28. François Seydoux, op. cit.

29. Dr Gerhard Schroder, in conversation with the author, March 1963.
30. General Lord Robertson, in conversation with the author, June 1969.
31. Professor Walter Hallstein, in conversation with the author, May 1971.
32. *Manchester Guardian*, 6 December 1957.
33. Dr Hans Globke, in conversation with the author, March 1971.
34. Hans-Gert Poltering. *Adenauer's Sicherheitspolitik 1955/63*, Düsseldorf, 1975.
35. Dean Acheson, "The Illusion of Disengagement", in *Foreign Affairs*, April 1958.
36. Helmut Schmidt. *Verteidigung oder Velgeltung*. Stuttgart, 1961.
37. Dr Erich Mende, in conversation with the author, May 1971.
38. John Mander. *Berlin. Hostage of the West*. London, 1962.
39. Ibid.
40. Curtis Cate. *The Ides of August*. London, 1979.
41. Terence Prittie. *Konrad Adenauer*.
42. *Manchester Guardian*, 13 January 1962.
43. Terence Prittie. *Konrad Adenauer*.
44. John Mander, op. cit.
45. Franz Josef Strauss. *The Grand Design*. London, 1965.
46. Willy Brandt. *People and Politics*. London, 1978.
47. Konrad Adenauer. *Memoirs*, Vol 3.
48. Professor Ludwig Erhard, in conversation with the author, March 1971.
49. Konrad Adenauer. *Memoirs*, Vol 3.
50. Dr Heinrich Krone, in conversation with the author, May 1971.
51. Adenauer's word was *Eigenschaften*, literally meaning "attributes".
52. Konrad Adenauer. *Memoirs*, Vol 3.
53. Georg Schroeder, in a private memorandum given to the author, March 1971.
54. Dr Erich Mende, in conversation with the author, May 1971.
55. Dr Gerhard Schroeder and Felix von Eckardt, in conversation with the author, March 1971.
56. Dr Hans Globke, in conversation with the author, March 1971.
57. Walter Henkels. *Bonner Koepfe*. Düsseldorf, 1968.
58. Rudolf Augstein. *Konrad Adenauer*. London, 1964.
59. Alfred Grosser. *Die Spiegel Affaere*.
60. Terence Prittie. *The New Republic*, 11 May 1963.
61. Golo Mann. *Encounter* magazine, April 1964.
62. Willy Brandt, op. cit.

Chapter Six

Free-Wheeling, Downhill

Succeeding a great man is a difficult business. When one of England's greatest Prime Ministers, William Pitt, resigned in 1801, his place was taken by an obscure gentleman called Henry Addington. The jingle at once became current:

> Pitt is to Addington
> As London is to Paddington.

Ludwig Erhard was fully aware of the lustre of Konrad Adenauer's mantle, even if it has been somewhat tarnished during the latter days of a fourteen-year long Chancellorship. His predecessor had made his inheritance as awkward for him as he possibly could. Needless to say, there had been not the slightest attempt to groom him for the job, and over all those fourteen long years Erhard had been given no say in any department of government save his own, Economics. There had, indeed, been a kind of unspoken agreement between the two men. Erhard believed that, not only did Adenauer show no consistent interest in the economy of the Federal Republic, but "he did not even want to know about such affairs".[1] For his part, Erhard scrupulously avoided interfering in any purely political issue.

Ludwig Erhard's origins can only be described as humble. His father came from Northern Bavaria, and as a 26 year-old farmer moved into Fürth and opened a haberdashery shop in 1885. Fürth has no claim to fame, but is only a very few miles from Nuremberg, which for a thousand years has lain on major east–west and north–south European trade-routes. Born in 1897, Ludwig was brought up in a God-fearing, hard-working, simple but friendly milieu. His father was Catholic, his mother Protestant; he and the other children were brought up in the mother's faith – although it was later said of Ludwig that "he knew the outside of his local church better than the interior".[2] Infantile paralysis, at the age of two, gave him a deformed right foot and slight curvature of the spine – that in turn, accounted for a short neck, a slight stoop and several chins.

He had a quiet upbringing and his early years were humdrum and utterly undistinguished; he inherited his mother's shyness, and expected to inherit his father's shop. But he went to the wars in 1916, was badly wounded two years later, and found the family business virtually on the rocks when he came out of hospital. He chose to study economics at Nuremberg's *Handelshochschule*, or School of Economics – was a keen and able student, and found a job in Nuremberg's Institute of Market Research. His most distinguished teacher, Franz Oppenheimer, had to flee the country when the Nazis came to power, and Ludwig showed real courage in refusing to *Heil Hitler* or join the Nazi Party in this most Nazi of all areas of Germany. This certainly lost him the chance of becoming a Professor.[3] He even resigned his post, with a staff of over one hundred working under him, when pressure was brought to bear on him to join the Nazi Labour Front. He made his own way, with his own market research office.

His rise to fame after the war was meteoric. On 19 April 1945, the American town-commandant of Fürth, a Major Cooper, asked him to take over its economic administration. In September, the US Military Government asked him to take over the Ministry of Economics for the *Land* of Bavaria. Hardly a success in that job, he moved on to do six months as a Professor of Munich University, where he expanded and adapted the thoughts on free initiative and a balanced economy given to him by Franz Oppenheimer. Then the Americans sent him to the Frankfurt Economic Council, and put him in charge of economic and financial planning. Photographs of him at the time show his clothes hanging loosely, his face haggard; he was a big man, but was down to about ten stone early in 1948. In March, he became Director of the Economic Administration of the US–British Bizonal Council, the most responsible post in the economic field held by any German at that time.

It is conventionally supposed that Erhard's career ran in a

comfortable groove from then on, for in 1949 he was the CDU's natural choice as Minister of Economics and he held that post until becoming Chancellor, fourteen years later. In reality, he had to go on making his way. One of his first administrative actions in Frankfurt was to declare the end of rationing and price controls on 21 June 1948, just two days after the Western Powers had announced the terms of Currency Reform. Only after a two-hour talk did he gain the support of the US Military Governor, General Lucius Clay.[4] British Military Government, under the influence of the Labour Government in London, remained bitterly, bitingly critical of him. One of its leading economists gave him a nickname of inordinate length[5] – "Euchen-Rieger-Hielscher-Abs-Roepke-Dummkopf". There was a protagonist of free enterprise for each letter of his name, save the last; "Dummkopf" equals "blockhead", and this particular British critic continued to expound the fallacies of Erhard's "social free-market economy" policies year after year.

Fallacies there may have been, but the positive results were spectacular. Under Erhard's direction, 12 million refugees were resettled and 7,700,000 new jobs created. The national income multiplied four times during the same period, and per capita income, in "real" terms of purchasing-power, nearly five times. The German mark became one of the three strongest currencies in Europe. In 1950, the Federal Republic was forced to ask for special credits from the European Payments Union, and in return was obliged to take measures to restrict domestic consumption and raise exports. By 1955, the Federal Republic had become the foremost creditor country in Europe, and by 1963 was the second largest trading country in the world. The so-called "Economic Miracle" began in 1948–9, and what was truly miraculous was that, apart from two moments of real doubt and hesitation – first when the Erhard administration fell, and secondly, in the aftermath of the oil crisis at the end of 1973 – it never really ended. The Federal Republic had to compete with all the same economic problems as did its European neighbours and, in addition, with huge war-debts, the influx of millions of refugees, and the destruction and dismantling of many key industries. Yet, having moved ahead of its major European rivals in the early 1950s, it has remained ahead ever since.

Figures tell part of the story; so, too, do the spectacular performances of the post-war millionaires, who carved out industrial empires for themselves. Given every encouragement to rebuild, communal cooperation was generally at a very high level. Reference has already been made to Jülich, the "town of three houses" (see p. 26). On 1 December 1944, the population of this market-town was officially listed as zero. When war ended, demolition and the repair of sewers, water mains, telephone lines and roads, alone cost over one million dollars. Only when most of this basic work had been done, did rebuilding begin; two-room buildings rose out of the ruins, growing horizontally as well as vertically, blocks of flats followed, then shopping streets.[6] By 1960, there were two sugar beet factories, half a dozen other smaller industrial plants and a population of 14,000. Or there was the case of New-Gablonz, the "successor" of the old, German-speaking centre of the glass industry in Northern Czechoslovakia. In 1945 its inhabitants became refugees, and early in 1946 a small group of them rented some sandy waste land and several disused hangars where Hitler's V.1 weapons had been built, outside the Bavarian town of Kaufbeuren. Twelve years later, the old glass industry had been re-created, with an annual turnover of 40 million dollars, supporting a population of 12,000.[7] There were dozens, even hundreds of parallels to the stories of Jülich and New-Gablonz.

What were the secrets of the "Economic Miracle"? One ludicrous myth, perpetrated by ignorant or biased observers, was that the Germans were "lucky" in having so much "outdated" equipment destroyed or dismantled; this, allegedly, forced them to re-tool and re-equip, and it was even suggested that this gave them an "unfair" advantage over European competitors. What arrant nonsense! Bombing, shelling and dismantling ripped the heart out of hundreds of major industrial plants, and after the war there was a desperate shortage of everything needed for their reconstruction. The real secrets of German success were very different: they were an immense will to work, a remarkable degree of industrial peace, and Erhard's decision to give the people of the Federal Republic their head, along with every possible incentive. These included interest-free loans, for everything from the rebuilding of modest homes to the reconstruction of giant steel and shipbuilding plants, massive grants to agriculture, the sweeping away of restrictions, and the liberalization of trade. Sometimes his policies may have looked like nineteenth century *laissez-faire*; in reality, their psychological content was the clue to their success – Erhard realized that the tremendous vitality of the German people, dissipated in the past in the political, colonial and military fields, and a will to win their way back, could be concentrated in productive work. What was more, Erhard realized that this was exactly what most Germans wanted.

Willy Brandt would later write: "Ludwig Erhard probably showed the right instinct when he urged that economic forces should be allowed to develop as freely as possible during the Federal Republic's early years. He was less well advised when he converted this into an ideology. It was his good fortune that things could not fail to improve after such a calamitous war."[8] Brandt was a political opponent, and perhaps nothing more than grudging praise could be expected from him. But he quoted the Danish Foreign Minister, Jens Otto Krag, as telling him that "he could not see how we Social Democrats had any chance of ousting Adenauer and Erhard under conditions of almost continuous economic growth. For all its social inequalities, the economic miracle was indeed a potent card in the government's hand".[9] This is nearer the mark, but there was more to it than that. Bruno Heck was probably right, when he wrote that Erhard was a fearless innovator: he actually changed CDU economic thinking, which up to 1949 was based on day-to-day improvisation to meet current social needs.[10] The CDU was ready to go far along the road to nationalization and a planned economy, in order to meet the wishes of the occupying powers. Erhard struck out on a line of his own.

It was generally imagined that he did at least have the unlimited support of Konrad Adenauer in carrying out his economic policies. After the first two or three years, this was not the case. One of his closest advisers, Alfred Müller-Armack, has written about the periodic clashes which took place between the two men.[11] The Chancellor was continually sending him memorandums, expressing doubts or giving directions, and Erhard was scrupulous in replying politely and in detail. Significantly, Erhard never gave way; where economic principles were concerned "he had the tenacity of a bulldog, the obstinacy of a mule, and the hide of an elephant".[12] He needed it, for Adenauer was persistent.

Thus in 1951 Adenauer became alarmed by the size of borrowings from the European Payments Union and by the scale on which Erhard wanted to liberalize imports. He formed a "private economics office" under Dr Friedrich Ernst, and instructed it to work out modifications of Erhard's free-market policies.[13] In the same year, he induced Erhard to accept as personal adviser Dr Ludger Westrick, whom he expected to keep the Chancellery informed of what was going on in the Ministry of Economics. Instead, Westrick became Erhard's right-hand man, extolling him as "co-founder", with Adenauer, of the Federal Republic.[14] Then Adenauer began to turn to Fritz Berg, the Chairman of the West German Federation of Industry (BDI) for advice. Berg, in return, sought to enlist Adenauer's aid in blocking anti-trust legislation.[15]

In 1956 Adenauer attacked Erhard in public. Speaking in the Gürzenich Hall in Cologne in May, he told an amazed audience that he disapproved of the bank rate having been twice raised, and had not been consulted before this was done.[16] He added that he would oppose Erhard's proposal to reduce tariffs by up to 30 per cent and threw in a gibe at his Minister of Finance, Dr Fritz Schaeffer, for approving 125 regulations for income tax alone. Later, Erhard would say of this incident that Adenauer's strictures were "beyond all reason".[17] At the time, he threatened to resign. In June 1957 he was once again talking of resignation, this time over Adenauer's sudden opposition to the lowering of import duties on basic materials.

After the 1957 elections Adenauer wanted Erhard to slap a high duty onto imported coal – not his own idea, but that of protection-minded German coal-mining interests. Both before and after the "Presidential Crisis" of 1959, Adenauer and Erhard were once again at odds, this time over the revaluation of the D Mark. Adenauer had the backing of both Dr Karl Blessing, the President of the Federal Bank, and Hermann Abs, Chairman of the Deutsche Bank, in opposing revaluation – both men belonged to the conservative body of thought in Germany which disliked any alterations of exchange-rates which might be avoided, and both men were concerned that raising the value of the mark could price German exports out of important markets. Erhard only got his way in March 1961, when Blessing changed sides, the Chancellor (for once) was overruled and the exchange-rate of the mark was raised from 23·8 to 25 cents.

Erhard was disgusted with France's refusal to go on negotiating with Britain over entry into the EEC in January 1961. It was thanks to him and the Foreign Minister, Gerhard Schroeder, that the Cabinet issued its subsequent statement deploring the end of negotiations. But he hesitated about going any further. Adenauer's view was that the composition of the EEC was a political, more than an economic matter – so he did not need to consult Erhard. Franz Josef Strauss summed it up: "Adenauer and Erhard never cooperated personally, in a political sense."[18]

At least, Adenauer's efforts to intervene in the economic field had been only spasmodic. Erhard must have hoped for a degree of cooperation when he, in turn, became Chancellor. He turned down the proposal that he should become Chairman of the CDU, thus leaving Adenauer undisturbed in an office which Erhard hoped he would regard as worthwhile consolation. In August 1963 Erhard pilgrimaged to Cadenabbia, to sit at Adenauer's feet – a friendly gesture indeed. He might have been mildly embarrassed by the Bundestag vote for him; it was 279 against 180 and he had collected 20 more votes than Adenauer in 1961. Adenauer could not have been pleased. His statement of Government policy, on 18 October, was awaited with keen interest; it was, after all, the first by anyone other than Adenauer in the whole of the Federal Republic's existence.

Erhard's statement was sound enough. Predictably, the new Chancellor had more to say about economic and social policies than about foreign affairs. The top economic priorities would be the maintenance of a strong currency and stable prices. Aid for the farmers would be increased; the "Green Plan", for rationalizing farm-holdings and agricultural production, was already costing more than 500 million dollars a year. Erhard promised greater social justice – he had been talking of a European society "of the free and the equal".[19] He proposed an "equalization law" for the benefit of the lower-paid which would involve a reorganization of sickness insurance benefits, better care for war victims, and better old-age pensions. Generally speaking, it was "no changes" on major problems – German reunification, West Berlin, European integration, defence, NATO. Indeed, how could it have been otherwise? Erhard took his advice from Schroeder. Perhaps the only change of tone was a heavier emphasis on military cooperation with the United States.

Erhard has been called an "interim Chancellor".[20] One understands why. He did not intend to change his economic policies by one jot. He inherited Adenauer's foreign policy, and its executor, Schroeder, was passed on to him. He would be just three years in office, and for the last year would be fighting an economic recession of a kind which frequently occurred in other European countries, but which was traumatic to Germans used to continuous progress. The Erhard administration has been almost universally written off as a failure. Its record deserves, at least, consideration.

The record was explicitly based on a policy of "no change".

One of the FDP's most vocal critics of Erhard maintained that he had, and missed, a wonderful chance of making a genuinely new start.[21] Germany, so the argument ran, was suffering from "spiritual anaemia"; what was needed was a "coalition of progress", with a real reformist domestic policy, an effort to understand youth and bring it into the democratic process, and a new and constructive approach to East–West relations. The judiciary should be purged of its ex-Nazi elements and given a true independence from the "establishment"; bureaucracy should be actively combated; lobbying by pressure groups should be stamped out; and a really social state should be created in place of a plutocracy in which 5 per cent of the taxpayers owned over 50 per cent of the wealth in private hands. These were revolutionary ideas, but mainly foreign to Erhard's empirical thinking. In any event, he was convinced that he had to proceed with caution.

In one respect, at least, he wanted and achieved progress. This was in East–West relations. In his declaration of Government policy, he stressed the need to secure better living conditions for the seventeen million people of the DDR, and linked this with the improvement of relations with East European countries, especially through the medium of trade. Schroeder fully agreed with him. Willy Brandt was later to criticize Erhard for a "lack of mobility" in this field.[22] But Erhard gave Brandt a free hand, in December 1963, to negotiate with the DDR on passes for West Berliners wanting to visit relatives and friends in East Berlin. The agreement which was reached enabled 1,200,000 visits to be made by West Berliners during an eighteen-day period over Christmas. In 1964 an even better arrangement was made, and West Berliners were allowed into East Berlin during four separate fortnightly periods. A more controversial "exchange" also took place in 1964: 800 East German citizens were, in effect, ransomed, and were sent to the Federal Republic against payment of 32 million marks' worth of goods and equipment.[23] This practice has continued ever since, for a long time in a clandestine atmosphere – for the Federal Government was genuinely anxious to rescue East German political persecutees from prison, or at the very least, surveillance and "house arrest". The East German regime for its part had no compunction about demanding "head money", and continues to do so.

Both Schroeder and Erhard were ready to establish closer relations with East European countries. A lot of nonsense had been talked in the past about the Federal Republic's economic strength forcing recognition and compromise out of the weaker East European satellites, and about "polycentrism" in Eastern Europe – meaning, the growing independence of Soviet satellites – giving the Federal Republic increased political leverage.[24] In fact, the Federal Foreign Ministry – even under Adenauer – had not waited for these things to happen and had negotiated the establishment of trade missions in Poland, Rumania and Hungary, with Bulgaria to follow in 1964. Erhard concluded a trade agreement with Yugoslavia and tried to do the same with Czechoslovakia, but the Czechs insisted on the 1938 Munich Agreement between Nazi Germany, France and Britain being declared null and void – whereas the Federal Government would go no further than express its rejection of that Agreement.

There were two horns to Erhard's dilemma. The first was that no Federal Government felt able so far to recognize the Oder–Neisse Line as Germany's eastern frontier. The future of the territories beyond that Line had not been settled at the post-war Potsdam Conference, and they still ranked as being "under foreign occupation". The second difficulty lay in the so-called "Hallstein Doctrine", under which the Federal Republic would not establish diplomatic relations with countries which recognized the DDR. The Doctrine actually produced a setback for Erhard in February 1965, when the impending visit to Egypt of the East German dictator, Walter Ulbricht, was announced. The Erhard Government acted with weird ambivalence: on the one hand, it declared Egypt's invitation to Ulbricht to be an unfriendly act, on the other it terminated military aid to Israel (admittedly, about 80 per cent of the agreed 30 million pounds' worth of arms had already been delivered). Ulbricht went, all the same, to Cairo as President Nasser's guest on 24 February, upon which the Federal Republic cut off development aid to Egypt. The result was that Egypt and nine other Arab states broke off diplomatic relations with Bonn. Nothing whatever had been gained; ten Arab states and their enemy, Israel, had been offended.

Quietly, almost surreptitiously, Schroeder continued to sound East European governments, particularly the Rumanian, on the possibility of closer relations – as early as June 1962, at the CDU Conference in Dortmund, he had advocated a "foreign policy of the possible", involving continual reappraisal of policies in Eastern Europe. In the spring of 1966, Erhard circulated a "peace note" to East European governments indicating readiness to consider arms limitations. He was urged to do more by Mende and the FDP, but criticized for doing too much by Strauss and the Bavarian branch of his own party. With such divided views within the coalition, it was not surprising that he hesitated.

Nor was the CDU divided on the subject of Eastern Europe alone. Konrad Adenauer was still Chairman of the CDU, and nothing that Erhard could do would convince him that he ought to remain Chancellor. He believed that Erhard was anti-French, a dogged "Atlanticist" who pinned all his hopes on the United States, and that he was forsaking the spirit of the Franco-German Treaty of Friendship. He announced his intention of standing again for the Chairmanship of the CDU. According to one commentator: "By clinging on to the party chairmanship until he is over ninety Adenauer is likely to establish a 'counter-government'. He is not going to like Erhard any better as Chancellor than as his deputy and Economics Minister. He will, at the very least, seek to exclude him from influence within the party. He is very likely to carry on a campaign of sniping and sabotage against him ..."[25] This, indeed, happened.

The official *Deutsche Korrespondenz*, published in Bonn, had warned against a repetition of Bismarck's departure from politics, which had left "an angry old man at Friedrichsruh".[26] This, the *Deutsche Korrespondenz* argued, should not happen again, with an angry old man at Rhoendorf, casting a baneful shadow across the Rhine. But Adenauer was implacable. To a young German journalist, he remarked: "Shall we discuss serious politics, or just Chancellor Erhard?"[27] And when someone said to Adenauer, "There is no government under Erhard", he replied: "That is quite wrong. There are at least three governments, and he's not in charge of any of them."[28]

He took a perverse pleasure in humbling or denigrating Erhard. When de Gaulle came to Bonn for talks with Erhard in July 1964, Adenauer invited him to come first to his office in the Parliament building. There he kept him until he was nearly half an hour late for his meeting with the Chancellor. On 1 November 1964 Adenauer gave an interview to the *Bild am Sonntag*, in which he stated that the Erhard Government was responsible for worsening relations with France, that de Gaulle had been treated with unnatural coolness when he had come to Bonn in July, and that France might be forced to turn to the Soviet Union as an ally. At the March 1965 CDU Party Conference in Düsseldorf, he sharply criticized government foreign policy and ostentatiously shunned Erhard personally. On his eighty-ninth birthday he talked to the press about the decline of Federal foreign policy, adding that he would do nothing to bring down the present government, since it would be defeated in the elections anyway.

Adenauer persistently refused to talk to Erhard, or even to Schroeder, who had worked so closely with him in the past – the latter had only one personal conversation with him after Adenauer resigned from the Chancellorship.[29]

Erhard would later remark sadly: "For my own part, I did my best to get on with him. I tried to give him the feeling that I valued his advice. I telephoned him often, and I went to see him before going to Paris to meet de Gaulle [in 1965]. He only occasionally reacted in a truly human manner. I believe he did great harm to his party and his country."[30]

Adenauer still had a tremendous following in the country, and his undisguised hostility helped to undermine Erhard's position. But Erhard had other crosses to bear; in his view, there were two "unholy alliances" against him, that of Adenauer and de Gaulle, and of de Gaulle and the so-called "German Gaullists".[31] While treating Erhard with urbane condescension, de Gaulle cared not a rap for him. By recognizing the Communist Chinese Republic in January 1964, he violated the Treaty of Friendship with the Federal Republic, which laid down that there should be joint consultation before any major foreign policy step. In the spring of 1964, de Gaulle sent a Parliamentary delegation to the DDR. Later, he received the Soviet leaders in Paris, and in the summer of 1965 visited Moscow. There were no consultations, and Erhard's muted protests were ignored. Meanwhile, de Gaulle continued to oppose any move to bring Britain closer to the European Six. In July 1965, France unilaterally withdrew from the Brussels negotiations on finance regulations for the European agricultural market. Then in July 1966, de Gaulle took France's armed forces out of NATO's integrated command structure – moves which conflicted directly with the German desire for maximum cooperation within the Six, and between the Six and the other NATO powers.

De Gaulle's "personal entente" with Adenauer made his hostility at least understandable, however uncomfortable it was. The attitude of the German Gaullists was much more puzzling to Erhard. For one thing, they disagreed diametrically with de Gaulle's East European policy, for they bitterly opposed détente of any kind and upheld the Hallstein Doctrine which, to de Gaulle, was childishly immature and totally outdated. The German Gaullists wanted a European nuclear deterrent, but de

Gaulle was not in the least interested in this, and simply went ahead with the creation of France's own "force de frappe" (one German commentator called it a "farce de frappe"[32]). Willy Brandt criticized Erhard for causing a "confrontation" between the CDU Atlanticists and Gaullists;[33] Erhard's natural rejoinder would have been that it was the Gaullist minority which sought the confrontation. About their only clear-cut demand was for a union with France, as a first step towards European political union. Erhard visited all Common Market capitals in 1964, found no enthusiasm for political union, and decided that union with France would merely split Europe. He was probably right.

There were other troubles. The East German regime was creating interruptions of traffic on the Berlin autobahn, on the pretext that the West Germans had no right to hold their first Bundestag meeting since 1958 in West Berlin. Then the presence of German scientists in Egypt, working on Nasser's rocket programme, caused considerable embarrassment, and they would eventually be cajoled into coming home. The SPD were making gains averaging 5 per cent in local elections in half a dozen *Laender*, and the party now had a Shadow Cabinet for the first time, with Brandt in charge after Ollenhauer's death in December 1963, and the formidable Helmut Schmidt looking after defence. There were rumblings of discontent over alleged discrimination against the Federal Republic in the field of nuclear weapons, and over outdated training methods in the Bundeswehr – as a result it was increased in strength by only 25,000 in 1964, and not by the planned 50,000, to a total of 450,000.

But Erhard and his Government remained as popular as ever; in mid-1964 a gallup poll showed that 71 per cent thought him a good Chancellor, while only 23 per cent thought Brandt would do better. The great bulk of the electorate were grateful to him for making them, and their country prosperous; they liked his *bonhomie*, his unruffled calm, and the atmosphere of healthy bourgeois comfort which he radiated. There were no clouds on the economic horizon: overall production went up by 8 per cent in 1964, wages by 8·5 per cent, while the cost of living rose by only 2·5 per cent. Prosperity was being "spread"; there was next to no unemployment, and 850,000 unfilled jobs. The purchasing-power of the D Mark was up by 6 per cent. The public did not have to know about these figures; they needed only to look around them. The atmosphere was one of quiet optimism far into 1965.

This had its effect in the Federal elections, which took place on 19 September. For by no means everything was going Erhard's way. The SPD were making even more headway in the *Laender*. In the Saar their vote was up by 10 per cent, and for the first time they beat the CDU in local elections in the strongly Roman Catholic North Rhine-Westphalia. In the course of the past four years the SPD had gained one and a half million voters in *Land* and local elections, and the CDU had lost two and a half million.

Then a number of leading intellectuals campaigned actively for the SPD, including Günter Grass, Heinrich Böll and Rolf Hochhuth. They compared the German worker to the slaves who built the pyramids and to the *Mitlaufer* (passive collaborators) of the Nazi era. Nothing could have been more counter-productive. The German worker did not want to be reminded of the Nazi past, and did not need to be a historian to know that he had nothing in common with the forced labour of the Pharaohs. Erhard, admittedly, was stung to unwise rejoinder; in July he declared "I must call these poets by their name; duffers and Philistines, who dare to pass judgement on matters they don't understand".[34] More operatively, there was no external threat to help the party in power; in 1953 there had been the East German rising, in 1956 the terrible story of Hungary, and in 1961 the Berlin Wall.

Adenauer helped his own side, in spite of his prophecies of disaster. He ignored Erhard totally and attacked the SPD with sardonic wit (in the 1961 elections he referred to Brandt's illegitimate birth; he did not repeat that mistake). Erhard's twice repeated message was: "Only the combination of proven economic genius and the diligence of the German people can guarantee continued prosperity."[35] The electorate evidently agreed, although this was the nearest Erhard ever came to personal boastfulness. Public opinion polls had been predicting a neck-and-neck race between CDU and SPD, but the CDU collected 246 seats against the SPD's 202. Brandt admitted that he had wanted something definitely better than that.[36] The FDP did fairly well, considering that they had been under the wing of a liberal Chancellor; with 49 seats, they were still a reduced "third force". Three manifestly democratic parties collected all but three and a half per cent of the vote. The outside world worries perpetually about "threats" to German democracy, but seldom draws appropriate conclusions from German election results.

The September 1965 Federal elections mark one of the most definitive caesuras in political history. Things had gone relatively well for Erhard so far; from now on, he would be in trouble, and not at once aware of the fact.

He was re-elected Chancellor by a 272 to 200 vote in the Bundestag. This meant that his majority had shrunk since 1963 from 99 to 72. However the public saw Erhard, Parliamentarians had their own view of him – admittedly coloured by the disclosures of the endless public opinion polls which are deemed necessary for a people stifled for so long from expressing views of their own. These polls generate their own impetus. In Erhard's case, they discouraged a careful reappraisal, within the CDU, of his political tactics. They simply confirmed him in power.

The economic recession which was already just beginning came as a total surprise and a shock to the people of the Federal Republic. One of Erhard's critics wrote that the only thing which could threaten the CDU administration in 1965 was an absolute CDU majority in the Federal elections; then, Franz Josef Strauss would emerge as the driving-force of the party and government.[37] The reaction would be violent. He was very wide of the mark; as Willy Brandt would point out,[38] the genius, even magician, failed in his own special field – "It was ironical that Ludwig Erhard should have foundered on the very rock, that of economics, whose avoidance had earned him such acclaim as a successful helmsman."

What was more, the German recession was independent of world trends and could not be put at any door save that of the Federal Government. The basic reason for failure was that the Government had been overspending. In the Bundestag, Helmut Schmidt attacked the Government fiercely for its immensely expensive programme to develop and modernize the railways, for allegedly accepting huge quantities of military equipment from the United States at inflated prices instead of "shopping around", and for readily agreeing to offset the American bill in foreign exchange for the upkeep of troops stationed in Germany.[39] The "Green Plan" for the support of agriculture was costing huge sums: one estimate was of nearly 4,000 million marks a year, plus an additional 2,000 million marks in 1965 to subsidize the farmers for the lower grain prices agreed with the EEC.[40]

Erhard did what he could. He ordered the 1966 budget to be cut by 10 per cent. He considered tax increases. Ministries were advised on the economies which could be effected, and the Chancellor even appealed, rhetorically, for everyone to work an extra hour a week – a proposal which fell on deaf ears, since the trade unions were tabling demands for wage increases of up to 12 per cent and for a shorter working week.

For the first time since the early days of the Federal Republic a trade deficit was forecast. Although there were still over 700,000 jobs waiting to be filled, a sharp increase in unemployment was forecast by the end of 1966. Government spokesmen hardly helped by explaining that some unemployment might be healthy for the economy, and Erhard's own party hindered actively by panicking when war victims began marching through the streets of Bonn, and voted for 30 per cent increases in their pensions. Erhard himself seems to have lost a little of that jaunty self-confidence with which he confronted all economic situations. He hesitated between imposing financial controls and gearing the economy up for another burst of expansion by means of investment incentives. His instinct, doubtless, was in favour of the latter, and he might have been able to ride the storm. But in the event there was no strategy, and the nation's confidence in him was rudely shaken.

There is a salient difference between German and other views about recession. In other countries, production and exports may stagnate quite seriously, and the main problem is to get people interested. The German people experienced economic near-catastrophe in the 1920s and again in the 1940s. They tend to regard a mere decreasing rate of expansion as a signal for alarm; economic stagnation is unthinkable. Only a slackening in the rate of growth is needed to produce foreboding. Erhard was the victim of what might be considered a psychosis in other countries, but which is regarded as justifiable concern by Germans.

Other things were going wrong too. The neo-Nazi National Democratic Party (NPD) was active, collecting over 8 per cent of the vote in *Land* elections in Hesse and Bavaria, and declaiming against "weak government in Bonn". In the North Rhine-Westphalia elections the SPD gained perceptibly, with 99 out of 200 seats. The coal-miners in the Ruhr were grumbling and there was open talk about the need for a "Grand Coalition" of the two big parties, to put the economy in order – two leading protagonists were ex-Chancellor Adenauer and Federal President Luebke. In August came a "crisis" in the Bundeswehr; both the Inspector General, Heinz Trettner, and the head of the Air Force, Heinz Panitzki, resigned. Trettner objected to trade-union canvassing in army barracks, and Panitzki to failure to improve the safety equipment of the F 104 Starfighter – he had some cause, for 66 Starfighters had crashed since the plane was introduced four years earlier, and 36 pilots had been killed. The British Chancellor of the Exchequer made his contribution to Erhard's troubles: Mr James Callaghan demanded that Britain's foreign exchange costs for the Rhine Army of about 100 million pounds a year should be offset in full. The only item on the credit side for Erhard was his election as CDU Chairman in succession to a reluctant Adenauer.

The crunch came in October. The FDP was alarmed by the looming recession and wanted no part in it. An inappropriate pretext for leaving the Government presented itself; Erhard proposed tax increases which were plainly in the national interest. On 27 October Mende told the Chancellor that his party could no longer serve in the Government – with some regret, for he was personally fond of Erhard. The Chancellor soldiered on, with a minority Government whose days were numbered. He toyed with the thought of inviting the FDP back into coalition, or even of turning to the SPD – there was, after all, virtually a bi-partisan foreign policy already in existence and talk of a Grand Coalition might even be regarded as mildly encouraging. But political decision was not Erhard's strong suit; he decided instead on the line of least resistance. On 2 November he announced that he was ready to resign, if an alternative government could be formed.

On 10 November the SPD called for inter-party talks on a change of Chancellor and the formation of a new government, and a fortnight of discussion began. Brandt meanwhile had a long talk with Adenauer, who stated flatly that Erhard had to go and supplemented this with the argument that Bonn's East European policy was not nearly active enough.[41] The irony of such a statement coming from the once staunch upholder of the Hallstein Doctrine could not have been lost on Erhard! As usual, he was behaving with impeccable modesty and restraint. He had served his country with deep dedication for nearly twenty years, and this time he was not to be "kicked upstairs" into the comfortable and prestigious office of Federal President, but was going to be kicked out altogether. Brandt, somewhat unkindly, considered him to have been "clumsily insensible to what lay in store for him"![42] For he was, later, to say sadly that he had expected a little more respect to be paid to him. But while the terms of his political demise were under discussion, he remained discreetly silent. On 26 November, it was all over. Kurt Georg

Kiesinger of the CDU was to become Chancellor, with Willy Brandt as his deputy and Foreign Minister. The Grand Coalition was in being.

Erhard's Chancellorship has been generally regarded as a failure. At the very least, it was a sad anti-climax to a career of previously uninterrupted success. Naturally, his Chancellorship should not expunge memories of his remarkable achievements, over a period of fourteen years, as Minister of Economics. But, up to a point, Adenauer had been proved right; long years as a specialist had helped to deprive him of the powers needed to run a government.

Brandt's view was that "Erhard had little experience of international affairs. It would not be unfair to call him an a-political politician".[43] It was his ill-fortune that he had, blamelessly, incurred the undying hostility of Adenauer, and that the latter remained a force on the political stage, almost to his death. Adenauer's continual sniping hurt him bitterly, and sapped his confidence. On being asked later what he thought Adenauer's salient characteristic to have been, he replied without hesitation "Contempt for humanity" (*Menschen-verachtung*).[44] It was his further ill-fortune that he had to deal with a statesman like de Gaulle, rigid, unbending and utterly unable to talk in terms of genuine compromise.

It may well be that Erhard laid too much stress on what he believed was a special relationship with the United States. He got on splendidly with President Johnson, commemorating his friendship in a remark of childlike candour – "I love President Johnson, and he loves me."[45] He had happy days with Johnson on his Texas ranch, and he liked recounting with a chuckle how he had told the President that Americans liked being in Germany, and the answer came pat: "They'd sooner be here in Texas."[46] But Erhard certainly shored-up a friendship with the United States which had been shaken by the building of the Berlin Wall and which Adenauer had latterly done little to nourish. And Erhard and Schroeder earned praise in some quarters for working quietly and simultaneously towards both détente and Western unity.[47]

Erhard, according to some critics, lost control over his own party by taking sides against the German Gaullists. Party discipline suffered as a result. In a sense, he was probably too nice a man for politics, and he would never have made a political ring-master. Of his personal honesty, fairness, humanity and fundamental decency there was never a doubt. He lived modestly, in a bungalow in the grounds of the Palais Schaumburg, warmly hospitable but entertaining only a few guests at a time. He was always kind, and his fatherly manner and interest in those who worked for him made him beloved in his own Ministry and even in the more impersonal atmosphere of the Chancellery.[48] One need not wax sentimental about such an attribute, but there is something salutary about a head of government who never loses his innate modesty and kindness of heart. Erhard retained his natural homeliness; perhaps the only other great contemporary politician who did so was Mrs Golda Meir of Israel.

Erhard gave his Cabinet his fullest confidence, and his Ministers as free a hand as possible. He encouraged team spirit and mutual trust, and he believed in the decentralization of authority. Here, at least, is a consolatory thought; the principles of Cabinet solidarity and Cabinet and Ministerial responsibility became, under Erhard, more firmly embedded in the practice of government. The Federal Republic probably needed Adenauer's paternalistic authority in its early years, but it needed a normalization of democratic procedure thereafter. The "interim Chancellorship" made that possible.

1. Ludwig Erhard, in conversation with the author, March 1971.
2. Walter Henkels. *Bonner Koepfe.* Düsseldorf, 1968.
3. Jess Lukomski. *Ludwig Erhard. Der Mensch und der Politiker.* Düsseldorf, 1965.
4. Ibid.
5. Fritz (E. F.) Schumacher, in conversation with the author, June, 1948.
6. Terence Prittie. *Germany Divided*, Boston, 1960.
7. Ibid.
8. Willy Brandt. *People and Politics.* London, 1978.
9. Ibid.
10. Bruno Heck. *Konrad Adenauer und seine Zeit.* Stuttgart, 1976.
11. Alfred Müller-Armack, op. cit.
12. Jess Lukomski, op. cit.
13. Ibid.
14. Dr Ludger Westrick. *Konrad Adenauer und seine Zeit.*
15. Ludwig Erhard, in conversation with the author, March 1971.
16. *Manchester Guardian*, 25 May 1956.
17. Ludwig Erhard, in conversation with the author, March 1971.
18. Franz Josef Strauss. *Konrad Adenauer und seine Zeit.*
19. Gerhard Schroeder. *Konrad Adenauer und seine Zeit.*
20. Arnulf Baring. *Aussenpolitik in Adenauer's Kanzlerdemokratie.* Munich, 1969.
21. Karl Hermann Flach. *Erhard's schwerer Weg.* Stuttgart, 1964.
22. Willy Brandt, op. cit.

23. Jess Lukomski, op. cit.
24. Ekkehart Krippendorf. *Survey* magazine. October 1966.
25. Terence Prittie. *Manchester Guardian*, 8 November 1963.
26. *Deutsche Korrespondenz*, November 1963.
27. James O'Donnell (American journalist), in private memorandum on Adenauer.
28. Hubertus, Prinz zu Loewenstein, in conversation with the author, September 1969.
29. Gerhard Schroeder, op. cit.
30. Ludwig Erhard, in conversation with the author.
31. Ibid.
32. Karl Hermann Flach, op. cit.
33. Willy Brandt, op. cit.
34. *Manchester Guardian*, 10 July 1965.
35. *Manchester Guardian*, 3 September 1965.
36. Willy Brandt, op. cit.
37. Karl Hermann Flach, op. cit.
38. Willy Brandt, op. cit.
39. Helmut Wolgang Kahn. *Helmut Schmidt*. Hamburg, 1973.
40. Jess Lukomski, op. cit.
41. Klaus Harpprecht. *Willy Brandt*. Munich, 1970
42. Willy Brandt, op. cit.
43. Willy Brandt, op. cit.
44. Terence Prittie. *Konrad Adenauer*. London, 1972.
45. Will McBride and Hans Werner Graf von Finckenstein. *Adenauer, Ein Portraet*. Starnberg, 1965.
46. Gerhard Schroeder, op. cit.
47. Walther Kiep. *A New Challenge for Western Europe*. New York, 1974.
48. The official chauffeur of the Palais Schaumburg served four Chancellors, but liked Erhard easily the best – "He treated us as if we were members of his own family".

CHAPTER SEVEN

Coalition, Grand or merely Big?

One of the most acute observers of the German political scene, and by now a major participant in it, noted that "Only if the Big Coalition does something big, can it justify its existence".[1] Helmut Schmidt would later lead a very different kind of coalition government but he was, on the whole, in favour of the establishment of the Kiesinger-led combination of CDU and SPD. He accepted the view of his party manager, Herbert Wehner, that "This state is ours too; we Social Democrats must never allow ourselves to be exiled to its fringes".[2] The SPD had spent 36 years in the relative wilderness of opposition or, under the Nazis, of total exclusion from active politics. Schmidt may have had his doubts; he turned down the offer of the Ministry of Transport, and decided instead to lead the SPD from the floor of the Bundestag. He explained this by remarking that there were twenty Ministers, but the chairman of the Parliamentary Party of the SPD stood on this own and made his own decisions.[3]

Doubts would have been natural. A few years back, nothing would have appeared more improbable than the "Grand" or merely "Big" Coalition. The CDU and SPD were deadly rivals: they stood for different ideologies, for completely different concepts of what the Federal Republic should become, and what sort of society it should produce. The only two great party leaders who had been thrown up so far, Konrad Adenauer and Kurt Schumacher, were not normal political opponents. They regarded one another as dangerous, baneful and misguided.

Adenauer, the realist, accepted the idea of a Grand Coalition and even propagated it himself – although his principal purpose was to end Erhard's Chancellorship. But the thought of alliance with the bourgeois "restorationists", the left-overs of the Nazi era, was surely enough to make Schumacher turn in his grave.

Wehner's fear that the SPD might be almost permanently "exiled" to the fringes of West German politics was a very real one. The "Adenauer era" might have ended, but Adenauer had built solidly and enduringly; ahead stretched an age of affluence of which all conservatives dream. Oddly, the man now called upon to lead the new government had, in a sense, himself been in exile. Kurt Georg Kiesinger was the CDU's most accomplished and articulate spokesman on foreign affairs in the Bundestag between 1949 and 1958. He had hoped to become Foreign Minister, which would have been no more than a just reward for his part in winning back West German sovereignty and bringing his country into Europe. But Adenauer took an ambivalent view of him. On the one hand, he thought that Kiesinger lacked real political acumen – once he remarked to him: "But, Herr Kiesinger, don't you want to be a politician?"[4] At the same time, Adenauer did not regard him as pliant enough, so he installed von Brentano as his first Foreign Minister instead. Kiesinger, understandably huffed, withdrew to his native, and beloved *Land* Baden-Wurtemberg, accepting the post of Minister–President and discharging his duties with an efficiency and elegance which turned Stuttgart, beside Munich, into one of the two provincial capitals of real political distinction and political weight. It needed nothing less than the Chancellorship to lure him back to Bonn.

Now, in 1966, Kiesinger was 62 years old, something of a dandy in appearance, always wearing well-tailored suits and neck-ties chosen with impeccable taste, his silver-grey hair always in perfect order, his manner suave and unruffled. He was born not far from Stuttgart, and was brought up a Catholic – he had a Catholic mother and Protestant father, and he believes that this, and his Swabian environment, encouraged tolerance and moderation.[5] He loved his native land; he wrote, simply, that "I have always regarded myself fortunate to have been born in Swabia".[6] Swabia, or Wurtemberg, lies across trade-routes of European importance for the last thousand years, but it has also lain in the path of armies endlessly on the march. It is a land of survival, and of acceptance in the course of survival, and the Swabians won a reputation for quietness and commonsense – the orderly and thrifty Swiss have often talked of them, and the

Badensers, alone among Germans as "our cousins", and one observer credits them with "zeal, cleanliness ... and a sense of direction".[7]

He was a sensitive child – one of his clearest memories was how his parents forgot about his sixth birthday, and did not give him his "birthday egg" for breakfast.[8] He remained sensitive all his life; at an advanced age he admitted that what hurt him most was that his "honour" should be doubted,[9] and agreed that he was "easily upset" – but, fortunately, "it never lasts long".[10] His family was poor, his mother died when he was very small, and his remarried father had a struggle to bring up him and his six step-brothers and sisters. Only a friend's help enabled him to study at Tübingen University. He trained to be a lawyer, and as a young man was active in Catholic youth groups. But in 1933 he joined the Nazi Party – he made no secret of the fact afterwards – and the National Socialist Lawyers' Association. In addition, he worked in the Nazi Foreign Ministry and his work involved radio monitoring and some liaison with Josef Goebbels' Ministry of Propaganda.[11] He remained a Nazi Party member up to the end of the war.

Kiesinger never took any active part in Nazi politics. The Nazis recruited many such non-active members essentially because they were efficient, hardworking, perhaps merely upstanding and good-looking, but always because they were well thought-of. Generally, they had to do no more than attend a single party meeting and pay their modest party dues. Kiesinger has claimed that he was quickly disillusioned, notably by the 1934 "Roehm Blood-Bath" when Hitler liquidated members of the radical wing of the Brownshirts. He claimed that he had "clean hands", and nearly emigrated in 1938.[12] Certainly, he asked one former Catholic Centre Party member, Dr Johannes Schauf, to help him emigrate to Brazil.[13] He had no difficulty in being "de-Nazified" after the war, and interesting information about his war-time activities came to light when he became Chancellor. It consisted of written evidence that two of his former Foreign Ministry colleagues had denounced him for expressing opposition to Nazi anti-semitic propaganda and refusing to disseminate it. This information was a useful boost to Kiesinger's morale; inevitably, there had been sharp criticism of the choice of an "ex-Nazi" in the West German press and in the SPD. This criticism, stimulated in particular from the other side of the Iron Curtain, did not of course come to an end. It was a reminder of the difficulty of coming to terms with the Nazi past.

Kiesinger, again, did what he could on a number of occasions to help Jews,[14] half-Jews and political opponents of the Nazis.[15] There is, indeed, plenty of evidence to show that he behaved courageously and honourably during a very difficult period.

His so-called "Nazi past" was re-emphasized when Kiesinger was elected Chancellor in the Bundestag. Although the executives of both parties in the coalition had approved his candidature, the vote was 340 to 109, with 23 abstentions. Over 80 CDU or SPD members either voted against him or abstained and at least half as many again stayed away. But he began work with two big advantages. The Grand Coalition commanded 468 votes in the Bundestag, against the 50 of the FDP, and would never need to worry about the size of its Parliamentary majority. And it was able to produce a Cabinet of "all the talents". Thus Brandt was Foreign Minister, Schroeder Minister of Defence, and Wehner Minister for All-German Affairs. Strauss came back into office, with the Ministry of Finance, and Karl Schiller, shrewd, able, professional, became Minister of Economics. Men of such talent and standing as Gustav Heinemann, Georg Leber and Carlo Schmid took on the relatively less important portfolios of Justice, Transport and *Laender* Affairs. It was an imposing line-up.

Of course, there were doubts, not just about the suitability of Kiesinger, but about the political morality of the whole idea of the Grand Coalition. The right wing of the CDU remained critical throughout its existence. But the SPD had much more reason for concern. The trade unions were suspicious, and the "new left" was frankly appalled. This applied in particular to its younger members, and a rift began to yawn between socialist youth and the party management. For the moment, Brandt was more worried by a section of liberal–left opinion taking offence; their fear was that every success would be exploited by the CDU, and every failure laid at the door of the SPD.[16] One critic even stated: "Since Schumacher's death German Social Democracy has renounced an independent foreign policy. The concept that a strong party could function as a political opposition sank with Schumacher into the grave."[17]

This was an extreme view; Schumacher had in fact died fourteen years earlier, and the SPD had continued to function as a steadily stronger and more efficient opposition. More reasoned criticism came from Ralf Dahrendorf, a leading liberal. He saw the Grand Coalition as an obstacle to the kind of social reform which he believed necessary – curtailment of bureaucracy, more equitable personal taxation, greater student participation in university affairs, and the end of the system of "interrogatory arrest". He complained of social stagnation, which he put down to the demand for "the security of a trapped rabbit".[18] Intellectuals like Günter Grass were furious; they tried to avoid castigating Brandt, and concentrated their fire on Kiesinger. There were gloomy prophecies of the dismantling of German democracy and the demoting of the electorate into a state of primal political ignorance.[19]

Still, the Grand Coalition had to get down to work, and Kiesinger's inaugural statement of Government policy, on 13 December 1966, heavily emphasized the economic developments which had forced Erhard out of office. Kiesinger outlined the threat, for the first time in over a decade, of unemployment – there were 700,000 unemployed already and 340,000 on short-time. He promised further cuts in government expenditure, but forecast a budgetary deficit of roughly 3,000 million marks for 1967. He pointed out that investment was falling off, building too, and that the national income had only increased by 2 per cent in the last year. He called for "controlled expansion"; bank loans would be limited and, for the first time since the creation of a federal state, the *Laender* and municipalities would be advised on ways of reducing expenditure. Such "interference" would only be temporary, since the Grand Coalition was only intended to last until the 1969 elections.[20]

Kiesinger had something to say about the dangers of right-wing radicalism. The NPD collected 665,000 votes in the 1965 Federal elections, not enough to give it a single Parliamentary seat. But it had won 8 seats in the Hesse Land Parliament and fifteen in the Bavarian, in *Land* elections which took place during the governmental crisis in November. The party had no real programme, only a list of complaints. The new Federal Government did not propose banning it, but instead suggested the introduction of a new electoral law, based as in Britain on direct election. This would make it virtually impossible for the NPD, or any similar neo-Nazi party, to win Parliamentary seats.

There was not much to be said about foreign affairs. The Erhard administration had carried on Adenauer's policies, the continuing build-up of the European Community, the maintenance of a strong NATO, the further development of close relations with France in the spirit of the Franco-German Treaty of Friendship. The Grand Coalition would do likewise. But East–West détente was becoming a subject of increasing interest; Kiesinger talked of establishing diplomatic relations with East European countries "wherever possible". The limitations, however, were obvious: Poland wanted prior recognition of the Oder – Neisse Line, Czechoslovakia wanted the 1938 Munich Agreement declared null and void, and Hungary sought explicit recognition by Bonn of the existence of two separate German states.

The Kiesinger Government managed to balance its first, crucially important budget in 1967. Careful husbandry produced cuts of nearly 2,000 million marks, and a revenue increase of about 900 million marks. Taxation on higher incomes went up, so did VAT, from 10 to 11 per cent, and further cuts in Government expenditure were agreed for the next four years. At the same time, investment in industry was encouraged and the exchange rate of the mark was kept steady. Strauss was an efficient and immensely active Minister of Finance; a useful bonus was that he got on well personally with Kiesinger. He was not "everybody's man".

By the end of 1968 the spectre of economic recession had been banished. Unemployment was down, while the industrial growth rate had been increased to 6 per cent. A big trading surplus was being built up, and the Government readily reduced import tariffs – but it resisted foreign pressure to revalue the D Mark once again. Brandt thought of Kiesinger as a politician who "was always on the look-out for a four-leaf clover".[21] Possibly, he was being less than fair. Kiesinger gave Schiller and Strauss their heads in running the economy, and they made a formidable team. Only over the revaluation of the mark did Kiesinger insist on having his way; he was one of so many Germans who instinctively recoiled from changing exchange rates and who felt that it was incumbent on countries whose currencies weakened to put their own house in order, instead of asking the Germans to make their exports less competitive.

The NPD continued to cause concern. In 1967 it made steady progress in *Land* elections, with an average vote of seven and a half per cent in four *Laender* (Schleswig-Holstein, Rhine-Palatinate, Lower Saxony and Bremen), and now held 48 seats in six *Laender* Parliaments. In 1968 the NPD scored its biggest success, a 10 per cent vote and twelve seats, in Baden-Wurtemberg – Kiesinger's own *Land*, and a slap in the eye for him personally. Its appealingly young and ardent Chairman, Adolf von Thadden (nicknamed "Boysie"), predicted that the party would win 50 seats in the 1969 Federal elections. It was already organized in 466 out of 500 urban and rural districts.

The supposed answer to the NPD, electoral reform, hung fire. Kiesinger was ready to agree to some transitional measure of reform, simply to keep the NPD out. In January 1968, he was asked what had come of his plans; he was forced to admit that they now depended on whether the Grand Coalition was renewed after the Federal elections.[22] The truth was that his SPD allies had quietly rebelled, their experts coming to the conclusion that any major change, to a more direct voting system, could cost their party upwards of 40 seats. The reason was plain: the CDU vote was well "spread" over the country, while that of the SPD was heavily concentrated in urban areas. Traditionally, the SPD scored bigger wins, in fewer constituencies. In what would be virtually a two-party system, the SPD would collect fewer seats. The issue of electoral reform produced one casualty in the Cabinet. The CDU Minister of the Interior, Paul Luecke, resigned in March 1968; he had taken the issue seriously.

The Franco-German *entente* needed refurbishing. Debonair and personable, Kiesinger made an excellent impression on de Gaulle. This did not prevent the General from declaring France's complete military independence of NATO in November 1967, one further unilateral violation of the Franco-German Treaty.[23] Nor did it discourage his adamant opposition to a British entry into the European Common Market. Kiesinger at least did rather more than Adenauer had done to support the British application. As de Gaulle's guest in the Elysée Palace in February 1968, he explained that he understood the French objections, but that friends had a right to differ. On his return to Bonn, he said that his Government wanted a British entry as soon as possible, in spite of the French reservations which he fully appreciated.[24] But he shared Konrad Adenauer's doubts about the validity of British intentions, as earlier speeches indicated. Thus, he showed understanding that a body of opinion remained in Britain which was much more concerned with holding the remnants of the Commonwealth together, and with maintaining the "special relationship" with the USA.[25] And he expressed sorrow that Britain had sought entry so half-heartedly, and with so many reservations.[26]

He was unimpressed by what he was told when he came to London. He was suspicious of Mr Harold Wilson's (British Prime Minister) intentions, and when visiting the House of Commons was amazed to be told all the reasons why Britain should *not* come into the EEC – opponents seemed to be far more voluble than supporters of entry. In Oxford he tried to get a candid answer from the man-in-the-street and was confronted by imbecile ignorance. One answer to his question about the Common Market was "Second turning on the right, and straight on" – this would (possibly) have taken him into the Corn Market. Back in London, at Bentley's in Swallow Street (Kiesinger is fond of oysters and Pimm's No. 1 gin-sling), he sat on one of the high stools at the bar and was bewildered by the insular atmosphere at such a fashionable restaurant – a specimen remark to him was "Oh, you're a German, are you? I suppose you're one of those Junkers". The last word was pronounced as in "junk-yard".[27] He came back from Britain in thoughtful mood, subsequently refused to ask de Gaulle to drop his veto on Britain's entry into the EEC, and instead proposed "commercial arrangements" between Britain and the Six.

East–West relations provided a potentially more fruitful field of endeavour. In January 1967 diplomatic relations were established with Rumania, by then already the first country of the Soviet Bloc ready to strike out an independent line in foreign policy. In August a trade agreement with Czechoslovakia resulted in trade missions being established in Prague and Frankfurt. Bonn now had representatives in all Communist countries, save Albania and Yugoslavia, and the decision was now taken to seek negotiations to re-establish diplomatic relations with the latter, broken off in 1957 when Marshal Tito recognized the DDR. They would be restored in January 1968. Kiesinger told the Bundestag that these and other moves were designed to relax East–West tension, that he was ready to establish full diplomatic relations with all East European countries, and would gladly agree a pact with the Soviet Union based on the mutual renunciation of the use of force.[28] In a magazine interview he said: "We have begun to build our bridges to the East. The opening of relations with Rumania and Yugoslavia is a beginning. We are prepared to open such relations with all our neighbours, in order to create a friendlier political climate in the whole of Europe."[29]

In July 1968 Kiesinger took a two hour press conference, dealing with East–West relations, easily in his stride – he was as masterly in producing illuminating answers as he was in fending off awkward questions. As so often before, he made it clear that a policy of détente did not mean neglecting NATO and lowering the West's guard – he was indeed worrying very much at the time over proposed withdrawals of Allied troops from Germany, totalling around 50,000 and coming at a time when Europe needed to stay strong and united. The Russian invasion of Czechoslovakia, a month later, proved his worries justified. Kiesinger told the Bundestag that he had protested to the Soviet Ambassador and had refused to accept the Soviet explanation that the Czechs had invited the Red Army in.[30] Later, he told the Bundestag that the Soviet invasion was a gross violation of human rights, that the Russians had sought to divert attention from this in a major propaganda barrage, and that he was especially disgusted by the participation of the DDR in the March on Prague.[31]

The Soviet invasion of Czechoslovakia put paid to any further attempts in 1968 to improve East–West relations, although Kiesinger continued to reiterate the need for peaceful détente. The jackal's role played by the DDR was a reminder that, whatever problems impeded Bonn's relations with other East European countries, there was a far more insuperable obstacle where the DDR was concerned. "The West", as one writer put it, "wanted to chip away at the division of Germany, and the East wanted to solidify and codify the status quo ... There would be no purpose in a meeting at the summit or any other official level as long as neither side was interested in what the other wanted to discuss."[32] The West Germans believed in the reunification of their country, however long that might take; the East German regime (not its people) wanted the permanent division of Germany. It was as simple as that.

What, then, could be done? Kiesinger was in agreement with Erhard's policy of increasing interzonal trade. But in April 1967, he expanded this theme by sending sixteen proposals to the ruling Socialist Unity Party (SED) annual Congress. Apart from increased trade, they included: technological cooperation, youth exchanges, free traffic in newspapers and other literature, the easing of travel arrangements and more frequent visits across the Berlin Wall by family relatives. Willy Brandt, who acted in complete concert with Kiesinger, put things in a nutshell: the aim was "to make the lives of people more bearable, as long as the division of Germany exists".[33] Small steps could be taken within the framework of "regulated coexistence". But the ensuing correspondence came to nothing, the East German Prime Minister, Willi Stoph, answering in May. For him, prestige and not people was what mattered. He demanded full recognition of the DDR by Bonn, the establishment of diplomatic relations between the two German States, and acceptance of the interzonal boundary as a State frontier. West Berlin, in addition, should be completely detached from the Federal Republic, and the two German States should join the United Nations.

This was a dialogue of the deaf. Walter Ulbricht, admittedly, continued to pay lip-service to the idea of German unity. At the SED Congress, for instance, he declared that Marxism–Leninism recognized the need for German unity, which had been destroyed by "imperialist machinations" in defiance of the wishes of the working class. German unity could be re-forged on the basis of the achievements of the DDR, whose "socialist" structure should extend to the whole of Germany. This was clap-trap; the Soviet Bloc conference at Karlovy Vary in the summer underlined the Soviet intention of keeping Germany divided. This was part of the Soviet Union's global policy. Its "European front" was to be shut down, while limited expansion could be achieved in the Middle East and Eastern Mediterranean (later in the Horn of Africa and Southern Africa too), and heightened vigilance observed in the ideological dispute with Communist China. The Soviet leaders knew that Ulbricht could be totally relied upon to do their bidding.

The Eastern Policy (Ostpolitik) which Brandt and Kiesinger were evolving took these sombre facts into account. They did not rule out the declared policy of "small steps", but they certainly made the Government's Ostpolitik far less credible in the eyes of the public. One newspaper, *Die Welt*, showed Brandt as a mouse emerging from his hole and saying to a gigantic Soviet cat: "Now can you hear me?"[34] The CSU *Bayern Kurier* had Brandt throwing food out of a barrel labelled "Concessions" to Ulbricht, the shark, with the caption: "If we feed him regularly, perhaps he will turn into a harmless carp".[35] And the *Donau Kurier* showed Brandt banging a tennis ball hopefully against the concrete wall of the Iron Curtain.[36] Brandt was known to have Kiesinger's backing, so another newspaper showed the two together under a tree in the Garden of Eden, with the snake of the DDR holding a letter in its mouth from Willi Stoph.[37]

Kiesinger did not give up. In the CDU paper *Rheinische Post*, he repeated his offer to the Soviet Union of the mutual renunciation of the use of force, and included the DDR in it.[38] On television he claimed that 75 per cent of the people of the Federal Republic were in favour of "our peace policy" – interestingly, CDU supporters in this gallup poll gave an 88 per cent vote – and suggested the need for quiet, steady pursuit of its aims.[39] What more could he have done? One critic suggested that a major gesture was needed, and an obvious possibility was recognition of the Oder–Neisse Line, since de Gaulle had already done so openly, and other Western leaders implicitly.[40] This critic felt that the CDU was still for "no experiments" and the SPD only for "small experiments"; this meant that the Grand Coalition was bogged down diplomatically.

Certainly, the East German regime did nothing to help détente forward. In June 1968, it announced that West Germans and West Berliners would require visas when passing through East German territory. In August, all ties between the East and West German Trade Unions were severed, following East German participation in the attack on Czechoslovakia. In the following year the East German Evangelical Churches were forced to withdraw from the Evangelical Church of Germany. Meanwhile, East German attempts to undermine West German democracy went on as before. East German agents were sent over the frontier into the Federal Republic, often in the guise of genuine refugees. Agents were busily recruited in the Federal Republic itself, with the help of the estimated 30,000 Communists who were driven underground when their political party, the KPD, was banned.[41] The DDR State Security services, with an estimated staff of over 20,000, maintained roughly the same number of agents in the Federal Republic. Their tasks were to collect information, to recruit helpers, to circulate communist propaganda, and sometimes to use blackmail or carry out kidnappings.[42] No details of West German or other NATO installations were too unimportant to note. This termite-like activity has been estimated to cost the DDR up to five million pounds a week, and in the course of it upwards of 2,000 East German agents are arrested each year in the Federal Republic.[43] All this was going on while the Grand Coalition was trying to evolve a sane policy of détente; all of this continues today. The outside world remains untroubled and uninterested, always readier to criticize the Federal Republic for measures taken to defend its democracy than to understand the situation which makes them necessary.

It says much for the liberalism of the Grand Coalition that it decided to allow an official West German Communist Party to be formed again, in September 1968. The KPD was banned in 1956; for twelve years West German Communists went underground and the thought may have prevailed that they were in fact more dangerous when working clandestinely than in the open. The new party was called the German Communist Party (DKP), and the possibly unkind thought has been aired that Kiesinger only allowed it to be licensed on condition that it changed its name – surely the least important factor in the situation![44] There was another, related, reason for licensing the DKP: West German youth, or a part of it, was showing an ever-increasing distaste of the Establishment and was creating its own form of extra-Parliamentary opposition. There was an obvious danger of young people who rejected the democratic West German State drifting into alliance with the Communist underground.

Kiesinger was later to claim, with some reason, that he took office in order to solve certain problems, and did his best with them. The revolt of German youth came as an unpleasant surprise. There were all sorts of reasons for it, none of them operative in isolation from the rest. Due to the Nazi era, there was a bigger generation-gap in the Federal Republic than elsewhere in Europe. If children did not blame their parents openly, they often did so in their hearts; and they were apt to blame them, not only if they had been Nazis themselves, but even if they had simply failed to oppose Nazism. A wave of anti-Americanism was beginning, which would become ever more formidable as the Vietnam War staggered on towards its miserable ending. Among some of the young, again, there was a growing revulsion against wealth, even the wealth of their own parents. Then there were legitimate grievances in the universities, where teaching methods and curricula were felt to be outdated and students wanted greater control of what they considered to be their own affairs. Some of the young believed that the ultimate crime was dullness, and hearkened to the siren voices of intellectuals proclaiming that the Federal State was dull, dreary and decadent. If only a small minority of the young went into open opposition against society at large, they certainly became alarmingly active. Germans, traditionally, never have done things by halves.

There is no clear starting-point of student revolt in Germany, but there are key dates. A student demonstration in West Berlin on 2 June 1967, directed against the Shah of Iran, resulted in a young man, Benno Ohnesorg, being shot and killed by the police. The official inquiry did not produce entirely conclusive findings, but left a strong suspicion that the police – quite apart from the shooting – had used unnecessary force. Without waiting for the findings, all sorts of people condemned the police out of hand; thus the writer Günter Grass called this "the first

Konrad Adenauer – the principal architect of the new West German democracy.

Konrad Adenauer addressing the congregation of the
Cologne Synagogue in 1959. He made reconciliation
with the Jewish people one of his primary objectives.

Konrad Adenauer, in ebullient mood, with Winston Churchill
during a state visit to London in 1951.

Konrad Adenauer
and Willy Brandt in
1962. More than
once, the former
warned that Brandt
was a young man in
"too much of a
hurry".

Ludwig Erhard,
regarded as the
creator of the
German "economic
miracle", with cigar –
as usual – in place.

Ludwig Erhard
speaking in the
Bundestag, with a
attentive Willy
Brandt, then
Federal
Chancellor, to his
right. Only a fair
orator, Erhard wa
masterly on his
own subject –
economics.

Kurt Georg
Kiesinger – not th
most famous
Federal
Chancellor, but
certainly the mos
handsome.

Willy Brandt – the Federal Chancellor who achieved international fame, entirely on his own merits.

Willy Brandt with his close friend Egon Bahr, the *eminence grise* of the Social Democratic Party and apostle of détente.

Helmut Schmidt –
commonsense and
toughness are his strong
points.

Helmut Schmidt and Walter
Scheel, then Federal
President, reaffirming the
Social Democratic–Free
Democratic compact which
began in 1969.

Helmut Schmidt – a
down-to-earth politician
who knows how to
relax.

Kurt Schumacher,
leader of the Social
Democratic Party from
1945 to 1952. His life was
an heroic struggle to
preserve German
democracy.

Herbert Wehner –
power-house of Social
Democratic
organization and
planning.

Walter Ulbricht, the late
East German dictator – a
pitiless, humourless
man.

political murder in the Federal Republic".[45] At the Socialist Students Union, a girl, Gudrun Ensslin, who was destined to become a ruthless terrorist, declared that the crime had been committed by "the generation of Auschwitz – you cannot argue with them".[46] The "police-murderers" had to be fought with their own weapon, violence.

Benno Ohnesorg's death resulted in the organization of the "June 2 Movement", whose members were committed in opaquely evocative terms to avenging his death. Although there had been plenty of student demonstrations before this date, this would seem to be the first West German group which decided that organized violence, on its own, was legitimate. It would spawn other groups, always ready to use violence in more terrifying ways but, significantly, becoming smaller and more compact as time went on. This is the classic mode of progress towards gangsterism; it all happened in Ireland in the nineteenth century, and then happened, all over again and in far more revolting form, in the twentieth. To do the "June 2 Movement" justice, it began with ideals, and some of its members wanted to maintain them.

The movement had a mouthpiece. The Hamburg magazine *Konkret* preached a far-left utopianism, and sold itself on a bizarre but by no means unique combination of political idealism and pornography. Its editor, Klaus Rainer Rohl, married Ulrike Meinhof, who was to be one of the founders of the "Baader-Meinhof Gang". Rohl and his associates all came from a well-to-do, middle-class background, for which they professed their disgust. They made a cult of living rough, offering a faint but fugitive resemblance to medieval hermits. Murder was not their immediately proclaimed method of launching revolution, but they defended all forms of "justified violence" and encouraged demonstrations without end, marches in the streets and the seizure of assembly and class-rooms in the universities. Lenin, as one commentator put it, would have included them in "the infantile left".[47]

Lenin's successors, however, felt differently. They saw in this incipient revolt of West German youth a very valuable tool for their campaign to undermine the West German State. Rohl would later confess that *Konkret*, and the activities which it promoted, had been financed with Soviet funds, filtered through Prague, to the tune of perhaps two million marks.[48] Thus, the Russians "for a couple of million marks ... helped disrupt whole areas of West German society, turn the German youth movement into a mass-force of anti-Americanism, and rehabilitate the theory and practice of Marxian revolution".[49]

The second key date in the history of student revolt was 11 April 1968, when a young anti-Communist tried to assassinate "Red" Rudi Dutschke, by now, along with Danny Cohn-Bendit, one of the two acknowledged leaders of the movement, in West Berlin. The outcome was violent student demonstrations all over the country, their principal targets being the newspaper offices belonging to Axel Springer, in West Berlin, Hamburg, Munich, Frankfurt and Essen. Springer controlled the biggest "newspaper empire" in Europe and had roundly condemned student violence. The Socialist Students League played a big part in this wave of demonstrations, causing embarrassment to Kiesinger's SPD partners in the Government and bringing the Chancellor's personal denunciation of "this planned political action of a revolutionary character".[50]

In 1968 and 1969 the students' revolt gained in momentum. Political gambits included the Vietnam War, the atom bomb and the two coalition parties in Bonn. But a distinction was still made between SPD and CDU. The SPD Minister of Economics, Karl Schiller, had been a member of the Nazi Party, but this was to some extent regarded as excusable. On the other hand, the CDU Chancellor was held to have no moral right to protest against student "resistance".[51] The student revolt was directed, in varying degrees, against all bourgeois society, but its esoteric nature has been explained in a single sentence: "It became a very popular front, uniting practically everyone on the left – except the proletariat."[52] The students, proclaiming their crusade for a more just and humane society, had no contact with the German working class whatever.

Kiesinger condemned student violence without reservation. "What is happening in Berlin," he said at the beginning of 1968, "and in various places in our universities, is the expression of the forces of anarchy."[53] In the Bundestag, he said that he had consulted all the Minister Presidents of the *Laender* in order to secure a common approach to the problems posed by the students. He had sympathy for their real problems, but they had not respected the patience and restraint shown by the Government in order to avoid embittering feelings any further. The situation had to be dealt with firmly, for unlimited restraint would only be regarded as weakness.[54] He repeated the need for firmness after the attempt on Rudi Dutschke's life,[55] and added that "Democracy is never guaranteed", and that the Federal

Republic had been a bit spoilt; its people had lived peaceably over the years, compared with those of other countries. But he was depressed by student responses. He had tried to discuss their worries with them, but all that he got back from them was slogans.

Student violence was to remain a serious problem for the Grand Coalition. When the police used what they considered to be necessary force, they and the Government were condemned for brutality. When students went on the rampage – arson had now been proclaimed "legitimate" by Ulrike Meinhof[56] – the Government was accused of weakness. Student unrest now became associated with a totally different issue, that of special legislation for an emergency, which would become operative only if "democratic order" in the Federal Republic was threatened. This legislation was, in fact, framed for quite different circumstances, such as a war situation or a real political campaign to destroy West German democracy. The students made no impact at all in the political field. In the Baden-Wurtemberg *Land* elections, all radical left-wing parties together collected only two per cent of the vote. The Emergency Law was passed in May 1968, and was supported by three-quarters of the electorate, but it led to fresh student demonstrations. The Soviet and East German press joined in, accusing the Grand Coalition of installing a political and military dictatorship.

There were worries in the political field, too, for Kiesinger. Federal elections took place every four years, but Presidential elections every five. In 1969, for the first time since 1949, they took place in the same year. In March, the Presidential candidates were Gerhard Schroeder of the CDU, and Gustav Heinemann of the SPD; as usual, election was by the "Bundesversammlung" of roughly 1,000 members. The candidates were well matched. Schroeder had served with distinction as Federal Minister of the Interior, as Foreign Minister and, finally, as Minister of Defence. Heinemann was an experienced politician too, a reformer and humanist, with close connections with the Evangelical Churches. The CDU had helped to place an FDP President, Theodor Heuss, in office in 1949; it was supposed that the FDP would repay this by supporting Schroeder. But after two inconclusive ballots the new FDP leader, Walter Scheel, brought his party over to Heinemann's side. There had been agreement behind the scenes between SPD and FDP that electoral reform, which would have effectively killed the FDP, would be dropped.[57] This was the beginning of collaboration between the two parties which has continued up to the present. Heinemann got in, by just six votes.

Willy Brandt had a number of talks with Scheel at this time. The FDP was still split between left-liberals who supported Scheel's personal preference for the SPD, and right-of-centre conservatives with an acute distaste for everything socialist. Scheel believed that he could carry his party with him, and Heinemann's election suggested that he was right. The FDP would stand to gain by alliance with the SPD; it would be able to maintain profile and Scheel believed that it would be seen as a brake on socialist policies which did not commend themselves to a majority of the electorate. By contrast, the FDP had always lost profile while in alliance with the CDU; middle-of-the-road voters tended simply to lump it together with the bigger, non-socialist party and to give their support to the latter.

The truth was that the SPD was becoming disenchanted with the Grand Coalition. They were losing ground in the *Laender* and there was an irritating tendency to regard them as junior partners. Brandt would later say that the risks of the SPD losing ground in office were outweighed by the advantages of sharing in government.[58] But this did not mean that he wanted the Grand Coalition prolonged beyond the Federal elections in September. He stayed that long mainly "because I could not be the one to bring the Grand Coalition down".[59] There had been surprisingly few disagreements between the two coalition parties. The SPD were still pressing for a revaluation of the mark, and Kiesinger was still resisting such a move. There were different views about extending the so-called Statute of Limitations, under which murderers could not be prosecuted if twenty years had elapsed since the crime. In the event, a majority was found for an extension from 20 to 30 years, and the SPD view prevailed. Wild-cat strikes in the coal, steel and ship-building industries, and in the public services, were a hint to the SPD that some of their loyal working class voters were losing patience.

In any event, the elections had to be fought, and fought primarily between the two coalition partners. Brandt was careful not to indulge in recriminations. Asked what the Grand Coalition had lacked, he replied: "There were practically no jokes about it."[60] He circulated instructions to avoid polemics and pay no attention to his opponents' style of fighting.[61] Kiesinger campaigned on the record of his Government, especially in having successfully combated economic recession and in opening the road to East–West détente. He played the small but useful trump-card of continuity; as one writer put it, he "represented the school of thought which Adenauer had left behind and which will have a lasting effect on German and European history".[62] He had been the last CDU politician to see Adenauer alive, just over a fortnight before he died on 19 April 1967. In his election speeches he hinted at the need to slow down Ostpolitik, mildly criticized Brandt for being prepared to accept a nuclear non-proliferation treaty, and denounced "leftist" tendencies in flowery, oratorical terms. He made it plain that he saw no reason why the Grand Coalition should not be renewed, but with the condition that it should in no event extend beyond 1973.

Voting took place on 27 September after what, for the Federal Republic, had been a low-key election campaign. It was clear early on that the FDP were doing badly, and the NPD even worse – the danger of neo-Nazis being returned once more to the Bundestag was banished, but the NPD vote of 4·3 per cent came rather closer to surmounting the "Five per cent clause" than was altogether comfortable. With only 5·8 against 9·5 per cent of the votes, FDP representation in the Bundestag was reduced to 30 – Scheel's approaches to Brandt had frightened off the party's right-wing supporters, probably for good.

Brandt's personality, Wehner's expert management, and the good showing of SPD Ministers entrusted at long last with the responsibilities of government – these were principal factors in the SPD's success. Its vote rose from 39·3 to 42·7 per cent, and its Bundestag seats were up from 202 to 224. The CDU had done by no means badly: its vote dropped only from 47·6 to 46·1 per cent, and its seats from 246 to 242. Kiesinger sat back for a moment, confident that he would have the option of re-forming the Grand Coalition or of taking the FDP back into the fold. After all, another 0·7 per cent would have given him an overall majority. A message of congratulations came from Washington; President Nixon had at that moment learnt only that the CDU was once again the strongest single party. His message, unwisely, was transmitted to the press.

Kiesinger waited a moment too long. There were members of the FDP waiting for a call from him, but Brandt acted too quickly for them. He telephoned Scheel, and just before midnight was able to confront the television cameras and announce that the SPD and FDP would form the next Government, with a Parliamentary majority of only twelve, but in the belief that they would successfully usher in a new period of German history. Kiesinger's surprise and chagrin were total. His pride was bitterly hurt. For the time being, he would remain Chairman of the CDU and he stayed on as a member of the Bundestag – ten years later he was still there. But his real political career ended on the night of 27 September 1969. He had none of Adenauer's desperate desire to cling to power. Maybe he lacked a sense of mission. Adenauer had said that he had "too thin a skin" for politics.[63] He was 65 years old, and had already had one heart attack; he was not prepared to try to make a comeback.

Historians have been inclined to write off both the Grand Coalition and its leader as failures. In fact, the Kiesinger Government succeeded in its main task, which was to overcome the economic recession. Any Briton can only feel envious of a Germany which had two political parties ready to make common cause and sink their differences in the national interest; Britain's Socialists and Conservatives have set their faces against doing the same, necessary thing for the past decade or more, and their country has suffered bitter, perhaps irretrievable loss as a result. Any Briton, again, can only admire the German statesman who returned from his own home to lead a completely experimental administration. Patriotism is too often derided; it is a saving grace of national existence.

The Grand Coalition encountered more problems than it had any right to expect. Two authors have outlined those that were predictable.[64] Much time had to be spent ironing out differences of opinion between the two parties, and decision-making was not always easy. The lack of effective opposition made it too easy to steam-roller legislation through, without searching examination and effective discussion. As an institution, the Bundestag suffered; debates became mere formalities, and it was an actual relief to listen to the rasping oratory of a Strauss or a Helmut Schmidt. The opinions of the two coalition partners about détente began to differ, and over electoral reform fell apart altogether. The two partners, again, became increasingly and uncomfortably aware that the compromises which they were obliged to make in Bonn were alienating many of their supporters all over the country. Obviously, the Grand Coalition was hindered by the uncompromising attitude of the DDR regime, which made even the smallest move towards all-German reconciliation impossible.

The 1968 Soviet invasion of Czechoslovakia was a severe and unexpected blow to détente. The rise of the neo-Nazi NPD was disturbing and unsettling. Far more damaging was student unrest and violence; its sheer irrationality made it impossible to deal with effectively. Like Kiesinger, his successors would be accused of fighting the students with repression and brutality. At least, they were able to profit from his experience; Kiesinger suffered from being the first to confront a frightening and inexplicable phenomenon.

He has sometimes been depicted as a light-weight among the post-war Federal German Chancellors. Some critics thought him vain and weak. Perhaps he lacked a true politician's killer instinct, but he always spoke his mind with a singular clarity and he was one of the very few CDU leaders who refused to be patronized by Adenauer, their "father-figure". Some thought him too fluent, too facile a speaker – Helmut Schmidt is credited with having called him "old silver-tongue", a tag which stuck.[65] But his speeches sounded superb, and today read excellently. Adenauer used him as the tireless champion in the Bundestag of the cause of European unity – and withheld his reward, the Foreign Ministry. He was accused of having affectations and foibles – an aversion to cigarettes, for instance, a habit of quoting Alexis de Tocqueville, a tendency to preach against blood sports. SPD interrupters in the Bundestag used to shout "Prima donna" at him. His speeches often irritated them; but most of all because they were both well-researched and eloquent.

Kiesinger presided over the Grand Coalition, at least until its final two or three months, with discretion and elegance. Brandt found him in no way hard to work with, "knowledgeable and intellectually stimulating".[66] He helped to give Christian and Social Democrats the chance of working together productively, understanding one another's thoughts, appreciating the fact that traditional opponents need not be lifelong enemies. How could this be other than a useful lesson? It was learned long ago in Britain (although in danger of being forgotten today). The experience of the Grand Coalition was necessary for Bonn; it took much of the previous supercharged animosity out of its political hot-house existence. Kiesinger's charm, wit and candour mark him out as a most civilized German. Some of his contemporaries would have preferred such a designation to that of a most successful statesman.

1. Helmut Wolfgang Kahn. *Helmut Schmidt*. Hamburg, 1973.
2. Walter Henkels. *Bonner Koepfe*. Düsseldorf, 1969.
3. Helmut Wolfgang Kahn, op. cit.

4. Walter Henkels, op. cit.
5. Kurt Georg Kiesinger. *Schwaebische Kindheit*. Tuebingen, 1964.
6. Ibid.
7. Roger Berthoud. The London *Times*, 15 November 1978.
8. Kurt Georg Kiesinger, in television interview, 13 December 1968.
9. Ibid.
10. Ibid.
11. Kiesinger evidently did his best to discourage anti-semitic propaganda and on more than one occasion brought down the fury of Josef Goebbels on his head, according to an Irish journalist, Anthony Crotty, who was in Germany at the time. Memorandum on Kiesinger in the Nazi era, by Dr Reinhard Schmoeckel. Bonn, 1977.
12. Heli Ihlefeld. *Kiesinger. Anekdoten*. Munich, 1967.
13. Johannes Schauf, in statement to Press, November 1966. Schmoeckel.
14. Deposition by Jutta Winter, November 1966. Schmoeckel.
15. Deposition by H. J. Unger, August 1969. Schmoeckel.
16. Fritz Lamm. *Die grosse Koalition und die naechsten Aufgaben der Linken*. Frankfurt, 1967.
17. Ibid.
18. Ralf Dahrendorf. *Fuer eine Erneuerung der Demokratie in der Bundesrepublik*. Munich, 1968.
19. Fritz Lamm, op. cit.
20. Kurt Georg Kiesinger, in speech to Bundestag, 13 December 1966.
21. Hermann Schreiber and Sven Simon. *Willy Brandt. Anatomie einer Veraenderung*. Düsseldorf, 1970.
22. Kurt Georg Kiesinger, in speech to Bundestag, 14 January 1968.
23. Aidan Crawley. *The Rise of Western Germany*. London, 1973.
24. Kurt Georg Kiesinger, in television interview, 16 February 1968.
25. Kurt Georg Kiesinger, in speech to Bundestag, 29 April 1965.
26. Kurt Georg Kiesinger, in speech to Bundestag, 7 June 1966.
27. A British diplomat, who accompanied Kiesinger, in conversation with the author.
28. Kurt Georg Kiesinger, in speech to Bundestag, 11 March 1968.
29. *Quick* Magazine, 1 May 1968.
30. Kurt Georg Kiesinger, in speech to Bundestag, 21 August 1968.
31. Ibid, 25 September 1968.
32. David Shears, *The Ugly Frontier*. London, 1970.
33. Willy Brandt, in television interview, 2 July 1967.
34. *Die Welt*, 14 October 1967.
35. *Bayern Kurier*, 26 August 1967.
36. *Donau Kurier*, 3 October 1967.
37. *Nuernberger Zeitung*, 26 May 1967.
38. *Rheinischer Post*, 27 July 1968.
39. *Sudwestfunk* radio, 25 August 1968.
40. François Bondy. *Die Weltwoche*, 20 October 1967.
41. Aidan Crawley, op. cit.
42. Heinz Hoehne and Hermann Zolling. *Network*. London, 1972.
43. Aidan Crawley, op. cit.
44. Ibid.
45. Jillian Becker. *Hitler's Children*. London, 1977.
46. Ibid.

47. Melvin Lasky. *New York Times Magazine*, 11 May 1975.
48. Ibid.
49. Ibid.
50. Kurt Georg Kiesinger. *West Deutscher Rundfunk*, 13 April 1968.
51. Jillian Becker, op.cit.
52. Melvin Lasky, op. cit.
53. Kurt Georg Kiesinger, to the *Verein Union-Presse*, 23 January 1968.
54. Kurt Georg Kiesinger, in speech to the Bundestag, 9 February 1968.
55. Kurt Georg Kiesinger. *West Deutscher Rundfunk*, 13 April 1968.
56. Melvin Lasky, op. cit.
57. Erich Mende. *Die FDP*. Stuttgart, 1972.
58. Willy Brandt, in conversation with the author, June 1972.
59. Willy Brandt. *People and Politics*. London, 1978.
60. Heli Ihlefeld. *Willy Brandt. Anekdotisch*. Munich, 1968.
61. *Abendzeitung*, 11 September 1969.
62. Thomas Dalberg. *Franz Josef Strauss*. Gütersloh, 1968.
63. Heli Ihlefeld. *Kiesinger. Anekdoten*. Munich, 1967.
64. R. B. Tilford and R. J. C. Preece. *Federal Germany. Political and Social Order*. London, 1970.
65. Helmut Wolfgang Kahn, op. cit.
66. Willy Brandt, op.cit.

CHAPTER EIGHT

Now, Hitler *has* lost the War

In one of the first press interviews which he gave after becoming Chancellor, Brandt remarked that he saw himself as the leader of a liberated, not a defeated Germany – he was, he said, aware of a feeling that now Hitler had finally lost the war.[1] A friend, Georg Meistermann, who painted his portrait, went even further back in history; in his view, Brandt's election "meant for me the rehabilitation of another Germany ... Bismarck ruled, until Kiesinger left".[2] The election, in fact, was a close-run thing. Brandt was given 251 votes, or just three more than half of the Bundestag, and two more than the bare minimum required. His own dry comment was: "Anyway, 300 per cent of Adenauer's majority" [in 1949].[3]

His election took place on 21 October, and during the three weeks which had elapsed since the Federal elections, Bonn had been a hive of political activity. The CDU leaders tried very hard to woo the FDP, and according to Brandt[4] offered them up to six Cabinet seats. For once, Kiesinger's customary good temper failed him; allegedly, he threatened the FDP with being kicked out of provincial Parliaments. The SPD, on the other hand, took over government with admirable unassertiveness. A cartoon in the *Sueddeutsche Zeitung* showed Brandt, in white tie and tails, making an uproarious entrance into the "federal box" in the political theatre, ejecting a scandalized Kiesinger and a sour-faced Strauss with: "You're sitting in our places".[5] It was not like that at all. Brandt himself admits to having felt "anything but exultant" in the hour of victory, and totally preoccupied with the problems which lay ahead.[6]

Within twenty-four hours of his election he was able to announce the names of his Ministers – easily a record in Bonn's short Parliamentary history – and his statement of Government policy, on 28 October, was a model of sobriety. He had, indeed, much more to say in a book, *Hundert Jahre Deutschland*, published just after the election. He told readers that the division of Germany was the consequence, not the cause, of the division of Europe, that the German Question could not be solved in isolation, and that it was no longer possible to demand progress towards reunification as a condition for improving East–West relations.[7] The future had to be faced without emotion, and in the understanding that the policy of the sword had failed the German people and that the legend of *Deutschland über alles* was over and done with. Brandt told the correspondent of the *New York Times* that he intended to be "the Chancellor of domestic reforms. There will be a lot of domestic policy-making".[8] His first administrative act was to revalue the mark, but he would, in fact, turn his attention increasingly to foreign affairs and very especially to Ostpolitik.

Like every post-war German Chancellor, Brandt was essentially a "self-made man". But there was a major difference between him and the others. They came from reasonably well-established families, even if none of them was brought up in luxury. Brandt's mother was poorest of the poor, and he himself, born Herbert Ernst Karl Frahm in December 1913, in Lübeck, was illegitimate – he only gave himself Willy Brandt as a "party name" after the Nazis came to power and the Socialist Workers Party to which he belonged was banned.[9] His Frahm grandfather helped to look after him when he was small, but he had to stand on his own feet from a very early age. Life was very tough indeed during the 1922–3 "inflation" – at one time he was earning a few pennies for every 10,000 million marks worth of useless Reichsmark notes which he collected and handed in – and again when economic recession took place in 1929. But he studied assiduously at school and at the age of fourteen was already active in political youth groups.

By 1931 he was, as he put it, *stark engagiert* – deeply committed – in the struggle against Nazism, and filled with an optimism which was only partly due to his youth. The Social Democrats underestimated Hitler – "Our leader in the Reichstag, Otto Wels, coined the phrase: 'rough fellows don't rule for long'. Like others, I too hoped that the Nazis might not last. It's easy to be wise after the event; but who guessed that the Nazis would be in for twelve long years or just what they would do in that time?"[10] Two years later, when the Nazis came to power, Brandt left the country. His name was on Nazi black lists and he would certainly have ended up, had he stayed, in a concentration camp. He sailed, hidden behind cases of stores and fishing gear, in a small cutter, from Travemünde on the Baltic to the Danish port of Rodbyhavn, on 1 April 1933. His total belongings consisted of a wallet with 100 marks in it and a briefcase, with a toothbrush, a couple of shirts and a copy of the first volume of Karl Marx's *Das Kapital*. The book, Brandt subsequently wrote with dry humour, "never succeeded in turning me into an orthodox Marxist".[11]

The writer, Heinrich Böll, has called Brandt's career "a legend, almost a fairy-tale which came true".[12] His life story is one of endless struggle and remarkable success in the face of adversity. He arrived in Denmark penniless; not only did he manage to make his way as a journalist – no easy matter in somebody else's country – but he continued his political work with the utmost determination. His Socialist Workers Party (SAP) stood to the left of the Social Democrats, and sought at various stages to help build a "popular front" of all left-wing forces and a Marxist International. Brandt's enemies have portrayed him as a crypto-Communist at this stage of his life, but in fact he was warning against Stalinism and wrote spiritedly against the Moscow trials, which brought death sentences for so-called "deviationists". He believed, certainly, in international cooperation among the working class, and he helped to found the International Bureau of Revolutionary Youth Organizations in February 1934. His views on cooperation were understandable; it was, after all, the schism of the parties of the left which did so much in Germany to let in, first Hindenburg and then Hitler.

A quality which Brandt showed from childhood onwards was courage. In February 1934, he narrowly escaped personal disaster when attending a rally of left-wing socialist youth at Laaren, in Holland. The pro-Nazi mayor of the place handed over four young Germans as "undesirables" to the police, and they were taken to the German frontier in handcuffs and handed over to the Gestapo. Brandt would probably have gone with them, if he had been at once recognized as a German;[14] but Norway was now his base, he had come from there and was at first mistaken for a Norwegian. He was taken instead to

Amsterdam by the police, interrogated there and expelled from the country.

In the summer of 1936 Brandt put his head in the noose of his own free will; he went to Berlin to re-establish contact there with the socialist underground, and was put temporarily in charge of the SAP organization of the "Metro". He carried the passport of a Norwegian friend, and admitted in later years to feeling some fear.[15] It could hardly have been otherwise; at this stage, the Nazis regarded the Communists and Socialists as their main enemies, and they probably comprised four-fifths of the population of the growing number of concentration camps. A great part of the work of the left-wing resistance against Nazism consisted in collecting information, and smuggling it abroad. Brandt and his friends were all too well aware that the inmates of the concentration camps were treated with ever-increasing brutality.

Information work was the essence of this "offensive of truth".[16] It included the printing or smuggling into the country of illegal newspapers and pamphlets, and their dissemination. All over Germany, small "cells" of resisters were formed, generally of no more than four or five people, to reduce the risk of incriminating others. They forged passports, produced cover-stories for the frontier-runners who took information abroad, stimulated criticism of the regime in the factories. Brandt left Berlin at the end of 1936; he has never boasted of this work, carried out under really dangerous conditions.

International conferences claimed much of his time. Then came the Spanish Civil War. Nazi support of Franco inevitably put Brandt on the other side, but his activities in Spain were mainly journalistic, and he left after four months, sadly disillusioned by the senseless sectarian quarrels which went on among Franco's opponents, and by the ruthlessness with which the Moscow-steered Communists sought to seize all political power. His fear was that even if the Republic should survive, it would turn into a communist dictatorship.[17]

Brandt was by now a remarkably mature young man, tough, outspoken, humorous, but at heart a "loner". He never complained of difficult days when he was a child, but illegitimacy is no easy matter and children can be cruel. Very early in life, he developed an ingrained reserve which his outward charm and candour never completely concealed. Somehow, an inner steel shutter separated him from his fellow beings; easy to get on with, easy to know, up to a point, yet he made no truly close friends. For self-revelation was utterly foreign to his character; without it, intimate friendship is next to impossible. Yet a fellow member of the SAP remembered best that "he was able to relax, loved a good laugh, had the gift of companionable silence too";[18] and a young British socialist found him "a very attractive character, and not just because he was friendly and exceptionally good-looking. He had a mixture of shyness and forthright resolution which immediately appealed. He said what he thought, yet remained friendly in spite of differences of opinion".[19] This characteristic stayed with him for life; more than thirty years later one finds the comment that Brandt "treats his political opponents with the dignity of an old-time aristocrat".[20]

The outbreak of war in 1939 found Brandt in Norway, busy with his journalism, with Norwegian youth affairs, writing his first book *War Aims of the Great Powers* and collecting material for another. The German invasion of Norway took him as much by surprise as it did both the Norwegian Government and people. He was lucky to be given a Norwegian Army uniform before being taken prisoner by the German Army near Trondheim; once again he narrowly escaped the net of the Gestapo and a Nazi concentration camp. He spent four weeks, ostensibly as a Norwegian prisoner-of-war, and was released in June 1940. The purely temporary wearing of Norwegian uniform later gave birth to the story that he fought against "his own side", a story which cropped up time after time during his political career and led to a number of lawsuits.[21]

Two further adventures lay ahead of him. In July, he escaped into Sweden, leaving his wife Carlotta and his infant daughter behind in Oslo, and then in December he stole back across the frontier to Oslo to make arrangements for them to join him in Stockholm – another act of remarkable courage. The war years in exile were frustrating, but by no means barren: between 1941 and 1945, Brandt wrote six books, carried on his political work with the SAP, and made friends among Swedish, and exiled Norwegian, Austrian and other socialists with whom he would stay in permanent contact when war ended.

Brandt's post-war career was as individualistic as what had gone before. He returned to Norway, and was given Norwegian citizenship. To a friend he wrote: "Now, I shall always feel intimately linked with Norway. But I have never forsaken the German working class movement. It would be more comfortable today to withdraw to a Norwegian base. But I can't bring myself to make this decision. I want at least to make the attempt to give my help so that the movement can be created afresh in Germany."[22] For the moment, he kept his options open, going first to Nuremberg to report the war-crimes trials for the Oslo *Arbeiderbladet*, establishing contact with the re-formed Social Democratic Party, then going to Berlin at the end of 1946 as Norwegian Press Attaché. This, as it turned out, was the crucial step; for in November 1947, he decided to reclaim German citizenship and in February 1948 he became the SPD's special representative in Berlin, in effect liaison officer between SPD headquarters in Hanover and the party's Berlin branch. With regret, but abiding gratitude, he renounced Norwegian nationality.

Brandt's work in Berlin, which took him to the chairmanship of the Berlin branch of the SPD and to the post of Governing Mayor of the city, is an intrinsic part of post-war German history. Here, I can give no more than an outline. First, his road to the top was a difficult one. He was working, initially, for the leader of the SPD, Dr Schumacher. Brandt found him unpredictable and temperamental – although he had a profound admiration for his deep idealism.[23] Brandt, again, was treated with some reservation by the leaders of the Berlin branch of the party. He was a returned exile and not a Berliner, whereas they had stayed in Germany and opposed Nazism with great courage and fortitude. Matters improved when Brandt changed his job, and began to work for the newly-appointed Governing Mayor of West Berlin, Ernst Reuter. An immediate empathy was established between the two men – Reuter, too, was a returned exile, having spent long years in both Russia and Turkey. During the 1948–9 Berlin Blockade, Brandt became his right-hand man, working often almost round the clock. The Western Powers, naturally, were given credit for the astonishing performance of the "Berlin Airlift", in which 2,325,000 tons of essential goods were brought to the beleaguered city in 277,800 flights over a period of nearly fifteen months. But credit should go, too, to the people of Berlin and their own administrators. The Berliners faced days of short rations, nights of cold and all sorts of shortages – electricity, for instance, was available only for a "staggered" four hours in 24, which could mean cooking and eating in the middle of the night. The Berliners were brave, loyal and humorous; their epic feat of endurance won them the admiration of their former conquerors who, for the first time since the war, began to visualize the possibility of treating

Germans as friends and allies. In this long and wearisome hour of trial, the SPD leaders – Franz Neumann, Gustav Klingelhofer and Otto Suhr, as well as Brandt and Reuter – were undaunted and dedicated.

One of Brandt's speeches at this time gives a good idea of his thinking.[24] He believed that the defence of free, West Berlin had checked the Communist advance in Europe. But its freedom would have to go on being vigorously defended in the future – "If Berlin, one day, becomes a solid component of the Federal German system, there will no longer be an isolated Berlin question." The survival of this free Berlin could even save the East Germans from being bolshevised, and it could be furthered by the integration of free Western Europe. Western Germany, meanwhile, must achieve true social progress, and combat – under the leadership of the SPD – the nationalism which was once again rising to the surface, thanks to "the unbelievably short memories of some of our compatriots". It was the sort of pep talk that the Berliners needed; the blockade was still on, the winter winds blew all the way from Siberia and in Berlin's bleak, ruined, unlit streets one would hear phrases like: "Look across the Potsdamer Platz, and you can hear the ripples of the Volga".[25]

Brandt took time off to join in the 1949 Federal election campaign and, like other members of the SPD, was horrified by its result. He claimed that Adenauer's CDU used Machiavellian tactics by depicting the SPD as the party of ultra-strict economic controls and as the stalking-horse of Bolshevism.[26] The election result had two important consequences for him; he turned down an offer of the safe SPD seat of Pinneberg in the Federal Parliament, and he became instead one of the non-voting Berlin members in Bonn and Ernst Reuter's confidential representative there. In Bonn he gained a working knowledge, not only of Federal government and institutions, but also of developments in Western Europe and, in particular, of the movement towards European unity. Brandt became the first leading member of his party to call for West German membership in the Council of Europe – he considered his party leadership's opposition purblind,[27] for the youth of the Federal Republic had already embraced concepts of European integration and were the first to demonstrate physically for the abolition of frontiers and all other barriers between nations.

Although commuting between Berlin and Bonn, Brandt's Berlin career progressed steadily. He became a borough chairman of the SPD, then edited the party newspaper, the *Stadtblatt*. At the end of 1950 he became a member of the City Parliament, and in 1952 ran as a rank "outsider" against Franz Neumann for the post of party chairman in the whole of West Berlin. Two years later, he ran for office again and was beaten only by 145 to 143 votes. Now, he was giving all of his time to Berlin, and became President (or Speaker) of the City Parliament. When in 1956 East Berlin was declared the capital of the East German State, Brandt made no secret of his belief that West Berlin should now be fully integrated with the Federal Republic and become its capital.[27]

In 1956 Brandt displayed nerve and judgement during the Hungarian Rising which was put down with such ruthless brutality by the Russians. He managed to divert a huge and infuriated crowd of West Berliners from marching through the Brandenburg Gate into East Berlin – they would have been confronted by Red Army tanks and there would have been appalling bloodshed. Brandt managed to turn them round and lead them back into the Tiergarten Park, where he induced them to sing the German national anthem – later he remarked dryly: "In political situations it is useful to remember that my countrymen are fond of singing."[28] He won gratitude and respect, and when the Governing Mayor died (Otto Suhr had succeeded the dead Ernst Reuter two years earlier), Brandt was elected to the post on 3 October 1957.

So much for the first phase in a remarkable success-story. The second related to his tenure of the Mayoralty, up to December 1966, when he became Kiesinger's Foreign Minister. Berlin was indeed lucky in its SPD Mayors – the city, up to very recent times, remained a stronghold of the party. Reuter led Berlin through the Blockade, Suhr through difficult days that followed, and Brandt through a whole series of crises. There was the Soviet ultimatum of 1958, demanding West Berlin's conversion into a "free city". There was continuous pressure on the city in the next three years. Then came the building of the Berlin Wall in 1961, and sporadic pressure thereafter. These were years in which the city's government could never relax, when there might be interference at any time with traffic on its life-lines, the autobahns and railways to West Germany, when desperate escapes across the Wall could bring murderous fusillades from East Berlin and touch off furious demonstrations of the West Berliners, and when the Soviet Union and the East Germans worked with the organized industry of termites to undermine the city's morale and sense of purpose. Yet in those years West Berlin's income was pushed up by 10 per cent annually, 30,000 new homes were built each year, unemployment was sharply reduced, trade and exports flourished, and a million visitors a year flocked to see a city which had recaptured much of its old care-free abandon. These are the sort of successes which go unchronicled, and it is easy to forget that the administration of a great city is probably the best of all preparations for the administration of a whole country – this was Adenauer's experience and it was to be Brandt's. West Berlin's progress was such that the East German SED (the ruling Socialist Unity Party) had to instruct its members not to shop there or attend its "filmstar-gazing" festivals.[29] West Berlin was not just a brilliantly successfully administered city; it became, under Brandt, the shop-window of the Western world.

Brandt was immensely popular, as well as successful. He never lost the human touch – one phrase of his was: "Here one is not faced only with problems of high policy; one deals with living people whom one can help."[30] But the problems of "high policy" were ever-present; chief among them was the problem of the Berlin Wall.

When its building began, in the night of 12 to 13 August 1961, Brandt was campaigning as SPD candidate for the Chancellorship in the Federal elections. He hurried at once to Berlin, leaving his election-train at Hanover and catching the first plane available. He sat in on the 9 a.m. meeting of the Allied Commandants, where one official found him "grave but statesmanlike. He never demanded rash action from the protecting powers nor reproached us for lack of firmness".[31] He would have had the utmost justification in doing so. Allied, as well as West German Intelligence had been caught completely unawares. Well, that can happen to the best Intelligence organizations in the world, although there had been numerous reports of suspiciously heavy traffic on roads into East Berlin, and it was well known that the East German rulers were becoming desperately worried over the flow of refugees into West Berlin, at a rate of over 1,500 a day.[32] The main Allied failure occurred after the Wall began to be built.

The Allied Commandants did nothing, beyond informing their Governments and waiting for orders. Their subsequent excuse was that the Wall was a unique event, and they were not empowered to do anything about it. But the 1953 East German Rising had been a foretaste, and the Allies had failed then too –

Allied Commandants and their staffs had done no more than go
down to the sector boundaries and peer across them through
field-glasses like dimly interested tourists. In 1961 it would have
been possible for Allied troops to have prevented the Wall from
being built, by physical means: neither the Red Army nor the
East German Army was there to stop them, only lightly armed
East German People's Police (see page 105). Yet the Allied
authorities remained inanimate, and initially mute.

This diplomatic paralysis was inexcusable, and left a deep
impression on Brandt's mind. He himself, indeed, passed
through a short interval of time when he appeared "stunned, in
the grip of a traumatic shock which had left him half-
paralysed".[33] But he went quickly into action thereafter, meeting
the press and speaking on Berlin radio tersely and to the point.
He pointed out that Four Power agreements on Berlin had been
grossly violated, that the sector boundaries had been turned into
a fortified state frontier, and that the unity of Berlin was in
process of being destroyed. He sent a personal letter at once to
President Kennedy in Washington, claiming that the Western
Powers were failing to take adequate action and were forfeiting
the trust of the Berliners. Later, he would be quoted as saying
"Kennedy cooked our goose",[35] and Kennedy himself was
reported as saying, of Brandt: "That bastard in Berlin is trying to
involve me in the upcoming German election."[36] Western nerves
were badly frayed, and Kennedy was addicted to rough language,
but what emerged was that the Western Powers were ready to
write off East Berlin altogether and would only defend their
rights in West Berlin, now and in the future.

British diplomats, indeed, readily admitted this.[37] The French,
with their usual diplomatic skill, managed to avoid saying
anything explicit, but were undoubtedly content to stand on
their rights in West Berlin. The Americans in Berlin, according to
one high-ranking Allied officer, castigated the British for being
"yellow" and for unseemly readiness to cordon-off the sector
boundaries and so avoid awkward incidents.[38] But in
Washington, President Kennedy and his advisers underwrote the
sacrifice of East Berlin after careful deliberations with the State
Department, the American Embassy in Bonn and the American
authorities in Berlin.[39] Kennedy was concerned only that there
should be no interference with the Allied access routes to Berlin.

One must, at this point, jump eight years in time, to Brandt's
succession to the Chancellorship. For although he had promised
to be the "Chancellor of domestic reform" he was very quickly

involved in foreign affairs, and his Ostpolitik and contribution towards East–West détente in Europe was to become the most striking feature of his Chancellorship.

First, it should be said that the building of the Berlin Wall had a profound and lasting effect on Brandt's thinking. It convinced him that confrontation was not enough – the West had foresaken its rights in East Berlin and over the German Question as a whole, and therefore an alternative policy must be devised.[40] All idea of a "roll-back" of Soviet power, as envisaged by John Foster Dulles, had gone for ever, years earlier. This left only one practical possibility, a policy of co-existence and détente. Brandt declared his support of these objectives when he became Foreign Minister; as Chancellor, he was to pursue them with the greatest determination and with a degree of success which is still today a matter of strong and sincere controversy.

Brandt himself has written: "It goes without saying that my so-called Ostpolitik was not first devised in 1966. The Adenauer and Erhard Governments had both, in their own way, striven to ease our relations with the Soviet Union and Eastern Europe."[41] Adenauer has generally been held to have done too little in this direction, but after his death, details of the so-called "Globke Plan" leaked out. Dr Hans Globke had in 1959 proposed mutual recognition of each other by the two German States, the establishment of diplomatic relations between them, then a referendum within five years on reunification, which would be preceded by free elections. The reunified Germany would have been free to join either NATO or the Warsaw Pact, or remain neutral. The SPD had, of course, published plans which were not too dissimilar, and there had been some interesting soundings behind the scenes – thus Herbert Wehner had paid secret visits in 1956 to talk to Marshal Tito of Yugoslavia, and in 1967 to meet President Kekkonen of Finland. It is somewhat paradoxical that, while the "Globke Plan" was shelved and SPD proposals denounced, the CDU-led administrations of Erhard and Kiesinger in fact went ahead with their own versions of détente and laid the groundwork for West German relations with all communist satellite states.

Of détente, Brandt wrote:

> It pointed to a common interest – a desire for survival in the nuclear age. There had long been indications that the United States and the Soviet Union aspired to a new relationship. The need for an accommodation had been dramatically highlighted by the Cuban crisis ... French

policy, with its different emphasis, sounded yet another warning note. We could not become the last of the Cold War warriors, the opponents of change and thus, perhaps, the world's leading troublemakers (and whipping boys).[42]

This statement sounds purely defensive, with the Federal Republic being pulled along in the wake of its allies, but Brandt had this to add:

> Above and beyond the German question, we felt it imposs-
> ible to persevere in a simple acceptance of prevailing
> conditions in Europe. What really mattered was to create a
> climate in which the status quo could be changed – in other
> words, improved – by peaceful means. I was unjustly
> accused, both then and later, of bowing to realities. I was,
> and still am, of the opinion that realities can be influenced
> for the better.[43]

And how to improve the political climate in Central Europe? Brandt had put this in the simplest possible terms a year before coming to power: "There is a threefold aim in our policy on the East; improved relations with the Soviet Union, normal relations with the East European states, and a *modus vivendi* between the two parts of Germany."[44] Here was the essence of his Ostpolitik.

Brandt always made something else clear, that Ostpolitik could not be conducted by the Federal Republic in isolation; it required the approval and support of the country's allies. The Western Alliance, moreover, needed to remain strong, united and active, if a West German Ostpolitik were to achieve progressively greater results. In May 1969, he said in Hamburg that the East–West confrontation in Europe could only be ended by first strengthening the Western Alliance and then by developing East–West relations and paving the way to the creation of a "European peace-order".[45] In June he explained that détente was a constructive, empirical process, and not a mere act of appeasement.[46] In the Bundestag on 30 October, he restated his readiness to negotiate with the East Germans "on a basis of equality and without discrimination"; but there should be a special relationship between the two states and they should not be "foreign countries" to one another.[47]

Three days later he gave an interview to the weekly, *Der Stern*, in which he said he was ready to meet Walter Ulbricht or Willi Stoph (the East German Prime Minister), to negotiate with East Germany, the Soviet Union and Poland, and to "put frontier questions on a normal footing".[48] There followed interviews with the *Stuttgarter Nachrichten* and the *Westfaelische Rundschau*. He told the former that a *modus vivendi* with the DDR would allow the East Germans to "live better".[49] He added, to the *Westfaelische Rundschau*, that the DDR might seek to create a smokescreen by merely asking for formal relations with Bonn; what was really needed were practical working arrangements which were beneficial.[50] Brandt summed up his Ostpolitik in his "Report on the state of the Nation" to the Bundestag on 14 January 1970: a moment of truth had arrived, human rights had to be won for all Germans, the two German states should move towards "cooperative togetherness", while limited détente would in no way diminish Western responsibilities in Germany or weaken NATO.

Brandt has since written that he was correcting the mistake of underestimating the strength of the DDR and of refusing to treat it as a "country of equal standing".[51] He had in fact already instigated preparations for a meeting with Willi Stoph, and on 25 February 1970 he confirmed this to the Bundestag and said that preparations were also under way for talks with the Soviet Union and Poland. Brandt kept all three East European Governments fully informed of what he was doing. The result was that Willi Stoph, who could have done nothing whatever without Soviet approval, invited him to a meeting. Brandt accepted on 8 March, and agreement was reached on 12 March to meet in the Thuringian town of Erfurt, just about the most central place in pre-war Germany. The meeting was fixed for 19 March.

Brandt told the press that this first meeting might do no more than "break the ice"; he knew that Stoph would be a tough negotiator and would have limited room for manoeuvre. There was no question of going to Erfurt with a "Brandt blueprint", and he was not interested in boosting his own prestige. He sought to tone down the euphoric mood of speculation, but he made no attempt to disguise the sensational nature of the meeting. As the weekly *Spiegel* put it, "What had for twenty years been either a nightmare or wishful thinking has entered the realms of reality".[52]

Sensational the meeting certainly was, although not in a diplomatic sense. Stoph's face, when he met Brandt at the railway station on the morning of 19 March, wore a glassy expression, and he led his visitor to the Erfurter Hof hotel opposite, across a full hundred square yards of red carpet – an outlandishly bizarre touch for a so-called "People's Democratic Republic". A huge crowd surged around them, chanting

"Willy", "Willy". There was no question whom they meant, and there was no answer to Brandt's joking remark: "Do they mean Willy, with a y, or with an i?" The crowd refused to go away after the two men went into the hotel, and continued to shout for Willy Brandt. So he came out onto the balcony of a second-floor window, and the cheers crescendoed into a tremendous tumult. Typically, the East German People's Police felt impelled to intervene. They brought up heavy reinforcements (the East German press claimed that they were there for Willy Brandt's "protection"!), thrust the crowds away from the building, and hustled any who protested out of the station square. Having cleared the area round the hotel, they ushered in a girls' choir, singing "Demand to Willy Brandt! The DDR must be recognized!" Typically, too, Stoph's speech at the principal meeting was broadcast word for word, but not a line was heard of those inimitable accents of Brandt's, in what one commentator once called "the voice of a very refined Louis Armstrong".[53]

From what Stoph said it would have been impossible to guess that this was the overture to agreement between the two German states – not real reconciliation, it is true, but at least a formal relationship in coexistence. Stoph's speech was ill-natured, at times insulting. He claimed that West German foreign policy had been animated by "forces of restoration and revenge", that attacks had been planned against the sovereign rights and the people of the DDR, and that political sabotage and economic sanctions had robbed his state of 100,000 million marks. He enunciated the myth that East Germany had been "occupied" by the Nazis – "we socialists have always fought against fascism and war" – whereas the Federal Republic, by "trying to reverse the results of the Second World War", had become the lineal successor to Hitler's Germany. Brandt had to endure moralizing, gibes and double-talk in a speech of inordinate length. He answered much more briefly, and to the point: his Government would do whatever was possible to modify the effects of partition and would operate on the basis of the "living reality of a German nation" rather than from territorial division. He laid down six salient principles for coexistence:

1. Both states should preserve the unity of the German nation. They were not "foreign" to one another.
2. They should observe the principles of international law –

respect for territorial integrity, peaceful means to settle disputes, no discrimination.

3. Force should not be used to change the social structure of either state.

4. There should be maximum neighbourly cooperation.

5. Four-Power responsibilities in Germany, and especially in Berlin, should be maintained.

6. The Four Powers should seek to improve conditions in and round Berlin.

The rest of the Erfurt meeting was a waste of time. An evening session was squandered by the East Germans repeating meaningless accusations against the Federal Republic. A mammoth banquet testified, once again, to the tasteless love of purposeless display of the communists. A visit to nearby Buchenwald concentration camp could only have been offensive to Brandt and his entourage. (The official communist guides there have an invariable patter ready, about the sufferings of "Comrade" Ernst Thaelmann and other communists, but never a word about the socialists, Jews and others who died in Buchenwald in their thousands. Naturally they never mention that Walter Ulbricht, the East German dictator, was in Moscow when Thaelmann was imprisoned and murdered in Buchenwald, when the Soviet Union and Nazi Germany were allies, and that Ulbricht never lifted a finger to save the "comrade" whom he regarded merely as a rival.) At Brandt's departure from Erfurt station, the train stood for twelve minutes before pulling out, with Stoph and his Foreign Minister, Otto Winzer, parading up and down the platform like robots, without even a non-committal word for their guests.

Back in Bonn, Brandt justified the Erfurt visit as "necessary and right". In the Bundestag the chief CDU spokesman, Rainer Barzel, expressed his doubts: was the Government about to recognize the Oder–Neisse Line, to establish relations with the DDR, to see two German states represented in the United Nations, and to seek the blessing of the Soviet Union for all this? Brandt was not perturbed. He believed that he could weaken the DDR's malign influence in Moscow, find areas of cooperation with his reluctant East German neighbour, and prove to other communist states that better relations were feasible.[54] He decided to go ahead with a second meeting with Stoph, this time at Kassel, in West Germany, on 21 May.

It took place under unpropitious circumstances. Members of

the neo-Nazi NPD, as well as Communists, demonstrated in the streets, giving Stoph and his companions the opportunity to make caustic comments about "so-called" West German law and order. A wreath-laying ceremony at the memorial for the victims of Nazism had to be postponed because the police could not guarantee the safety of the East German "guests", but Brandt took Stoph to the memorial after all and stood beside him there. Then, in the first working meeting, Stoph interrupted Brandt before he had read more than two sentences of his speech and himself read out a prepared statement accusing the Federal Republic of interfering in his country's affairs.

Brandt kept his head and his temper, returned to his speech and listed twenty proposals for an overall East–West all-German agreement. Apart from the six principles laid down at Erfurt, they included increased movement of persons and goods between the two German states; eventual complete freedom of movement; the reunion of members of families; cooperation over posts, telephones, information, culture, education and the environment; expansion of trade, and finally, the exchange of chargés d'affaires and membership of both states in international organizations. Stoph, predictably, did not attempt to discuss any of these points, and returned to some of the already time-worn, tiresome and intensely silly accusations against the Federal Republic. On the face of it, the Kassel meeting was a flop and Brandt's twenty-point programme might have been supposed to have become a dead letter.

But, as Brandt has himself pointed out, "Though not until eighteen months after the Kassel meeting, all the essential ingredients of this twenty-point programme were included in the settlements ultimately reached".[55] He achieved this by sheer diplomatic skill. In the first place, he pushed ahead with negotiations with the Soviet Union and Poland, thereby placing the onus of responsibility for failure to reach an all-German agreement on the East Germans. In the second place, he insisted on an amelioration of the Berlin situation, through Four Power talks. In the third place, he demanded, and secured a linkage between the different sets of talks, by making signature of treaties with the Soviet Union and Poland dependent on prior Four Power agreement over Berlin. He offered, in fact, a "diplomatic package" and he banked, quite rightly, on the Soviet Union's desire for détente in Central Europe ensuring its acceptability.

He was proved right by the swift progress of negotiations with the Soviet Union. His Foreign Minister, Walter Scheel, was of considerable help, with a gift of sociability which even the Russians found hard to resist, an equability which they failed to shake, and a clear idea of aims. The Russo-German Treaty was signed on 12 August 1970. The two countries agreed to renounce the use of force against each other, and undertook to respect the territorial integrity of all European states and the "map of Europe" as it existed. The Soviet Union waived its spurious "right" to intervene, as victor nation, in the affairs of the Federal Republic. This was a purely ocular concession; what was more important was that the Soviet Union had necessarily to revise its image of the Federal Republic as a tailor-made bogeyman, a "militaristic", "fascist" and "revanchist" state. Brandt called the Treaty "just business"[56] but he was well satisfied. The Treaty was the clue to the success of his whole package, and in a press conference in Moscow he alluded to its impact on the negotiations with the DDR and to Four Power agreement on Berlin. Equally important, the Soviet Union could now be relied upon to encourage satellite states to mend their fences with Bonn.

This quickly proved to be the case with Poland. The first round of talks with that country began in February 1970, and the Poles offered one startling concession: they dropped their demand for West German recognition of the DDR as a precondition for any Polish–West German agreement. There has never been any real friendship between Poland and East Germany – many Poles have an open contempt for East German politicians who so slavishly do the bidding of Moscow. But it was probably more operative that the Polish Government felt absolved of any need to sponsor the DDR, in the light of the Soviet desire for détente. The Polish Government was, at the same time, deeply anxious to secure West German recognition of the Oder–Neisse Line as Poland's western frontier. As long as it was not so recognized, the Soviet Union might conceivably do a deal with the Federal Republic at Poland's expense, while Poland remained uncomfortably dependent on Soviet patronage. In any case, the Poles wanted to break out of relative economic isolation and the strait-jacket of the East European "Comecon" imitation of the European Common Market, and expand economic and technological contact with the West. Their leaders realized, too, that Brandt could be trusted, even liked; like them, he had fought against Nazism.

Recognition of the Oder–Neisse Line was a major political risk for Brandt. Its unacceptability had remained an article of faith with millions of refugees from the lost territories to the east of it; their votes could be crucial in Federal elections. For many years, it was a taboo subject: the German claim to these eastern territories was regarded as irrevocable. The climate had, indeed, been changing; many Germans realized that there could be no possibility of regaining these territories, or dispossessing the large Polish population which had resettled them after the expulsion of more than 90 per cent of their German inhabitants (who, incidentally, suffered cruelly at the time, apart from losing everything they possessed). Brandt argued that recognition of the Oder–Neisse Line was a recognition of realities – "It accorded with simple truth when we said that nobody can give away what he no longer possesses. Nobody can dispose of that which has already been disposed of by history."[57] He would quote a woman who had lost her home in East Prussia as saying: "The treaty with Poland lays a wreath on Prussia's grave, but the grave has existed for many years."

The Treaty with Poland was signed on 7 December 1970, and Brandt travelled to Warsaw for the occasion. He was acutely aware of the implications of the visit of the head of a German Government – the Nazis had murdered six million people in Poland, including four million Jews, and the gallant Polish people had been left isolated and helpless by the outside world while the Jews of the Warsaw Ghetto rose in revolt, the Polish National Resistance staged its own unutterably courageous rising, and Polish freedom-fighters kept up a running battle through five long years of hateful and brutal occupation. Brandt laid a wreath at the Tomb of the Unknown Soldier, and inscribed the visitors' book: "In memory of the dead of the Second World War and of the victims of violence and betrayal, in the hope of an enduring peace and of solidarity between the nations of Europe."[58] At the Warsaw Ghetto memorial, he made an unforgettable gesture, going down on his knees in that great, empty space in which and round which not a single Jewish family survived. It was a gesture totally unrehearsed; not one of his entourage expected it. Afterwards he said: "I did not plan it, and I'm not ashamed of it."[59] Later still, he would write:

> My gesture was intelligible to those willing to understand it, and they included many in Germany and elsewhere. The tears in the eyes of my delegation were a tribute to the dead. As one reporter put it – Then he knelt, he who has no need

to, on behalf of all who ought to kneel, but don't, because they dare not, or cannot, or cannot venture to do so. That was what it was: an attempt, through the expression of fellow-feeling, to build a bridge to the history of our nation and its victims.[60]

Brandt's historic gesture was bitterly criticized by Germans who thought it theatrical, unnecessary or even inappropriate – since he was one German who had no need to feel shame or guilt. What a misunderstanding of Brandt's motives! The Poles understood them, as the Polish Prime Minister, Josef Cyrankiewicz, made haste to explain. In a sense, his gesture overshadowed the treaty, which was a fairly mundane document. It established that the Oder–Neisse Line was Poland's western frontier, and that Poland's frontiers were inviolable and could not be altered by force. Because the Federal Republic could not formally accept borders which were not its own, this boundary between Poland and the DDR was not formally recognized, and the treaty included the reservation that its terms should not be an obstacle to an eventual all-German peace settlement. The Poles took some persuading; at one stage Dr Duckwitz, the chief German negotiator, told the Poles: "We are playing our cards in the open; you can trust us. More important, Brandt really wants peace with Poland, and you can trust *him*."[61] Brandt had, knowingly, made one very big concession. There were several hundred thousand "ethnic" Germans still living in Poland, and their future repatriation was not dealt with in the treaty. Many individual cases were tragic.[62] Brandt believed that Poland would gradually relax restrictions on the emigration of these people, forlorn remnants of an indigenous German population.

There remained the Four Power agreement on Berlin, and the East–West, all-German agreement. Obviously these were the hardest nuts to crack. The East German regime had, in large measure, actually depended on its hostility towards the Federal Republic. Any closening of relations between the two German states could endanger it: the "other", richer, free Germany had to be kept at arms length. For the East German regime depended on faked elections, rigorous surveillance of all "dissidents", the consequent maintenance of a vast secret police apparatus and other familiar trappings of a totalitarian state. A sincere reconciliation with the Bonn Government, and between the peoples of the two German states, was out of the question.

Brandt was always aware of this situation. His aim, as he so often said, was to improve the lot of the people of the DDR and safeguard the existence of the 2,300,000 inhabitants of free, West Berlin. He knew that even these modest objectives would be hard to achieve. In his "Report on the State of the Nation" of January 1971, he gave four reassurances. The German people's basic right of self-determination would continue to be upheld. So would the reality of a single German nation. He would only seek a written agreement with the East Germans on the basis of the twenty points put to Stoph in Kassel. Finally, he would maintain the legal status of Berlin.

He faced all sorts of difficulties. The CDU Opposition was now determined to destroy his Ostpolitik, believing it to be dangerous and unpopular – on the latter score they were proved wrong. East European interest in promoting Brandt's Ostpolitik was also waning; the Soviet Union's interest was turning towards a European Security Conference, where the apprehension and apathy of the West could be profitably exploited – possibly this could even be done without making any concessions over Berlin. Soviet pressure on the DDR, therefore, was relaxed, and without Soviet pressure its rulers could defer agreement with Bonn indefinitely. Brandt's best card was the linkage of the treaties with the Soviet Union and Poland; but ratification of those treaties, instead of being mere routine, now looked more questionable. Brandt's small majority in the Bundestag could well crumble away altogether.

The Four Powers exchanged papers for the first time on 25 September 1970. In October they reached agreement on procedure; it would be three-stage, towards Four Power agreements, implementary German arrangements, and a final quadripartite treaty. There were big differences in the Western and Soviet positions at the outset. The West wanted the easing of conditions in Berlin, guaranteed access to West Berlin from the West and increased personal movement between West and East Berlin, whereas the Russians wanted the West German presence in West Berlin curtailed and a Soviet consulate-general established there. There was a Western draft ready by February 1971, and a Soviet draft a month later. In May, Walter Ulbricht resigned as first secretary of the SED. He was seventy-seven years old and as violently hostile to the Federal Republic as ever; he would probably have been a stumbling-block to agreement had he remained politically active.

The Four Powers reached agreement on 3 September; on the

whole it represented a reasonable compromise. The Soviet Union guaranteed the unimpeded movement of people and goods between West Berlin and the Federal Republic and undertook to facilitate such traffic. At the same time, the Soviet Union promised not to change "the situation in the area" unilaterally, and recognized all ties between West Berlin and the Federal Republic. Less explicitly, it declared that "communications between the Western sectors of Berlin and areas bordering on these sectors, and those areas of the German Democratic Republic which do not border on these sectors, will be improved. Permanent residents of the Western sectors will be able to travel to such areas for compassionate, family, religious, cultural or commercial reasons, or as tourists, under conditions comparable to those applying to other persons entering these areas."

This offered firmer guarantees than ever before on access to West Berlin from the Federal Republic, and some easing of movement between West and East Berlin. In return, the Soviet Union was allowed to install its consulate-general in West Berlin – its only foothold there, other than its participatory guard on the ageing Rudolf Hess in Spandau gaol – and asserted its right of sanction of the consular and representational services of the Federal Republic in West Berlin. In addition, the Federal Republic would no longer send the Bundestag to Berlin to hold plenary sessions there, nor assemble the "Federal Assembly" of over 1,000 delegates in Berlin to elect a new President. West Berlin, then, lost something of its symbolic and representational character.

One formidable hurdle remained, although this is moving ahead of the other events described in this chapter, the securing of agreement on the implementary German arrangements. These were negotiated between Egon Bahr, on behalf of Brandt, and Michael Kohl of the DDR. Brandt explained their relevance: "It is, of course, particularly important how our Ostpolitik progresses after the treaties have been ratified. Some pessimists believe the Russians will now back off and take no great interest in the treaty we have to negotiate with the DDR ... the Basic Treaty will give us a lot more trouble yet."[63] This was in August 1972, and the Basic Treaty was not signed until 21 December. It included mutual renunciation of the use of force, the validity of all existing treaties signed by both states, mutual acceptance of sovereignty, and of the principle that neither state could represent the other internationally. Permanent representative missions would be exchanged, and joint commissions would be formed to deal with such subjects as trade, communications and the demarcation of the existing borders.

So perished two doctrines which had at one time been fundamental to the all-German policy of the Federal Republic, and to which the Western Powers had subscribed. The first was the already semi-defunct "Hallstein Doctrine", under which the Federal Republic could not enter into relations with governments which recognized the DDR. This was not much of a loss, as successive Federal Governments had indicated. The second doctrine which was abandoned was that of the illegality of the East German State. This, indeed, was of tremendous importance, for it meant that the division of Germany was recognized by the whole Western Alliance, and that all future talk of reunification would be illusory and unreal. Brandt himself has sought to explain how this renunciation of German unity could be regarded as acceptable. He wrote:

> We clung to historical reality. I was well aware that, throughout its phases of historical development, Germany had never entirely corresponded to the "classical nation-state". On the death of those eager hopes which had flourished immediately after the war, it became clear to me that there could be no return to a nation-state on the nineteenth century pattern. I nevertheless remained convinced that the nation would live on, even under differing political systems, because nationhood is a matter of awareness and resolve. Although the identity of nation and state had been destroyed, its existence in Germany had in any case been brief. Germany had always existed as a "cultural nation", and it was as a "cultural nation" that it would retain its identity ... to me, this has always been an objective which should not preclude the western part of Germany from seeking a wider political home in the European community of the West.[64]

This was, of course, written some years after the Basic Treaty between the two German states, and it reads like an epitaph for German unity. Even Adenauer, while fully subscribing to the last sentence of Brandt's statement, would scarcely have dared to utter such a thought publicly. Had the "identity" of the German nation, then, really been destroyed? In that case, how could the nation "live on" in a spirit of "awareness and resolve"? And how would "cultural" unity be preserved, when the rulers of

East Germany were busily creating a culture founded on Marxist-Leninism and the goose-step? There are no ready answers to such questions.

At the time, however, the Basic Treaty and the agreements with the Soviet Union and Poland were seen in a rosy light. Thus the SPD Mayor of West Berlin, Klaus Schütz, was completely confident – he said of the Four Power Agreement that his city now had "*status quo* plus", the first written agreement which guaranteed its communications.[65] Even ex-Chancellor Kiesinger admitted that what mattered most to the Berliners was concrete advantage. One dissenter was the former US High Commissioner in Germany, Mr John McCloy; he wrote, "I see no indication that the Soviet Union has given up its plan to drive the USA out of Europe."[66] But the American State Department and the British Foreign Office were both delighted with the treaties, especially that of the Four Powers, and the press of the Western world talked of "a break in the clouds",[67] and – somewhat less convincingly – of the Russians being still able "to tread on West Berlin" but of being "less likely to; they have more to lose".[68] The *Sunday Telegraph* struck a warning note which was apposite: "Good may come of this, but it would be as well to realise that we shall never again, from an American President, hear John Kennedy's affirmation of faith – *Ich bin ein Berliner.*"[69]

The Basic Treaty was only signed some months after the Treaties with Poland and the Soviet Union were ratified by the Bundestag, and the Four Power Agreement on Berlin simultaneously received confirmation. It is dealt with here, because it was the last and in some ways most significant part of Brandt's "Ostpolitik package". Whatever the advantages or disadvantages – and these will be discussed later – Brandt had shown ingenuity, courage and staying-power in pressing ahead. His negotiators, Foreign Minister Walter Scheel, and the enigmatic and controversial *eminence grise* of his Federal Chancellery, Egon Bahr, had displayed skill and persistence. One of his critics called Brandt a "mystic" in his foreign policy.[70] But he was always an essentially practical man; he knew exactly what he was doing. Not long after the Basic Treaty was signed, he remarked: "I may have to leave reunification to the next generation."[71] This was an understatement: German re-unification had been indefinitely deferred, perhaps abandoned for ever.

1. Willy Brandt. *People and Politics*. London, 1978.
2. Georg Meistermann. *Gedanken ueber einen Politiker*. Edited by Dagobert Lindlau. Munich, 1972.
3. Heli Ihlefeld. *Willy Brandt. Anekdotisch*. Munich, 1968.
4. Willy Brandt, op. cit.
5. *Sueddeutsche Zeitung*, 5 October 1969.
6. Willy Brandt, op. cit.
7. Hans Adolf Jacobsen & Hans Dollinger. *Hundert Jahre Deutschland*. Berlin, 1969.
8. David Binder. *Willy Brandt. A German Life*. New York Times Brochure, November 1969.
9. Terence Prittie. *Willy Brandt*. London, 1974.
10. Willy Brandt, in conversation with the author, February 1972.
11. Willy Brandt. *In Exile*. London, 1971.
12. Heinrich Böll. *Typisch Brandt*. Edited by Hermann Otto Bolesch. Munich, 1972.
13. Willy Brandt, as told to Leo Lania in *My Road to Berlin*. London, 1960.
14. Willy Brandt, in conversation with the author, February 1972.
15. Willy Brandt. *In Exile*.
16. Otto Bauer. *Die illegale Partei*. Paris, 1939.
17. Willy Brandt. *Marxistische Tribüne*, July 1937.
18. Herbert George (formerly SAP), in conversation with the author, December 1971.
19. Walter Padley MP, in conversation with the author, December 1971.
20. Professor Dr Werner Forssmann. *Gedanken ueber einen Politiker*.
21. Rolf Italiander. "Die neuen Herren der alten Welt", *Akzente des Lebens*. Bremen, 1970.
22. Letter to Herbert George, 23 August 1945.
23. Willy Brandt, in conversation with the author, December 1971.
24. Willy Brandt, in speech to the SPD borough conference, Berlin, 14 January 1949.
25. Ewan Butler. *City Divided*. London, 1955.
26. Willy Brandt, as told to Leo Lania.
27. John Mander. *Berlin. Hostage for the West*. London, 1962.
28. Willy Brandt, as told to Leo Lania.
29. Terence Prittie. *Manchester Guardian*, 5 July 1958.
30. Willy Brandt, as told to Leo Lania.
31. Geoffrey McDermott. *Berlin. Success of a Mission?* London, 1963. On the other hand, Curtis Cate claims Brandt said that, if the West did not act, "the entire East will laugh, from Pankow (E. Berlin) to Vladivostock".
32. Curtis Cate. *The Ides of August*. London, 1979.
33. Ibid.
34. Willy Brandt. *Begegnungen mit Kennedy*. Munich, 1964.
35. David Binder. *New York Times*, November 1969.
36. James O'Donnell (of the *Saturday Evening Post*), in letter to the author.
37. Geoffrey McDermott, op. cit.
38. The name of the British General must, for reasons of discretion, be withheld.
39. Curtis Cate, op. cit.

40. Willy Brandt. *People and Politics.*
41. Ibid.
42. Ibid.
43. Ibid.
44. Willy Brandt. *The Policy of Détente.* London, 1970.
45. Willy Brandt, in speech to Overseas Club, Hamburg, 7 May 1969.
46. Willy Brandt, in speech at Congress of 11th Socialist International, 16 June 1969.
47. Willy Brandt, in speech to Bundestag. 30 October 1969.
48. Willy Brandt, in interview with *Der Stern*, 2 November 1969.
49. Willy Brandt, in interview with the *Stuttgarter Nachrichten*, 3 December 1969.
50. Willy Brandt, in interview with the *Westfaelische Rundschau*, 9 January 1970.
51. Willy Brandt. *People and Politics.*
52. *Der Spiegel*, 16 February 1970.
53. Hans Georg von Studnitz. *Typisch Brandt.*
54. Willy Brandt. *People and Politics.*
55. Ibid.
56. Lothar Reuel. *Die Welt*, 15 August 1970.
57. Willy Brandt. *People and Politics.*
58. Heli Ihlefeld. *Willy Brandt. Anekdotisch.*
59. The London *Times*, 18 May 1972.
60. Willy Brandt. *People and Politics.*
61. Willy Brandt, in conversation with the author, February 1972.
62. Willy Brandt. From his own notes, 26 August 1972. *People and Politics.*
63. Willy Brandt. *People and Politics.*
64. Ibid.
65. Klaus Schütz. Speech in the Berlin City Assembly, 7 September 1971.
66. John McCloy, in letter to the West German publisher, Axel Springer, July 1971.
67. Sebastian Haffner. *New Statesman*, 3 September 1971.
68. Michael Lake. *The Guardian*, 24 August 1971.
69. Douglas Brown. *Sunday Telegraph*, 29 August 1971.
70. Hans Georg von Studnitz, op. cit.
71. Quoted in *Typisch Brandt.*

CHAPTER NINE

End of a Dream

The immense amount of work required to launch his Ostpolitik meant that Brandt had only limited opportunities of implementing his promise to be "the Chancellor of domestic reform". During his Chancellorship, home affairs were indeed never neglected, but sometimes they seemed to be pushed into second place. This may have been an illusion; sound administration is always the reverse of spectacular, and twentieth century society in industrialized countries has developed a habit of never being satisfied and, like Oliver Twist – but with far less reason – always asking for more.

Even so, Brandt's sternest critics would have to admit that his Government got through a lot of work. One of his dearest wishes, as he often explained, was to bring true social justice to Germany – not in the form of spectacular hand-outs, but gradually and by persistent effort.[1] His government's first budget gave practical expression to these wishes: retirement pensions were raised by 5 per cent, pensions for war-wounded and war-widows by 16 and 25 per cent respectively, and sickness benefits by 9·3 per cent. Pensioners ceased to pay a 2 per cent health insurance contribution; tax-free allowances for children were raised across the board; and one million families could now claim an allowance for the second child, against 300,000 previously. A fund, of 100 million marks, was set up for handicapped children.

A law was passed for the creation of property for workers. This led to a big majority of workers keeping up to 95 per cent of their pay, and to graded tax remission for married workers applying up to a wage of 48,000 marks (6,400 pounds at the time). There were increased allowances for training and re-training, and special allowances for refugees from the DDR. Expenditure on education and scientific research was raised, progressively, by a total of nearly 300 per cent between 1970 and 1974. The school-leaving age was raised to sixteen, giving ten years compulsory schooling, 30,000 more places were created in the schools, and an extra 1,000 million marks allocated for new school buildings. The 1970 programme provided for 5,000 new scholarships for graduates, and double that number again were being awarded three years later.

The Brandt Government set out to create 44,000 new jobs, with a special emphasis on West Berlin and backward areas close to the sealed interzonal frontier. The budget for social housing was at once increased by 36 per cent, that for communications by 14 per cent. The Federal Republic's roads and railways were becoming choked, one of the results of prosperity. Incentives were offered to bring goods traffic back onto the railways, and at the same time a long-term programme was launched to create 28,000 kilometres of new and converted motorways (it was fulfilled to the letter). There were increased grants for sport (the Government was painfully aware of the huge strides in the field of sport made in the DDR and of resulting increased East German prestige). A "Federal reserve" of ten million tons of crude oil was approved – although this plan was not implemented in time to overcome all the effects of the 1973 Arab oil embargo – and already existing stockpiles of all vitally needed supplies in West Berlin were built up, just in case there should be another blockade. Other measures included a town-planning act, allocations for the protection of the environment, and the reduction of the voting age to eighteen – thus giving the vote to an additional two and a half million young people. In January 1972, a Factory Management Law (Betriebsverfassungsgesetz) established co-determination on the shop floor. Brandt would have gone out for full copartnership rights in industries other than coal and steel, but for once his Free Democratic allies were able to act as the "brake" on socialist policies which they were meant to be.

What is indicative about Brandt's social policies is that they were outlined, and began to be implemented, at the very beginning of what should have been a four year term in office.

Most governments keep tax and other concessions in reserve for election year. The Brandt Government, moreover, was not operating during an easy period of economic expansion. Europe was moving into an era of ever more damaging inflation, and in July 1971 the Bundestag had to be recalled in order to approve anti-inflationary measures; wages had risen in a year by 14 per cent, the cost of living by over 4 per cent, and the Government had to raise income and corporation taxes by 10 per cent. In 1971 the Government had to let the mark "float", and the result was a second upwards revaluation, this time by no less than 13·5 per cent against the dollar. The weakness of the dollar was now endemic – mainly the result of the huge costs of the Vietnam War and poor American husbandry – and in 1973 the Federal Bank had to buy up more than 6,000 million marks worth of dollars to prevent it going below the "floor level" of 3·15 marks. Thanks to the spendthrift American Policy of printing more and more money to cover the costs of war, the richest country in the world was undermining its own financial position. In June 1973, the Federal Government in Bonn had to revalue the mark yet again, this time by 5·5 per cent.

Yet the West German economy forged steadily ahead. Brandt was well satisfied:

> The Federal Republic compared favourably not only with the past but with current conditions in other countries. The gross national product had risen by 3 per cent in 1971 and 3·4 per cent in 1972, while 1973 showed a growth of no less than 5·3 per cent. Industrial peace was being preserved by good relations with the unions and an improved social security network. Prices had risen appreciably, but far less than in almost all comparable countries. The Mark was consolidating its status as one of the hardest currencies in the world ... the international monetary crisis in spring 1973 had been checked.[3]

Brandt never ceased to urge moderation in wage demands, although his primary aim was "greater justice, to ensure that more true freedom exists in our society".[4] Even in this phase of controlled economic expansion, he called repeatedly for all wage demands to be kept down to single figures. This insistence on moderation was needed even more after the oil crisis at the end of 1973, bringing an increase of unemployment to over 400,000 and – something almost unthinkable for a prosperity-conscious West German public – a temporary ban on Sunday motoring.

Economic problems lost Brandt one of his key Ministers. Karl Schiller, Minister of Economics, was opinionated and sometimes supercilious, but undoubtedly able. In 1972 he unilaterally proposed tax increases without consulting his Cabinet colleagues – critics called him "utterly tactless" and wrote of his "bullying tactics".[5] In June he opposed foreign exchange controls, at a time when the floating of sterling was driving a great deal of "hot" money into Germany – Schiller insisted that he had French backing for a joint float of European currencies, but it transpired that the French Government had said only that it would cooperate in this, if currency controls were first tried out in Germany and proved ineffective.[6] Schiller resigned, in a letter which ran to four thousand words – something of a record in inter-departmental correspondence. Brandt transferred Helmut Schmidt from the Ministry of Defence to take Schiller's place, a move of some significance. Earlier there had been pressure on Brandt to name Schiller as "crown prince" in the SPD party hierarchy. Brandt had refused precisely because he believed that Schmidt would be the better choice. Experience in the economic field would help now to groom Schmidt for future leadership. As for Schiller, Brandt's view was that he had too much of an artist's temperament; "for him it was Beethoven's Ninth Symphony, and then for him alone".[7]

Brandt faced other difficult domestic problems. The first was the apparent decline of his coalition running-mates of the FDP. In 1970 they failed to get the needed 5 per cent of the votes in the elections in the Saar and Lower Saxony, and ceased to be represented in these *Land* Parliaments. Three right-wing members of the party in the Bundestag switched their allegiance to the CDU, and Brandt's slender majority of twelve was halved. The FDP decline appeared to continue in 1971. The reason for it was clear: its right-wingers, especially in prosperous centres of industry, suspected Brandt and the SPD of moving too far and fast along the road of social reform. Franz Josef Strauss was expressing their thoughts when he said: "Brandt is straying always further to the left. And when he pauses, that's the new middle-position for him."[8] Brandt himself treated the FDP with respect, and not at all as an obviously junior partner. But he must sometimes have been somewhat taxed by the FDP's efforts to assert its supposed role as a "brake"; when an FDP Minister in *Land* North Rhine-Westphalia pompously stated that his party was the SDP's "pill", the Chancellor countered caustically with "a coalition is not a bedroom affair".[9]

The FDP did, however, manage to maintain profile. When in coalition with Adenauer's CDU this had been difficult; the man-in-the-street saw the smaller party only as a pale reflection of the larger. In reality, the FDP very rarely acted as a brake on Brandt's policies, but the possibility of doing so was always there. Brandt skilfully used the FDP for his own ends; its vital votes gave a sound reason for resisting demands from his own SPD left-wingers. Walter Scheel, at all events, had made up his mind that the FDP could only survive in partnership with the SPD, which eased his task of steadily organizing a genuinely liberal, mainly middle class and propertied party. The FDP no longer had anything to fear from the neo-Nazi NPD, which had earlier taken away some of its right-wing voters and which now itself went into a decline with all the marks of permanency.

More serious than the troubles of the FDP was the continuing growth of dissatisfaction among sections of German youth. Brandt was probably the most sympathetic Chancellor that young Germans could ever expect to have. He had never forgotten that he had himself been very much of a rebel when he was young. His eldest son, Peter, was going through a phase of adolescent assertiveness and revolt against all authority, and the Chancellor never failed to show him sympathy and understanding. Brandt recalled that "In 1930 and 1931, as a sixteen and seventeen year-old, I chanted: 'The Republic, that's pretty tame; let socialism be our aim'. Yet the Weimar Republic was quite something compared with what preceded it and, above all, what came after it."[10] He made a point of never talking about *the* students, or even *the* left-wing students; he believed that those in authority "must speak out in favour of reason" and explain that social problems "cannot be dispelled with a wave of the wand".[11]

But reason was sometimes ignored. For much of the term of his Chancellorship Brandt was engaged in a running battle – admittedly waged generally with kid gloves – with the "Jung-Sozialisten" or "Jusos", the youth movement of the SPD. Thanks to the late age at which many Germans leave university, there is nothing unusual about 30 or 35 year-olds regarding themselves as "youth". The 250,000 Jusos included some formidable debaters and there was a perpetual danger of many of the young drifting into well-meant but barren "extra-Parliamentary opposition". It says much for Brandt's tact and patience that this did not happen.

Far more alarming than the outspoken complaints of the Jusos was the readiness of a very much smaller section of German youth to resort to violence. When taking office, Brandt spoke of "the need for an immediate programme to modernize and intensify crime protection".[12] Three years later, he felt obliged to pass a law which expanded the powers of the Federal Investigation Bureau, tightening up regulations for prosecution for carrying arms, possessing stocks of ammunition, peddling drugs and uttering threats against politicians, and imposing surveillance of foreigners and investigation of all activities which might be hostile to the Constitution. His Government was bitterly criticized for allowing mails to be opened and telephone lines tapped (in Britain, it transpired in March 1978, the tapping of telephone lines is in fact legal).[13] Legislation passed during Brandt's term of office also tightened up procedures for screening candidates for jobs in government service. The way in which this legislation was implemented would lead to major political controversy in 1978–9.

In private conversation, Brandt said that the most dangerous threat of all to civilized society was "the availability of fearsome weapons of destruction in the hands of irresponsible people".[14] He was, he agreed, thinking of two particular groups of such irresponsible people: so-called "revolutionary youth" within the Federal Republic, and international terrorists who moved freely and lethally across state frontiers. The two sets of enemies which proved particularly menacing were the home-grown "Baader-Meinhof Gang" of young West Germans, and the terrorists of the Palestine Liberation Organization.

The revolt of German revolutionary youth had already taken shape during the Kiesinger administration. According to one authority, the universities provided the most obvious focus, because the Marxists saw them as "a springboard for their campaign to effect radical changes in the present structure of society".[15] Radical militants operated, as in other countries, by creating chaos – one outside observer in Berlin put the trouble down to "an alliance between a mindless, pink administration which makes a virtue of appeasement, and a violent radical group of students who use Nazi tactics".[16] The practical result was that students were learning too little, or next to nothing.[17] Frustration bred increased frustration; violence became an end in itself. On television, Brandt said that it could not be tolerated – what was needed was factual information, cool evaluation, appropriate action to counter hatred and injustice, but not "sterile excitement".[18] As he put it: "Blind hitting-out is not the politics of our Constitution." A future Federal Chancellor, Helmut Schmidt, called the campaign of violence, "the most serious challenge in the history of our democracy".[19]

No warnings could avert the catalysation of violence. The Baader-Meinhof Gang became active only after the Brandt Government took office, and there was no connection between these two events. Its activities up to mid-1972, when five of its leaders were arrested and a dozen others "went underground", were fearsome indeed: the gang murdered librarians, night-watchmen, police, American soldiers. They murdered indiscriminately, to strike terror into the hearts of ordinary citizens – one of their leaders, Georg von Rauch, explained that "We must, I must, quite simply liquidate human feeling".[20] Brandt had no doubt about the seriousness of their menace; in his words, "The underground arsenals of the Baader-Meinhof group contained the most formidable private collection of ordnance in post-war Germany".[21] The Chancellor ordered a nation-wide manhunt in which 150,000 police took part. Naturally, there was an outcry on the extreme left against alleged police brutality; naturally, too, well-meaning intellectuals claimed that all that was needed was social reform: radicalism could be killed by kindness. Kindness and reason meant nothing to the young gangsters. The use of force was the only language which they understood. The police action of the summer of 1972 sent them underground for the next three years.

The Palestine Liberation Organization posed a very different kind of threat. In February 1970, its members attacked an Israeli aircraft at Munich, killing one passenger and wounding eleven. On 6 September 1972, the PLO perpetrated a far more gross and horrifying crime, at the Olympic Games in Munich. Eleven Israeli athletes were murdered, nine of them after having been held prisoner, trussed up like chickens for the slaughter. Vast sums of money had been spent on the Munich Olympics; they were to have been a special feather in the German cap. For Brandt, this disgusting mass-murder was particularly poignant. He had always stood out for maximum restitution to the Jews who had survived Hitler's ghastly persecutions and for maxi-mum efforts to secure a reconciliation between the State of Israel, which had become the home of most of them, and his own German people. He had visited Israel in 1960 and had been one of the first leading Germans to express his contrition and desire to make amends – he expressed his unfeigned admiration too, and said of the Israelis: "They are in the same camp as we are."

The "Munich massacre" had an unhappy sequel. Brandt's Government was bitterly criticized for what seemed bungled efforts to set the Israeli athletes free from their captors. Five of the Palestinian terrorists were killed by the German police, three were captured and held in gaol. They would have been brought to justice, but in October a German Lufthansa plane returning to Frankfurt from Beirut was hijacked. It and its passengers were held hostage until the three imprisoned Palestinians were released. Brandt had flown to Munich, but admitted that, once there, there was nothing that he could do.[22] He was saddened, but philosophical: "Instead of letting disappointment get us down, we strove to learn from this grievous experience. It pointed to the need for police reorganization, for the establishment of a special anti-terrorist unit, and for numerous measures designed to promote cooperation in the fight against terrorism and the taking of hostages ... One lesson of Munich was that pacifism must cease when confronted by terrorism".[23] The special anti-terrorist unit, at all events, would come in useful some years later, at Mogadishu.

The Munich massacre could hardly have come at a more inopportune moment, for Federal elections were only two months away. One of Brandt's Free Democratic colleagues, Hans-Dietrich Genscher, had coined the election slogan, "Out of the stadium, and into the election!"; it was thought that this would now boomerang.[24] Fortuitous circumstances, certainly, seemed to be militating against Brandt's election chances. Karl Schiller had left the Government, and had taken some grumblers with him. The Jusos were complaining about the way in which the Baader-Meinhof gangsters had been harried and hunted down, although they would probably vote for the SPD when the day came. Muck-raking always takes place when an election is in the offing, and Brandt had been under fire for having his private swimming-pool rebuilt, allegedly at a cost to the tax-payer of the equivalent of 7,000 pounds.

Above all, the Government – thanks to further defections – had lost its majority in the Bundestag. This produced a ludicrous situation from mid-April onwards. Ratification of the treaties with Poland and the Soviet Union was blocked, and votes of no-confidence in the Bundestag narrowly failed. When two Free Democrats left their party and joined the CDU, complete Parliamentary deadlock resulted, and when the budget was debated there was a 247 to 247 votes stalemate. Feeling in the country was strongly in favour of ratification of the treaties, and there were massive demonstrations in big cities, particularly Essen, where schools packed up altogether on 25 April and hundreds of thousands of Ruhr workers marched through the streets. "In that moment," the Editor of the *Neue Ruhr Zeitung* said, "I realized that Brandt meant more to the ordinary people of Germany than Adenauer ever had done."[25] In the Bundestag Brandt defended his policies in a fine, fighting speech, without one word of rhetoric but redolent of his belief that he was safeguarding the national interest. The London *Times* wrote: "Herr Brandt is not the world's leading political orator, but he lived up to his reputation that he is at his best with his back to the wall, by making a resounding defence of his Ostpolitik and his Government's economic and social record. It was a memorable performance by the Chancellor, who revealed not the slightest sign of anxiety over his political fate."[26]

The debate on the ratification of the treaties took place on 10 and 17 May. The CDU could still have blocked ratification, by opposing the agenda. But they made an elementary procedural blunder, in introducing a motion to alter the agenda and postpone ratification. The result was a tie, and their procedural vote was accordingly deemed to have lost. Had they voted against the agenda, there would doubtless have been another tie, the agenda would not have been carried and ratification would have had to have been postponed until after the elections. A group of Christian Democrats now decided that they could not carry out a last-ditch resistance against the treaties, particularly in view of the amount of support for them in the country at large. Both treaties were ratified. Aware, at last, of the popular dislike of their procrastinations, the CDU cooperated in giving Brandt the no-confidence vote which was still needed, before the Federal President could order the elections to take place. This was on 22 September, and the elections were ordered for 19 November.

The CDU's manoeuvres damaged their election prospects, rather than enhancing them. When Brandt made his first big election address, in Dortmund on 12 October, he pulled no punches. The CDU, he said, had put party before country, had held up international treaties which were in the national interest, and had sought to make political capital out of the tragedy of the Munich massacre. He called the CDU a "party of Sancho Panzas", but with a "secret Chancellor", Franz Josef Strauss, the "last Prussian from Bavaria". He dealt briefly with Karl Schiller, who had been working – albeit with little enthusiasm – in the

CDU interest, as having resigned in "a victory of vanity over commonsense". Brandt promised a resolute and progressive partnership of Social Democrats and liberals which would represent the expanding "political centre" with imagination and compassion.

The SPD set out to exploit Brandt's personality; election posters showed him sun-tanned, healthy and handsome, smiling broadly or deeply reflective – the Chancellor had the natural advantage of being highly photogenic. "If this were a presidential election," one paper wrote, "there is no doubt that Chancellor Brandt would win hands down. He has come to bestride Germany – East and West – like a colossus. He has completely taken over the mantle from Konrad Adenauer of statesman and father figure."[27] Favourite slogans were "Willy must stay!" and "Vote for Willy! Who else is there?", and wherever he went he attracted huge crowds. There could be little doubt, too, that the Soviet Bloc would do what it could to help him. Shortly before the elections, the East German Government allowed the first family reunions and announced that more former political prisoners would be free to leave, too, by the end of the year – 7,000 had already been amnestied and 300 of them allowed to cross into the Federal Republic. The Soviet Union undertook to give exit permits to 1,800 "ethnic" Germans who wanted to leave the country, and Poland confirmed its readiness to let its Germans go home at last. Here were some of the first fruits of Brandt's Ostpolitik, and they were exactly those that made the most popular appeal.

Thus, when violently heckled on 18 November in Paderborn, an old Nazi stronghold, Brandt countered by bringing a young woman from the East German town of Erfurt, who had just arrived in the Federal Republic, onto the platform. "What matters to me," Brandt told his dour Westphalian audience, "is to improve the fate of human beings in a divided Germany."[28] On the eve of the elections he announced that a "hot line" would in future link his Chancellery office with that of the East German Prime Minister in East Berlin. Of some help, too, to Brandt was the announcement on 17 November that talks between NATO and the Warsaw Pact would take place on 31 January 1973 on mutual balanced force reductions – an esoteric subject, maybe, but another indicator that détente was working. Even so, public opinion polls seemed to suggest that a neck and neck race was taking place, and that the CDU would in any case retain its place as the strongest single party. A heavy question-mark hung over the FDP; it needed only a small further loss of votes for it to disappear from the Bundestag. In that event, Brandt would be left without a coalition partner and his courageous election campaign would have been in vain.

A survey carried out by *Der Spiegel* a week before polling day showed that voters gave Brandt 75 points for trustworthiness, against 50 to Rainer Barzel, the CDU candidate for the Chancellorship, and 42 to Strauss, Bavaria's favourite son. Brandt scored a commendably low 13 for aggressiveness, with Barzel on 49 and Strauss a staggering 76. The survey made plain that the man-in-the-street valued Brandt's sound qualities as much as his charisma. One of Brandt's admirers saw in him "everybody's elder brother";[29] he radiated responsibility and protectiveness, as well as modesty and loyalty.

The election result was a complete vindication for his policies. The SPD vote was up from 42·7 to 45·8 per cent, and it emerged, for the first time in the history of the Federal Republic and, indeed, the first time in over forty years, as the strongest Parliamentary party. The CDU vote was down from 46·1 to 44·9 per cent, and its seats from 240 to 225. The FDP vote rose from 5·8 to 8·4 per cent, and its seats from 30 to 41. With the SPD returning 230 members to the Bundestag, Brandt's coalition majority, which had been whittled away from 12 to nothing at all, rose to 46. It was a famous victory, and Brandt was re-elected Chancellor a few days later by 269 votes to 223.

Commentators unhesitatingly predicted a third term in office, in four years' time. Everything, indeed, seemed to be going his way. The signing of the Basic Treaty between the two German states was only a few weeks away, and however questionable its long-term strategy, there was no question that more than two million West Berliners would sleep more soundly in their beds. Diplomatic relations were opened with Communist China, and Brandt was establishing increasingly close contact with both the French and British Governments. He got on particularly well with Britain's Conservative Prime Minister, Edward Heath; he found him "uncomplicated" and did not feel his "reputed lack of personal warmth".[30] Paradoxically, he was not at home with the British Labour leaders and had been startled by George Brown's (later Lord George Brown) remark in 1967, on the subject of the European Common Market: "Willy, you must get us in, so we can take the lead".[31] But his fellow-feeling for Heath undoubtedly helped Brandt to ease Britain into the EEC – even France had come to regard her entry as inevitable, in face of a degree of popular enthusiasm in Britain which would later prove deceptively misleading.

1973, as it happened, turned into an increasingly frustrating year for Brandt and his government. True, diplomatic relations were established with Czechoslovakia, Hungary and Bulgaria, and Poland showed good faith in allowing ethnic Germans to leave the country. But wherever one looked otherwise, there were difficulties. The Soviet leader, Leonid Brezhnev, was in Bonn in May – it was necessary to supply a guard of 5,000 police and 1,500 Federal Frontier Guards. He proposed long-term economic cooperation, with exchanges of Soviet raw materials and West German technology, but nothing came of an over-ambitious project. There was a cooling of relations with France; the French Minister of Agriculture, Jacques Chirac, complained that Bonn was "turning away from Europe", and President Georges Pompidou, with whom Brandt got on surprisingly well, was already a sick man. The British were making a slow start in Europe, and the Copenhagen Conference of the EEC showed that the Nine were going to find it more difficult to reach decisions than the Six had done in the past.

The outbreak of the fourth Arab–Israeli war in October brought one major diplomatic problem. With Israel fighting for its very existence, after being attacked and taken unawares, only the United States showed any readiness to ship Israel the arms which were essential for that country's survival. The Federal Republic refused to allow arms to travel to Israel from United States bases in Germany – Brandt explained that "we expressly protested against the use of our territory without notification, let alone consultation, as if NATO did not exist."[32] In particular, the Brandt Government would not allow Israeli ships to carry arms from German ports. The British Government adopted the same attitude, even to the point of refusing overflying and refuelling facilities to US planes engaged in the emergency arms-lift to Israel. The American administration was angered; it was not only left on its own helping Israel, but was openly cold-shouldered.

All the European powers were seriously alarmed over the possibility of a major Arab oil embargo being applied against them. Their weak-kneed diplomatic postures did not, in the event, save them, first from sporadic boycott and then from sensational increases in the price of Arab oil. Brandt sought to defend his own attitude, but admitted that "the Europeans cut a far from impressive figure during the war that heralded the oil crisis. Various governments allowed themselves to be played off against each other by countries determined to use oil as a weapon. They cannot, however, be blamed for taking their immediate worries as seriously as the fate of their citizens demanded."[33] They could, however, be blamed for a palpable display of irresolution. Israel's Prime Minister, Mrs Golda Meir, was particularly bitter about the total lack of response at the meeting with other socialist leaders in London on 11 November 1973. She subsequently claimed that after she had addressed the meeting, no-one was prepared to say anything, and that a man sitting behind her said: "Of course they can't talk; their throats are choked with oil".[34]

At the end of 1973, too, Brandt found himself less than popular with the three EEC countries which had requested the setting up of a considerable fund for development aid – the United Kingdom, Ireland and Italy. Brandt has somewhat ingenuously admitted since that he was placed in an embarrassing position by his economic and financial advisers, who wanted the fund kept down to "reasonable" proportions. He considered that he extricated himself successfully by proposing a figure "so low that those present could not have taken me seriously",[35] but he was forced to admit that although "the road to Europe was not blocked, progress remained slow and arduous". It did, indeed, and the obstacles on that road which began to multiply were those created by purely selfish national self-interest. This, indeed, is in danger of becoming the leitmotive of the EEC.

On September 26 1973, Brandt made an important speech at the United Nations General Assembly.[36] He was, in fact, introducing the two German states to the Assembly, and he repeated his belief that "my people inhabit two states, but have not ceased to regard themselves as a nation". The future for the German people lay in peaceful coexistence of the two states, neighbourliness and cooperation, although "I cannot promise that this will always be easy". Brandt appealed for such a spirit of coexistence to be applied on a world-wide basis, entailing the combating of racism and unbridled nationalism, the defence of human rights and, eventually, the triumph of reason. Coexistence and détente, he made clear, was not a matter of localized tactics in Germany, but a principle which could bring happiness and peace to the world.

It was in this spirit that the Federal Republic entered the European Conference at Helsinki in the autumn of 1973. The principal aim of the Conference was to promote East–West security and cooperation. Perhaps its most important component was the so-called "Basket Three", dealing with human rights and cultural contacts. Brandt may have set his hopes higher than was justified. The end of the Stalin regime had not, as had been vaguely hoped at the time, brought the dawn of a new era of freedom in the Soviet Union. The new Soviet leaders, from Khruschev and Bulganin down to Kosygin and Brezhnev, did not feel themselves strong enough to take risks in this direction. Government by consensus of the Central Committee of the Communist Party, although less ostentatiously brutal than that of Stalin, has remained based on the repression of human freedoms. Believing as he did in "progressive" détente, involving an ever-freer exchange of people and thought between the Western and Communist worlds, Brandt must have been sorely disappointed by the demise of a "Spirit of Helsinki" which was never more than imaginary. He subsequently admitted that "the East European leaders did not make things easy for themselves" by approving Basket Three at Helsinki: "Having checked to see what their systems could tolerate, they must have been surprised that the West so largely ignored their own considerations and so often yielded to the illusion that all agreements would be promptly and unreservedly implemented."[37] The short answer to this soliloquy must be that it is only natural to expect agreements to be implemented; otherwise they have no practical value whatever.

Frustrating though some of the events of 1973 were, Brandt's Government remained firmly based, successful and popular. There was a setback for his party in the local elections in Hamburg in March 1974, but public opinion polls showed some diminution in the strength of the two coalition parties. Brandt was downcast; he wrote that:

> No serious investigation of causes (for some loss of support) could overlook my own mistakes and weaknesses. In many people's minds, expectations of success had become transmuted into an obsession with success which no government, far less a coalition, could hope to satisfy in full. Exaggerated demands and verbal excesses contributed to this weakness, but the decisive factor was the economic pressure to which the Federal Republic had been increasingly exposed since the end of 1973.[38]

The Germans were suffering from the same symptoms of

uncertainty as other Europeans; the spectre of eternal inflation haunted them. In Germany, inflation was kept down to manageable proportions, but its psychological implications were far greater for a people who had suffered so terribly from it in the past.

Still, Brandt's personal popularity and prestige were undiminished. He had been awarded the Nobel Peace Prize two years earlier and the congratulations showered on him by the outside world were reminders of the extraordinary esteem in which he was held there – in Britain, for instance, he was far and away the best-liked German in human memory. He had received the freedom of the city of Berlin in 1970; to this was added the freedom of his native Luebeck in 1972, where he found himself in somewhat strange company – the past freemen of Luebeck had included Bismarck and three other minor pillars of the old Conservative order, and Hitler and three of his most villainous Nazi followers. These tributes only underlined his continuing success, and it was hard to imagine the CDU mounting a serious challenge to the coalition for years to come. In the summer of 1973 their candidate for the Chancellorship and chairman of the Parliamentary Party, Rainer Barzel, resigned. The sting went out of CDU attacks in the Bundestag, and when the worthy but uninspiring Helmut Kohl became CDU chairman, commentators began predicting an unending period of SPD–FDP rule.

In April 1974, Brandt was on a visit to Cairo. Returning to Bonn he learnt on the morning of 24 April that one of his closest advisers in the Federal Chancellery, Günter Guillaume, had been arrested as a spy in the service of the DDR. Guillaume, a former officer in the East German Army, had come to Western Germany as an ostensible refugee in 1956. After working as a photographic salesman, he joined the SPD in 1957, and made steady progress as a party, and then a government, official before being appointed to his post in the Chancellery in 1970. An outwardly jovial, earthy character,[39] he seemed to have none of the characteristics of a conventional spy. He handled secret and confidential documents, and enjoyed Brandt's fullest confidence. He was situated at the key, pivotal point for obtaining information on all policy matters of crucial importance.

Guillaume had been sending information to East Berlin by courier, radio and via dead-letter boxes. Brandt would later admit that Guillaume even collected information assiduously from him while holidaying with him in the summer of 1973. It was after this summer holiday that he came under the suspicion and surveillance of the West German counter-intelligence services. They reported their views and information to the Chancellor – among other things, Guillaume had failed to state that he had been an East German Army officer when applying for West German citizenship and enrolling in government service. But the Office for the Protection of the Federal Constitution recommended that Guillaume should be kept on in the Chancellery, even after his guilt had been proven beyond doubt. Their argument was that Guillaume would incriminate his masters.

Brandt himself has consistently refused to say more than the bare minimum about the "Guillaume affair". He had not expected the man's arrest, and admitted that it was "a severe blow".[40] But, he went on: "It did not immediately occur to me that considerations of personal responsibility would force me to resign. I continued with my work. Next day I participated in the Bundestag debate ... There followed speeches in Saarbruecken and Hamburg, a visit to Heligoland and election meetings in Ostfriesland. I conferred with the Minister of Finance on the problems presented by the new budget, supervised other aspects of cabinet work and attended a private meeting with trade union leaders." And so, "my decision to resign matured without undue haste". Perhaps over-ready to blame himself, Brandt admitted that: "I took advice which, looking back, I should not have taken. I was right to shoulder the political responsibility ... I could not have soldiered on with an easy mind."

He resigned on 6 May 1974, and the next day newspaper posters all over London carried the slogan "Brandt shakes Europe". The German public was stunned. Brandt himself made arrangements for government to continue with his usual matter-of-fact commonsense. Walter Scheel carried on with a caretaker administration until 15 May and on the next day the Minister of Finance, Helmut Schmidt, was elected Chancellor in the Bundestag – "In a surgical sense, a quick, clean operation had been performed, and a protracted, nagging crisis avoided."[41]

Brandt denied the lurid stories which were circulated about his private life – one theory was that Guillaume had obtained information about it and had threatened to blackmail the Chancellor. He insisted that he had resigned to maintain his personal integrity, and in accordance with the unwritten rules of democracy. His only complaint against the counter-intelligence services was that they could have informed him of their suspicions and information about Guillaume much earlier. The independent commission of inquiry which looked into the affair agreed on this point, and put the main blame on those services.

Why, then, did Brandt need to resign at all? There had been reports that he was weary and disappointed, others that his health was causing problems. Another "explanation" which was widely believed was that he was disillusioned by the lack of results from his Ostpolitik, by the divisions within the Western Alliance and the EEC, a further falling-off of support for the SPD in elections in Schleswig-Holstein, the Saar and the Rhine-Palatinate, and by increasing economic problems. But Brandt was a thoroughly experienced politician; he recognized that there would always be periodic political setbacks as well as successes. He had never expected his Ostpolitik to bring instant results, and his government had coped better with the energy crisis than those of other major European countries. Paradoxically, the biggest recent source of worry to him had been the Labour victory in the British elections in March. The Labour Party had committed itself to renegotiating Britain's terms of entry into the Common Market, and to holding a national referendum which might easily have resulted in the British people opting for economic isolation.

But it is probable that psychological factors played the key role in Brandt's decision to resign. One writer noted that, "He has built an elastic wall round himself, which protects him, and he needs protection: he is very sensitive and easily hurt."[42] Another, with the same womanly prescience, found herself often on the verge of warning him to take care of himself.[43] He had always wanted and tried to believe in human decency and – this was perhaps a failing for a politician – to give his total trust to people close to him. The man who painted his portrait, Georg Meistermann, felt that this instinctive "fairness" was sometimes shamefully exploited and equally shamefully misinterpreted.[44] Brandt set very high standards of loyalty and team-work; those who served him sometimes failed to match up to his expectations.

This undoubtedly happened at the very moment when he most needed solid support. Government officials, and even Ministers, hastened to disassociate themselves from the "Guillaume Affair". There was a notable lack of readiness to come forward to defend Brandt. He had always, at heart, been a loner and now he was, indeed, left very much alone. In a biography of him I wrote:

A self-imposed loneliness can make for extreme vulnerability under such bizarre circumstances. Brandt certainly,
was very vulnerable. All his life he had bottled up feelings,
doubts, emotions, above all his inmost thoughts, whenever
his own person and interest were concerned. It is
understandable that a man who had, throughout life, to
fight every inch of his way for what he wanted and what he
believed in, would be bitterly and totally disappointed when
forsaken, so brazenly and at so critical a moment. The view
that he was only waiting for an excuse to quit is ...
untenable. His personal crisis of confidence was forced upon
him.[45]

There was no need, in May 1974, to write a last line about
Brandt, the statesman. He remained Chairman of the SPD and
five years later was still carrying out his duties with firmness and
a circumspect discretion. He helped his party win another
Federal election in 1976. He became a thoroughly successful
President of the Socialist International, where he employed his
talents in promoting the North–South dialogue of the rich and
needy nations, as well as East–West détente. In November 1978,
he was re-elected to this post in Vancouver in such a boisterous
vote by acclamation that the translation headphones, "unable to
adjust to the decibels, let out a banshee wail in response".[46] He
continued to speak with the responsibility and imagination of a
true statesman. Thus we find him proclaiming the urgent need
for arms limitation, for the rocketing costs of ever more
sophisticated and ever more deadly weapons is today threatening
even highly developed economies with collapse.[47] Then, again,
Brandt took a pragmatic view of events in countries like Spain
and Portugal; they had, he pointed out to the London *Times*, to
find their own roads to constitutional government. In Spain, for
instance, the Army had to keep "a say and a responsible role in
society. It is not what we are accustomed to – we expect our
soldiers to keep out of politics – but to these countries it may be
important".[48] As chairman of the independent Brandt
Commission on international development issues, he has been
tireless. He promised, in addition, to run as a candidate for the
European Parliament. With typical manliness, he refused to
worry about how things could have turned out, had he remained
Chancellor – "I'm like a peasant doing his work. He doesn't look
over his shoulder. He looks ahead."
How should one assess Brandt's Chancellorship? His fall, as

dramatic and as tragic in its way as the assassination of President John Kennedy, ended a golden dream. But it should in no way blind anyone to his solid, and sometimes spectacular achievements.

Nothing is so salutary as a change of government. Probably only Brandt was capable of bringing the SPD to power. From 1959 onwards he was the most influential member of the party engaged in capturing the floating vote and in making the electorate understand that the SPD was no longer a party of revolution and the ostentatiously raised and clenched fist. One of his advisers had this to say:

> First and foremost he made people understand that a modern party was needed. In conferences he was the unifying factor. He had time for all shades of opinion and showed tolerance and understanding. He did not allow himself to be over-worried by the new left or younger members who wanted radical change – he regarded this as natural for younger people, a phase of their lives which they would grow out of. The most important thing about his wise, middle-of-the-road philosophy was that it gave the SPD the chance to expand – the party came to terms with the churches and business circles. They stand a good chance now of getting a bigger share of the women's vote, which has been solidly conservative since the war.[49]

Having obtained power, the SPD did well with it. Their social and economic record was good: one thinks of the doubling of the educational budget from 3 to 6 per cent, of the expansion of secondary education and the increase of university students by 100,000 to 650,000, and of rational steps to deal with the energy crisis. German social democracy has now helped to establish a pattern for Europe, which may have a positive effect in time on countries like France, Italy and perhaps Spain (but which, sadly, has so far been rejected by the British Labour Party). Brandt passed on a rich legacy of sound and sensible domestic administration to his successor, Helmut Schmidt.

In the second place, Brandt did something very special towards developing a new image of the Germans in the outside world. The enormities perpetrated by Nazi Germany left an abiding impression; never is an occasion missed of recalling them. To Germans, this may seem regrettable, for a new Germany has been created since 1945. But is is inevitable; the Nazi era has sometimes been depicted a "Twilight of the Gods", but it was, rather, the twilight of Satan and the fallen angels, lurid and spectacular. Brandt was, unmistakably, the representative of the new Germany, and accepted as such by the outside world. Part of the sadness of his fall was that it seemed, to many outside Germany, that he had been rejected by his own people. But this did not erase the many positive effects of the earlier election of a man who had opposed Nazism as Chancellor. Chief, perhaps, among them was his propagation of democracy in action. Brandt never read lectures on the subject, but he put his thoughts pithily and, like the Norwegians among whom he once lived so happily, as shortly as possible. One phrase of his was "The best citizen is the best patriot";[50] another, "The State, that's the lot of us".[51] In the view of the writer, Heinrich Böll, Brandt was "the first Chancellor who led us away from our tradition as a Herrenvolk, a so-called master-race ... using the spur and the whip".[52]

In a personal interview, Brandt gave some idea of what he wanted for his people.[53] He wanted them to recognize materialism as the worst enemy of all, to look at their country as an integral whole and not merely as a well-run economic entity, to expand their interest in things of the mind and to maintain the mind's independence, to develop human assets and extol human values. He wanted Germans to combat the cult of violence, and also the sense of insecurity which fathered it: "Society must make itself more effective, and must always be prepared to act." Ideals should be brought back into daily existence – "Our nation," Brandt had said some years earlier, "needs fewer phrases and more veracity."[54] He was the symbol of the search for a more rounded, complete, self-aware German identity – but he would never have said so in pompous or dogmatic terms.

His Chancellorship will be remembered most of all for his Ostpolitik. There has been a tendency to take too extreme a view of it, one way or the other, to acclaim it as a brilliant success or condemn it as a shameful surrender to Soviet Communist pressure. The first thing that has to be said about his Ostpolitik was that it was intended to be the rational coefficient of the Westpolitik instituted by Konrad Adenauer twenty years earlier. Adenauer was strictly rational in believing that the Federal Republic had to have friends, and become an integral part of the European community. Brandt sought to extend this rationalism, by recognizing the realities of the situation in Central Europe. One British newspaper explained this in simple terms:

It can be argued that Herr Brandt surrendered a principle and got little in return. The East Germans, and behind them the Russians, have made only a few slight concessions in the matter of human, administrative and trading contacts across the borders. But they are real concessions, whereas the reunification of Germany, short of some new world cataclysm, has become an impossible dream. Post-war international relations are difficult enough, but it is better that they should be based on present realities than on a vanished past or an imaginary future.[55]

Brandt believed that he was jettisoning dogmas which no longer had any practical application, and ending diplomatic and ideological trench-warfare in the heart of Europe. Immediate objectives were to safeguard West Berlin's communications, increase contact between the two halves of the city and between the two German states, and relax tension locally. Brandt achieved all this, in greater or lesser degree. He sought, in addition, a real thaw in East–West relations. Here he was only partly successful. At least, the Soviet Union could no longer slander the Federal Republic with the impunity and abandon of the past; as Brandt pointed out to one German historian, even the teaching in Soviet schools about present-day Germany changed as a result of the Soviet–West German Treaty.[56] Movement between the Federal Republic and East European satellite states was facilitated, and visas abolished. Human contacts were taking place without one chronicled case of unpleasantness.

All of this was to the good, but détente has drawbacks. A former British Ambassador to Moscow, Sir William Hayter, has explained that the Soviet Union operates in the diplomatic field unilaterally and "on all levels",[57] knows what it wants and sets out ruthlessly to get it – the Russians "always negotiate for victory. It never occurs to them that the proper object of negotiation is not to defeat your opposite number, but to arrive at an agreement with him which will be mutually beneficial". Soviet diplomacy suffered, according to Sir William, from certain disadvantages – "a clumsiness, amounting on occasion to an alienating brutality; an inability to inspire confidence in anyone; above all, an almost total, perhaps incorrigible, lack of understanding of the real character, motives and feelings of the foreign countries and peoples with whom it has to deal".[58] Russian persistence, the same writer pointed out, easily made up for these defects; the Russians persisted until they got what they wanted, and at the same time knew that the West would give up when its own demands or plans were rejected.

The first drawback about the détente secured through Brandt's Ostpolitik was that the Soviet Union did not for one moment recognize his claim that détente should be "progressive", with one positive, forward step leading to another. Brandt has since explained that détente allowed thousands of ethnic Germans to be brought back from Poland and the Soviet Union.[59] To the Soviet leaders this was a very minor "sacrifice"; they were after immensely bigger rewards. The first was an armistice in Central Europe which would enable them to hold on to all of their post-1945 territorial gains, and for these gains to be explicitly recognized by the West. The second was to undermine the awareness and resolve of NATO, first by creating a sense of false security and secondly by offering the bait of arms-limitation agreements which would save the Western Powers money but would leave them in a position of increasing military inferiority. The third, and most dangerous Soviet aim of all was to free their hands for action in other parts of the world. The armistice in Central Europe has enabled the Russians to move into countries like Ethiopia, Algeria, the South Yemen, Afghanistan, Angola, Mozambique, and Iran. The global strategic advantages for the Soviet Union have been gigantic, and they have in turn encouraged the most alarming development of all, the creation of a vast and ever-growing Red Navy. Britain once visualized her Navy's role as maintaining the freedom of the seas, and protecting trading interests and serving the cause of peace; the Soviet Union sees in its navy an instrument of power.

West Berlin's gain has been the loss of peoples all over the Asian and African continents. Yet should Brandt be blamed for this? He has never ceased to explain that détente can only be truly successful if the Western Alliance remains militarily strong, politically firm but flexible, and above all united. He saw détente as an organic process, requiring steady Western pressure and consistent Western purpose. These elements have been lacking, and have endangered the whole concept of Ostpolitik. Ironically, Brandt's enemies in the Western world accused him of betraying the Western Alliance, after encouraging him to go ahead with détente – intent only on ridding their minds of worries about West Berlin's communications and incidents on the Berlin Wall.

One of Brandt's most trenchant critics was Axel Springer, the newspaper tycoon. He claimed that Brandt, and the Western

Powers, wrote-off East Berlin ("If we are discussing Berlin, we should talk about the whole of Berlin"[60]). He considered that the Soviet–West German Treaty confirmed the division of Germany and made permanent frontiers out of demarcation-lines, and that the Treaty with Poland totally ignored the gulf between the Polish people and their Communist regime.[61] In his view, it was wrong to recognize the loss of the eastern territories; all that this did was to forfeit a useful card in negotiating a future all-German settlement.[62] Another critic wrote that Brandt "was flying in the face of all post-war experience. There was really no evidence that the nature and purpose of the Soviet Government had changed".[63] What Brandt had done, he added, was to grant *de facto* recognition of frontiers which included those through the middle of Germany and of Berlin, recognize the Oder–Neisse Line, and clothe the DDR in a "cloak of legality".

Brandt left the impression of an enigmatic personality. He was warm-hearted, compassionate, sentient as a person; his political assets were clarity of thought, commonsense, instinctive moderation and the same gift that Adenauer possessed of setting himself definite objectives and pursuing them with great patience and persistence. He chose often to reveal his thoughts, but never himself. One can only sympathize with an innate shyness which difficult circumstances had implanted in his character. When he stepped down from the Chancellorship, he had worked for forty years to make a happier future possible for his people and for Europe, and he proved himself the right man to lead the Federal Republic towards it. Among many memorable sayings, one perhaps stands out: "We are condemned to peace, for life. There are worse things in life than that."[64] Certainly, he sought to make his own contribution to peace, with all the power of his intellect and imagination, and with that instinctive underlying human compassion which has made him the most attractive political personality of his generation, perhaps of the twentieth century.

1. Willy Brandt, in conversation with the author, December 1971.
2. Federal German Press Office. *Aufbruch in die 70er Jahre.*
3. Willy Brandt. *People and Politics.* London, 1978.
4. Ibid.
5. The London *Times*, 5 June 1972.
6. *The Economist*, 22 July 1972.
7. Quoted in *Typisch Brandt*. Edited by Hermann Otto Bolesch. Munich, 1973.

8. Franz Josef Strauss. Ibid.
9. Quoted in *Typisch Brandt*.
10. Willy Brandt. At SPD Congress in Bad Godesberg, January 1969.
11. Willy Brandt. *People and Politics*.
12. Sebastian Cobler. *Law, Order and Politics in West Germany*, London, 1978.
13. Ibid.
14. Willy Brandt, in personal conversation with the author, March 1972.
15. *Washington Post*, 2 April 1972.
16. Professor Hugh Trevor-Roper, in letter to the author, March 1972.
17. Professor Helmut Jaesrich, in conversation with the author, February 1972.
18. Willy Brandt, on nation-wide television, 4 February 1972.
19. Melvin Lasky. *New York Times*, 1 May 1975.
20. Ibid.
21. Ibid.
22. Willy Brandt. *People and Politics*.
23. Ibid.
24. Norman Crossland. *The Guardian*, 8 September 1972.
25. Jens Feddersen, in conversation with the author, 25 April 1972.
26. The London *Times*, 25 April 1972.
27. Malcolm Rutherford. *Financial Times*, 17 November 1972.
28. Boris Kidel. *The Observer*, 19 November 1972.
29. Dorothée Sölle. *Gedanken ueber einen Politiker*. Edited by Dagobert Lindlau. Munich, 1972.
30. Willy Brandt. *People and Politics*.
31. Ibid.
32. Ibid.
33. Ibid.
34. Mrs Golda Meir. *My Life*. London, 1975.
35. Willy Brandt. *People and Politics*.
36. Ibid.
37. Ibid.
38. Ibid.
39. Terence Prittie. *Willy Brandt*. London, 1974.
40. Willy Brandt. *People and Politics*.
41. Terence Prittie, op. cit.
42. Luise Rinser. *Gedanken ueber einen Politiker*.
43. Dorothée Sölle, op. cit.
44. Georg Meistermann. *Gedanken ueber einen Politiker*.
45. Terence Prittie, op. cit.
46. Hans-Joachim Noack. *Frankfurter Rundschau*, 6 November 1978.
47. Willy Brandt, in interview with Hans Gerlach, of the *Koelner Stadt-Anzeiger*, 15 September 1978.
48. The London *Times*, 12 July 1978.
49. Dietrich Spangenberg, in conversation with the author, March 1973.
50. Heli Ihlefeld. *Willy Brandt. Anekdotisch*. Munich, 1971.
51. Ibid.
52. Heinrich Böll, in a letter to the author. March 1972.
53. Willy Brandt, in conversation with the author, March 1972.
54. Heli Ihlefeld, op. cit.
55. *Sunday Telegraph*. 12 November 1972.
56. Golo Mann. *Gedanken ueber einen Politiker*.
57. Sir William Hayter. *The Diplomacy of the Great Powers*. London, 1960.

58. Ibid.
59. Willy Brandt. The London *Times*, 12 July 1978.
60. Axel Springer. *Von Berlin aus gesehen.* Stuttgart, 1971.
61. Ibid.
62. Axel Springer. *Die Welt*, 12 January 1971.
63. Aidan Crawley. *The Rise of Western Germany.* London, 1973.
64. Jens Feddersen. *Gedanken ueber einen Politiker.*

CHAPTER TEN

The Perils of Plenty

In spite of the scandal and sadness of Willy Brandt's resignation, he left his successor a rich legacy – a government based on real trust and partnership, a handsome majority in the Bundestag, a degree of economic prosperity which was the envy of most other Europeans, excellent foreign relations, and coexistence with the other German State which seemed at least to have defused the Berlin situation. Brandt left behind, too, a reputation for political integrity; he had resigned because he believed it was the honourable thing to do. German politics as a whole benefited, and his own SPD in particular.

One cynical commentary on Brandt's political career was that "It is still a major political crime to have supported the Nazis, but it is better to have done nothing than to have openly rebelled".[1] There was some truth in that: anti-Nazis like Brandt incurred animosity, not only from ex-Nazis, but from a great many Germans who had indeed "done nothing" during the Nazi era and who would spend the rest of their lives trying to justify this. In this respect, Helmut Schmidt started with an advantage over his predecessor; he had, indeed, done nothing to oppose Nazism, but he should hardly be blamed for it.

He was born only in December 1918, and was thus under twenty-one years old when war broke out. His father was a schoolmaster in the Barmbek borough of Hamburg, renowned for the sauciness of its young. Splendidly situated on the river Elbe, Hamburg – along with Bremen – is one of the two most "outward-looking" cities of Germany. Both were formerly free cities of the Hanseatic League of trading communities. Both are ports, with close connections with Scandinavia, Britain, the Low Countries and the world overseas. Hamburg is a city brimming with self-confidence and independence of mind. These were characteristics which Schmidt inherited in full measure, with Barmbek sauciness thrown in – he would earn the nickname of "Schnauze", difficult to translate, literally meaning "snout" but implying extrovert cheekiness and "lip".

Schmidt was only fourteen when the Nazis came to power. He joined the Hitler Youth, but didn't discuss its activities with his family – "Red" Hamburg was a citadel of social democracy and his parents would have nothing to do with the Nazis. He has claimed that he knew nothing about politics before the war, and his sheer lack of interest had more to do with him leaving the Hitler Youth at the age of seventeen.[2] He was artistic, played the organ, wrote poetry and painted a little; and he worked hard, and was usually top of his class at school. He had time only to take his school examinations, do his six months in the civil national labour-service (Reichsarbeitsdienst), and his two years in the Army, prior to being called up for active service when war broke out. His failure to have been in any way concerned with political opposition to the Nazis has never worried him – his own phrase was that he "was four or five years too young at the time".[3]

He has said, too, that he took part "readily" in the defence of his country – curiously, this statement has often been held against him.[4] But Hamburgers are honest and direct – sometimes it may even seem that they are being brashly assertive, but that is not their intention. Schmidt was an excellent soldier, ending the war as a Lieutenant and battery commander in an anti-aircraft unit. In the meantime, he had seen service in Russia, had won the decoration of the Iron Cross, and took part in the brilliantly executed if localized Ardennes Offensive in the winter of 1944–5. He never had any contact with the German Resistance against Hitler, but has expressed sympathy and admiration for those who took part in it; he himself fought to the end for his country, for the simple reason that he could see no alternative to doing his duty.[5] His abiding memory of war was not of the snows of Russia or the Ardennes, or of his Hamburg home destroyed by British bombs, but of the comradeship of the men with whom he served.

It followed that Schmidt, after being taken prisoner by the

British, was classified as non-Nazi and was quickly released. Married by now, he studied for four years at Hamburg University and took a degree in economics, while his wife worked for part of the time as a seamstress to help pay his fees. One of his teachers was Karl Schiller, a future Cabinet colleague, who claimed him as his prize pupil. Schmidt early on joined the social democratic student movement (SDS) and the SPD, and on leaving university found a job in the economics and transport department of the Hamburg city administration, the Senate. Commanding men in battle is not a bad preparation for a future administrator; Schmidt had all the qualities which were needed, sense of responsibility, reliability, confidence and quickness of intellect. In four years he rose to be head of his department of the Senate, and in 1953 was elected a member of the Bundestag. He was now fairly launched on a political career, but set his sights low – he was already taking an interest in military matters, but determined to establish a reputation as an expert on transport and communications.

His first eight years in the Bundestag brought no hint of a meteoric career. The SPD was run by an "old guard", men whose political careers had started in the 1920s and many of whom had gone into exile in the early days of the Nazi era. It was very difficult to break into this closed circle, and Schmidt's progress was unspectacular. He had begun as a left-wing socialist, advocating nationalization of as many industries as possible, and preaching the popular pacifism of the day – "Nie wieder Krieg!", "Never again war!", was a phrase on many lips. Schmidt would change his views very drastically as he went along. He would become a right-winger in his party – as one commentator put it, "a Social Democrat whose philosophy is more akin to that of Democrats in the United States than Socialists in Europe".[6] And he was among the first Social Democrats to decide that the Federal Republic would have to play its part in the defence of Western Europe.

This did not happen all at once. Campaigning in the 1957 Federal elections, Schmidt attacked the CDU for seeking to arm the Bundeswehr with the most modern weapons; in particular, he was violently opposed to the stationing of American nuclear weapons on German soil. In the Bundestag in 1958 he claimed that putting nuclear weapons into Germany was as bad as the Enabling Act which gave Hitler the powers of a dictator. He supported the proposal of a nuclear-free zone, which would include both German states, Poland and Czechoslovakia, and he advocated the step-by-step withdrawal of American and Soviet forces from Germany. Later, he would admit in his book *Verteidigung oder Velgeltung* (Defence or Reprisal) that he had been "jointly guilty" for preaching a mistaken policy.[7] He was changing his views by the time of the SPD Godesberg Conference in 1959, reluctantly admitting that German reunification was no longer a practical possibility and that the most that could be done in the way of arms limitation in Central Europe would be to create military "thinned-out" zones on both sides of the interzonal frontier – something, in fact, akin to the proposals of Anthony Eden and, later, Harold Macmillan.

In 1961 Schmidt resigned his Bundestag seat. He had become disenchanted with what he regarded as the stale and stuffy atmosphere of Bonn,[8] and – even more – with his lack of progress in the ranks of the SPD hierarchy. He was offered a job in Berlin, but went back instead to his native Hamburg, as Senator for Internal Affairs (the equivalent of Minister in other *Laender*). This move was the making of him, politically. For in February 1962, Schmidt took complete charge during the damaging and dangerous Hamburg floods. The sea-defences – the Elbe is tidal at Hamburg – were breached during the night of 16–17 February, but the alarm was given only at 6.20 a.m. Within twenty minutes Schmidt was in his office and when, hours later, Hamburg's Mayor, Paul Nevermann, arrived back from holiday, Schmidt told him to keep out of the way.[9] By general consent, Schmidt's organizational ability probably saved several thousand lives. He became something of a national figure overnight, but he was, in addition, a thoroughly successful administrator during his four years in Hamburg, and would certainly have been able to run for the Mayor's office. But in 1964 Willy Brandt appointed him Shadow Minister for Defence, and in 1965 he was back in the Bundestag. In 1967, when the Grand Coalition was formed, he became Chairman of the SPD Parliamentary Party, and in 1969 Brandt appointed him Minister of Defence in his first Cabinet.

A year earlier he had become Deputy Chairman of the SPD, and his progress would from now on be smooth and inexorable, along the two parallel lines of Ministerial office and of position in the party. Any new Minister is "on trial", but Schmidt made the Ministry of Defence very much his own. From now on, he was Brandt's logical successor.

There had been, in the course of the years, a complete metamorphosis in his thinking on defence. He had completely discarded his earlier pacifism. In 1958 he advocated a volunteer army, but three years later became a supporter of conscription. He still, for a time, opposed the stationing of American nuclear weapons on German soil, but would become the strongest supporter of full military cooperation with the United States. Up to 1966 he was warning against the "neurosis" of dread of the Soviet Union, but was later the total advocate of maintaining NATO's deterrent strength.[10] The brutal Soviet attack on Czechoslovakia undoubtedly had an effect on him; certainly, it discouraged any ideas which he still entertained of creating nuclear-free or militarily thinned-out zones in Central Europe.

He was an outstandingly successful Minister of Defence. He had done a recent spell of training as a reservist, the only Minister in the history of the Federal Republic to do this. He felt utterly at home with the men of the Bundeswehr, and visits to them were comradely occasions in which he could relax and at the same time learn about their problems. He was a liberal Minister; he allowed soldiers to grow their hair long – at the Aachen Carnival he was called the commander of the "German Hair Force". His own comment was: "What matters is what goes on *inside* a man's skull". He was an able administrator; he reorganized the Ministry and divorced the civilian administration from the chain of command, speeded up training of NCOs – there was a shortage of 30,000 when he took over – and ironed out inequities over conscription.[11] Of course, there were troubles too. More than 100 Starfighters had crashed, and Schmidt was criticized for ordering 50 more of these planes – even though modifications had been carried out on them. He was accused of bureaucratization – Defence Ministry staff increased from 5,200 to over 6,000 in two years – and of allegedly selfish defence of his budget (Schmidt's answer was that the Federal Republic's credibility as partner and ally depended on fulfilment of commitments to NATO). In October 1971, he caused wild excitement when he announced that private cars would be "called up" for the 1972 military manoeuvres. The public, with eight out of ten families owning a car, were horrified. Schmidt hastily made clear that only 400 cars would be called for and, in the event, only 160 took part, and on a purely voluntary basis.

His directness of speech and sometimes abrasive manner made him enemies. He called Franz Josef Strauss "so dangerous, because so talented" and remarked that he was "the toad we had to take into our bed" – the bed of the Grand Coalition. He may have horrified the daughter of the Federal President, Gustav Heinemann, when she asked him if the use of napalm in aerial bombing could not be stopped – his blunt answer was that its tactical value on the field of battle was unquestioned. He fell out with his old teacher, Karl Schiller, and was reputed to have said that Frau Schiller told him her husband had reached the carpet-biting stage. French critics found something "censorious" in him, and nick-named him "Le Feldwebel", the sergeant-major.[12] A master of invective and prickly irony, Schmidt had no time for friendly repartee, not even for the sort of gentle sarcasm used by Konrad Adenauer.[13] Nor could he ever suffer fools gladly, or to be beholden to anyone.[14]

As already suggested (see page 186) Brandt regarded him from 1972 onwards as his probable successor. Schmidt's service from 1972 to 1974, first as Minister of both Economics and Finance, and then of Finance alone, was the last part of a process of "grooming" which began when he took charge of the SPD Parliamentary Party in 1967. By the time that he became Chancellor he had, in addition, written several books. One deserves brief mention here. In *The Balance of Power*[15] Schmidt wrote of political as well as military equilibrium. He declared himself in full favour of détente, but added: "It would be foolish to strive for détente while neglecting to provide for the military protection of one's own existence."[16] Détente in Europe was "impossible without the balance of power provided by NATO". Always a realist, Schmidt recognized that "the conventional forces at the disposal of NATO in Western Europe, after allowing for certain US troop withdrawals [shamefully called 'rotations'], and for the withdrawal of all French forces, are inadequate for defending the NATO territories in Europe".[17] Schmidt recognized, too, that not one of the Federal Republic's allies was prepared to interest itself in German reunification, and France, at least, actually feared such a prospect. His country would have to set itself the limited aim "of preserving what is worth preserving".[18]

The book gives a good idea of Schmidt the pragmatist, realist and conservative social democrat. One writer felt that it was a weakness that he was "no spiritual leader",[19] and argued that what the Germans wanted was a head of government with a clear-cut and acceptable ideology. Schmidt would think exactly the opposite; ideologies have never helped the German people and they have often suffered from the lack of sound and sensible administration. Commonsense was sure to be the keynote of the leadership of a man who called himself "the leading employee of the West German Republic".[20]

With both Brandt and Scheel, now Federal President, leaving at the same time, a minor Cabinet reshuffle was needed. Schmidt had in the past argued for the "rejuvenation" of German politics, and pointed out that Ebert, Stresemann and Bruening – as well as Kennedy in the United States – all took office in their mid-forties.[21] So it was not surprising that the changes which he made resulted in the youngest Cabinet in the history of the Federal Republic, with an average age of 49. The new Chancellor's inaugural statement of Government policy made it plain that there were plenty of problems to be solved. Those which he listed were deficiencies and differences in the EEC, the monetary turbulence arising from the weakness of the dollar, considerable increases in the prices of a range of raw materials besides oil, and rising unemployment. The message was clearly "Back to work", following the emotional atmosphere created by Brandt's departure. Good husbandry – and Schmidt had installed a first-class Minister of Finance, Hans Apel, from his native Barmbek, in his place – brought its due reward in November, when a Government programme was launched to reflate the economy, create more jobs and stimulate investment. There were tax reductions, increased child allowances, bonuses for employers and for workers prepared to move to new areas for jobs.

The rate of inflation was held down to 6 per cent, the lowest of any major industrialized country, and an economic growth rate of 4 per cent was just acceptable. But there would be no simple solutions, during Schmidt's Chancellorship, to his country's economic problems. In 1975 unemployment rose to over one million, and Schmidt had to offset a budgetary deficit by raising VAT by 2 per cent and so angering the Trade Unions. In addition, 400,000 foreign workers left for home during the year, when their work-permits were not renewed. Even so, 2·2 million remained, creating special social problems and a certain amount of grumbling. In 1976 Schmidt was under heavy fire when 10 per cent increases for eleven million old-age pensioners were first promised, then cancelled and, finally, grudgingly honoured. Unemployment was up to 1·2 million, and the Unions were for ever demanding strongly reflationary policies. Consolation for the Government was the rate of inflation falling below 4 per cent, at a time when it was in double figures in countries like France and Britain. But no German government can convince an inflation-conscious electorate that all is well, save by banishing inflation altogether. And that was clearly impossible.

Unemployment was slightly reduced in 1977, and again, to 900,000 in 1978, but Schmidt now faced a new difficulty – the really pressing demands for reflation were coming, not from the Trade Unions, but from outside the country. Both the American and British Governments began to press for German reflation during 1977; Schmidt countered initially by pointing out that the Federal Republic was increasing its imports, while other European states were cutting back. Pressure only increased, and at the London Conference in May, Schmidt was forced to promise appropriate measures in the autumn. These were announced on 14 September. Budgetary expenditure would be raised in 1978 by 10 per cent, and capital expenditure by 16·5 per cent. The railways would get an additional 1,000 million marks, there would be tax-free Christmas bonuses for all employees of 400 instead of the usual 100 marks, basic tax allowances would be increased as well as grants for research and development. An additional 730 million marks would be pumped into the building industry, and new jobs would be created in two particular sectors. There would be 1,600 new posts in the Federal Institute of Labour, and 2,200 in the security services. Paradoxically, the Government was pushed into expanding its civil service bureaucracy and its even more unpopular security arm! These measures, moreover, would increase the budgetary deficit from 21,000 to 28,000 million marks, at a time when any provident administration would want to be balancing its books!

Here, indeed, was a strange situation. No government likes to be told by outsiders how to run its own affairs. Least of all does it like to be forced into doing things which can cause consternation and criticism at home. In other European countries a curious notion persisted that their own troubles would be solved if the Germans would only "consume" more and thus, hopefully, reduce their exports, so leaving the field open for less efficient competitors. This notion was based on the fallacy that domestic consumption can be turned on from a tap, and exports turned off in the same way. The experience of any well-run industrialized country is that the broader the base of domestic consumption, the more likely industry is to expand both its output and its exports. Instead of asking the Federal Republic to increase its already swollen budgetary deficit, other Europeans should have been working out plans to increase output and the competitiveness of their own products in export markets. It says much for Schmidt's increasing ability to maintain a philosophical calm that he reacted so seldom and generally so mildly to unsolicited advice.

One revealing analysis of German economic success was published by *The Times*.[22] The paper compared the performance of the Federal Republic and of Britain, the first with 62 million inhabitants and Britain with 56 million. The West German gross national product (GNP) was more than double the British. Its production of motor cars was three times bigger. Defence expenditure was 50 per cent higher. Its social services, one might add, were immeasurably better. Its people enjoyed a far higher standard of living than the British, and to ask many of them to "consume" more was rather like inviting Strasbourg geese to burst their livers twice as quickly. The secrets of German success, as compared with Britain, were far better labour relations – over a four year period an annual average of three working days per thousand employees were lost, against a staggering 253 in Britain – higher working morale, and immensely higher capital investment.

One is mildly surprised that the Federal Republic's competitors did not ask that Germans should work less and go on strike more often. But, in any event, salt was readily rubbed in the wounds which Schmidt was asked to inflict upon himself. One British newspaper produced an article entitled "Myth of export boom exposed", which explained that the Germans were "running out of steam" and faced "export-led stagnation".[23] The writer (incredibly, the "Economics Editor") concluded with the thought that "Other countries, like Britain, could doubtless follow the example of Japan and Germany, and enjoy booming foreign trade. But it does not necessarily lead to higher growth, in the long run. The myth of export-led growth has at last been exposed."

In March 1978, the British Budget Commissioner for the EEC, Mr Christopher Tugendhat, claimed that the Federal Republic was contributing less to his budget, per head, than Belgium or Holland, and that the Germans were being obstructive over European agricultural policies and, because of the strength of the mark, were buying fertilisers and agricultural machinery abroad on favourable terms (there was pressure at this time on the Federal Republic to revalue the mark *upwards*, which would have made these foreign goods even cheaper!) Tugendhat concluded with the bizarre thought that "any losses sustained by Germany on the EEC budget were vastly outweighed by the benefits of 20 years of unfettered access to the markets of its main customers".[24] The implications of this accusatory statement were that partners in the EEC were by no means equal, and that the Federal Republic should be deeply grateful for arrangements which all other Europeans accepted as of right. Small wonder that Schmidt, and his Government's representatives, have sometimes exploded in wrath.

Two days after the Tugendhat *démarche*, mollifying words were published in a leading British newspaper.[25] The British Prime Minister, the article explained, "does not wish to join in the chorus demanding that Japan and Germany expand faster. He believes that public pressure is counter-productive". The article went on to stress that "the rate of growth in Germany is critical for the economic expansion of all other European countries". But the original statement was subtly untrue; Mr James Callaghan was indeed pressing for faster German expansion, in private; the way in which to indicate this, in public, was by means of an "inspired leak" to the Press. Once again, the Chancellor may have fumed in Bonn – and who should blame him? Once again, he hid his feelings – in public.

In any case, the Federal Government did what it could to help in 1978. Another "Summit" Conference in July, this time in Bonn, brought a DM12,500 million "pump-priming" West German programme, with cuts in income and corporation taxes, increases in child allowances, and grants for technological development. The payroll tax was abolished, at a cost of 2,300 million marks, and there were increased allowances for small firms (which of the Federal Republic's critics considered that such allowances increased the capacity and competitiveness of these firms, which would then be reflected in export markets?). The Federal budgetary deficit was geared to rise from 28,000 to 35,000 million marks. It would, of course, be easily covered by public borrowing. But what country invites pressure upon itself to increase its own borrowing, when such borrowing is not strictly necessary?

Apart from what one can only characterize as nobility in increasing its own national debt, in the interest of others, the Federal Republic raised its development aid budget by 23 per cent, and proposed to write-off its aid-grants to the world's 30 poorest countries. This would cost an estimated 4,000 million marks, which would have been due in repayments and interest. The proposal[26] was unnoticed by other European countries, possibly because they may, for once, have been mildy conscience-stricken – not so much over useful concessions to help the poorest of the Third World, but because they were fundamentally opposed to giving any credit to the Federal Republic for doing likewise.

One is confronted with a most unpleasant syndrome. In a sense, it is a left-over from the last war and the Nazi era. But the usual pretexts for "blaming the Germans" are very obvious, and there may be residual reason in them. They may have to do with war-crimes, with present-day anti-semitism (although there are very few defenders of the Jews in the world today, but plenty of people ready to lambast anti-semites for their own diversionary reasons), with neo-Nazism in Germany itself and in the global context of a "Hitler cult". Today this syndrome relates German unacceptability to German riches – one example is the perpetual complaint that the rich Federal Republic contributes too little within the EEC. The Germans deny this, and figures which they published in April 1979 bear them out;[27] they showed that the Federal Republic had paid more than it received, in the course of EEC adjustments, to the tune of 3,885 million marks (about £1,000 million). France was the only other much smaller creditor, and the other seven EEC countries shared out about £1,220 million between them.

As Chancellor, Schmidt had the strictly political task of keeping the government which he led and in which he believed – in fact, the SPD-FDP coalition – in office. In the *Laender*, this was an uphill struggle – however well the FDP may do in government in Bonn, its organization and following in the country at large are eternally battling for the 5 per cent of the votes needed for Parliamentary representation. In several *Laender* it failed to achieve this. The result has been an increasing majority for the CDU in the Bundesrat, the second chamber of the Federal Parliament. The crunch came with the *Land* Hesse elections in October 1978. The CDU looked likely to emerge as the strongest single party. This meant that the failure of the FDP to surmount the 5 per cent hurdle would have put the CDU in power. And that, in turn, would have given the Opposition a two-thirds majority in the Bundesrat, and the right to block all Government legislation passed up to it. In the event, the FDP scraped in, and the situation was saved.

The same consideration, the viability of the FDP, governed the 1976 Federal elections. The SPD vote dropped from 45·8 to 42·6 per cent, that of the CDU rose from 44·9 to 48.6 per cent. Fortunately for Schmidt, the FDP were in once more, with nearly

8 per cent of the vote, but the coalition's Bundestag majority was cut from 46 to a mere 10. There was no escaping the fact that the SPD had lost a million votes to its rivals, and that the CDU slogans of "Freedom in place of socialism" and "Less power for the State" had been popular. Predictably, inflation played its part; the tendency persists among German voters to blame the government in office if there is any inflation at all, regardless of how much lower it is than in other major industrialized countries.

Schmidt, then, will face a critical situation in the 1980 elections. He remains personally as popular as ever – in a recent public opinion poll 73 per cent thought that he was doing a good job.[28] Only Adenauer has rivalled this figure. His Free Democratic allies will, for sure, be hard put to it to secure representation in the Bundestag; they have badly missed the sparkling personality of Walter Scheel since he became Federal President and their present leaders are worthy but unexciting men. In fact, Schmidt's main hope lies in the equivalent lack of personality at the top, in the CDU. Helmut Kohl, its leader, is sound but colourless, and its three outstanding personalities are in the *Laender*. Two of them, Franz Josef Strauss in Bavaria and Alfred Dregger, stand well to the right of centre in the party and are not the men to pick up the floating vote, estimated at about a quarter of the electorate. The third, Richard von Weizsaecker, is somewhat isolated from Federal politics in West Berlin.

Another factor, which could be either a threat or a boon for Schmidt, is the possible divorce of the Bavarian Christian Social Union (CSU) from the CDU. In November 1976, the CSU decided to form its own Parliamentary group, separate from that of the CDU. In December, Strauss, influenced by the CDU threat to fight elections in Bavaria in opposition to him, rescinded this decision. But the possibility remains of the CSU declaring itself as a separate party, essentially for tactical reasons. The argument in favour of doing this goes as follows: in Bavaria the CSU would hold its own, while in the rest of the Federal Republic the CDU would be well shot of Strauss in its bid to pick up more of the floating vote. The CDU and CSU would, of course, cooperate to the full, as Strauss has made clear when he disclaimed "narrow-minded ambitions" and insisted that he was not "an Aladdin running around with another magic lamp".[29] The possible separation of the CSU from the CDU, and the mounting of a two-pronged assault against the Government parties, remains one of the imponderables of the 1980 elections. Were such an assault successful, the FDP could be blotted out; then, even Schmidt's popularity would not be enough to keep the SPD in power.

Another imponderable has been created by the emergence of completely new parties. Germans have decisively rejected radicalism of both the right and the left, in fact of orthodox communists and neo-Nazis. But since the beginning of 1978 two groups of environmentalists emerged, and one of the so-called "Green Lists" – with virtually no funds and no organization – made a surprisingly good showing in the Lower Saxony and Hamburg *Land* elections, with about 4 per cent of the vote. For the time being, at least, these groups did not pose a serious threat to the principal parties, but their members are – broadly speaking – "progressives" and the thought of possible votes lost for the SPD must be a nagging one for Schmidt.

In the 1976 elections Schmidt's party campaigned with the slogan "Moddel Deutschland", in fact, on its good social and economic record. But his Governments have been beset with problems which were none of their making but are the products of a contemporary *malaise* which exists in a great many countries, and which takes its distinctive forms in the Federal Republic. Right- and left-wing radicalism, as already suggested, are not among them. There are about a hundred right-wing and perhaps three times as many left-wing groups, but estimates of total membership are of only about 20,000 and 80,000 respectively. Members of the small neo-Nazi groups desecrate Jewish cemeteries, daub swastika slogans on buildings, and occasionally resort to violence – generally while carrying out robberies or trying to steal arms and ammunition. The Federal authorities are less worried by these activities than by the links maintained with similar groups abroad, like the "Vlaamse Militante Order" in Belgium, the "Front de la Jeunesse" in France, and the "NSDAP" in the United States.[30] A "Nazi International" could finance treasonable activity within the Federal Republic, and could do much to stimulate the "Hitler Cult" and the incipient anti-semitism which exists everywhere in Western Europe.

Treasonable activity is very clearly the main danger posed by the extreme left. It is deliberately promoted and financed from the other side of the Iron Curtain. In the five years up to the end of 1978, 100 spies working for the East German security services were detained.[31] Estimates of the number of East German agents working in the Federal Republic in 1979 varied between 8,000 and 10,000.[32] One of the most damaging spying cases since the Guillaume Affair was that of Frau Ursel Lorenzen, who worked for the British Director of NATO's Operations Directorate in Brussels. She took information with her to East Berlin on NATO contingency planning of the most crucial nature.[33] Her ostensible reasons were that NATO crisis planning involved laying the greater part of both German states waste, and that the NATO Secretary-General, Dr Joseph Luns, had belonged to a Dutch Nazi movement as a student in the 1930s. This malicious accusation was a reminder of the incidental damage done by left-wing spying; not only political leaders but ordinary, decent citizens are tainted by suspicions which are unjust and unfounded. One East German gambit is feeding false information to the West German authorities in order to wreck the careers of innocent people. This was almost certainly done in the case of Dr Luns.

The Federal authorities will continue to deal with right- and left-wing radicals with the correct blend of firmness and moderation – they discovered long ago that the best way of dealing with relatively harmless East German agents was to send them home, as inept but marked men who would no longer be of any use to their masters. A much more serious problem for Schmidt has been the activities of the small section of West German youth which had reverted to gangsterism. The student violence of the late 1960s waned to some extent during Brandt's Chancellorship, but reappeared in an even more brutal and vicious form than before, from the end of 1974. On 9 November of that year a terrorist of the Baader-Meinhof gang, Holger Meins, died in Wittlich gaol. There were immediate riots and demonstrations at a number of universities, and on 11 November the President of the West Berlin Supreme Court, Guenter von Drenkmann, was shot dead – the "Red Army Faction", the re-named Baader-Meinhof gang, claimed credit. Lawyers acting for imprisoned terrorists were suspected as acting as link-men between them and their friends outside.

In February 1975, the Chairman of the West Berlin CDU, Peter Lorenz, was kidnapped and freed only after the Government agreed to release five convicted terrorists from gaol, give them each 20,000 marks of "pocket-money", and fly them out of the country. Early in April, terrorists seized the West German Embassy in Stockholm, murdered the military attaché, and held the Ambassador and members of his staff hostage. They demanded the release of 26 terrorists, including all the leaders of the Baader-Meinhof gang, and when their demand was refused, they murdered another embassy official and blew up the Embassy. Five terrorists were caught, and one killed. In Bonn, Schmidt said that there could be no surrender in such cases; the release of more than two score proven criminals would cause unimaginable danger to the German public.

In May, the trial began in Stuttgart of the four ring-leaders of the Baader-Meinhof gang, Ulrike Meinhof, Andreas Baader, Gudrun Ensslin and Jan-Carl Raspe. They were charged with complicity in five murders, in 71 cases of attempted murder, and in extraneous bank-raids and bombings. After weeks of legal wrangling, their defence lawyers claimed that they were in need of medical care. When the trial was resumed, the court decided to exclude the accused from the proceedings, but the Federal Supreme Court ruled against this. The claims of the defendants that the terms of their detention amounted to torture were rejected by the Federal Constitutional Court, by Amnesty International and the European Commission on Human Rights. They were eventually sentenced to life imprisonment in April 1977.

But the imprisoned gangsters intended to make their point, at once and at all costs. With legal proceedings taking an interminable time, Ulrike Meinhof committed suicide on 9 May 1976. Vengeance would follow, and it must surely have been directed from the prison-cells of the murderers. On 7 April 1977, the Chief Federal Prosecutor, Siegfried Buback, was murdered, along with his 29 year-old driver. A few days previously he had spoken at a press conference of "disquieting and alarming indications" that the terrorists were planning multiple actions.[34] He could hardly have known that his name was the first on the list, nor that the utterly ruthless murderers would kill his poor driver.

On 30 July, Juergen Ponto, the Chairman of the Dresdner Bank, was murdered when resisting an attempt to kidnap him, not far from his home, near Frankfurt. There were three assailants; as he lay dying, one of them put a gun to his head and blew his brains out. Later, one of the most wanted terrorists, Michael Baumann, gave up crime and explained why his former friends murdered so cold-bloodedly. He said: "It gives one a feeling of superiority. The gun takes all fear away, and even the puniest man feels stronger than Cassius Clay. You only have to know how to pull the trigger; any idiot knows that. Many succumb to this fascination."[35]

On 5 September 1977, the President of the Employers Association (BDI), Hans-Martin Schleyer, was kidnapped. His driver, and three bodyguards, were murdered during a brief, futile struggle. The murderers demanded that eleven prisoners, including the three surviving Baader-Meinhof gang-leaders, should be released, that each should be given 100,000 marks, and all of them flown to countries of their own choice. Schmidt, once again, refused to surrender. This was a most difficult decision for him to take – not a popular one at all. With Schleyer being held by the kidnappers, a battle of wits ensued. But the terrorists, who were in close touch with the Palestine Liberation Organization, had another trick to play. On 13 October, PLO and German terrorists hijacked a Lufthansa Boeing 737, with 86 on board, during a flight from Majorca to Frankfurt. The plane was forced to fly to Rome, Cyprus, Dubai and Aden, where the pilot was murdered in cold blood in the supposition that he was trying to transmit messages which could have endangered the kidnappers.

No country wanted to give asylum to the terrorists and their victims, and the plane flew on to Mogadishu, in Somalia. There, on 17 October, a brilliant rescue operation was carried out, by the German Federal Frontier Police unit formed after the Munich Massacre of 1972. Help and advice were given by Britain, France, the United States and Israel, which had executed the only previous long-range rescue of Entebbe. For once, there was a degree of international cooperation, in the interests of civilized society. Three terrorists were killed, and the fourth wounded. All the hostages were set free.

These, and other contemporary terrorists, were young and cruel – they "deprived people of the use of their limbs, had blown off one man's jaw, another's hand, had blasted two of their victims into fragments, shot another and thrown him down a flight of stairs, to let him lie bleeding to death".[36] In the Mogadishu kidnap, harmless passengers were treated with total brutality, knocked about, mocked and left lying in their own excrement.

Within hours of the rescue, the three Baader-Meinhof terrorists were found dead in their cells at Stammheim prison, near Stuttgart. Two had shot themselves, and Gudrun Ensslin had hanged herself. They had smuggled in weapons and ammunition; Raspe even had a transistor radio in his cell. Yet again, the terrorists still at large acted at once; on 19 October the corpse of Schleyer was found, near Mulhouse, in Alsace. Schmidt, in a statement on television, explained that this sort of total terrorism was an international problem. The Federal President, Walter Scheel, spoke with feeling of "this animosity against all established order ... this naked barbarism".[37] One British newspaper wrote: "What has the Federal Republic done to deserve this agonizing trial? It appears to have done everything to deserve the opposite ... After years of dictatorship, destruction and foreign occupation, the West Germans built a democratic federal state with a vigorous economy – a country which is a key pillar of the Western Alliance ... How easily it might have been otherwise."[38]

There was, briefly, a wave of sympathy for Schmidt and his Government. The murders, as it happened, stopped for the time being, for the terrorist "General Staff" had done away with itself in Stammheim gaol. A number of leading terrorists left the country – thus Gabrielle Rollnick would be arrested later in Bulgaria, Stefan Wisniewski in France, Astrid Proll in London, Christoph Wackernagel in Amsterdam, Knut Folkerts in Utrecht, Rolf Wagner and Brigitte Mohnhaupt in Yugoslavia. For the moment, at least, the menace of the Baader-Meinhof gang was checked. But nobody could tell what new cadres were being built up, and what new outburst of violence might take place in a year or two. By mid-1979 perhaps 60 to 80 convinced terrorists were still at large, able to persuade, able to recruit.

Shortly before Mogadishu, the Chairman of the British section of Amnesty International, the Rev Paul Oestreicher, wrote that the German terrorists were totally alienated from all German society.[39] Their "theory, avidly studied but little understood, comes from Marx and Lenin. But not their desperado terror, which is a product of their own idealistic mythology, their deep-seated hatred of our kind of society and their desperate need to live dangerously and spectacularly." In his view, "Their perverted idealistic passion is like Hitler's. So is their deep hatred". And the effect of their terrorism was "to strengthen substantially every reactionary tendency in German society ... They probably hate the whole social system so much that they could not care less whether Helmut Schmidt or Franz Josef Strauss rules Germany".

The writer, Günter Grass, added his thoughts after Mogadishu was over. He had this to say: "A group elevates itself to élite level, says – we speak in the name of the people – passes judgement in the name of the people, has received a mandate from no-one to do so, but also murders in the name of the people".[40] Grass saw posters in Amsterdam University which showed a picture of Ulrike Meinhof, with the caption "Died in the fight against fascism". Grass told the students that this was "a lasting insult to every individual who truly died in the fight against fascism". He himself believed that the terrorists were left-wing fascists and, like the Mafia, planned further acts of terror from their cells, with the help of their lawyers.

A terse comment on the terrorists came in the *Financial Times*, with the signature "J. C." It was: "If they can be compared to anything, it is to Dostoyevsky's devils – people who by their own admission are ready even to throw acid in a child's face, if it will help their cause. What is that cause? Beyond destroying society, it is impossible to say".[41]

The terrorist explosion was a traumatic business. Significantly, little sympathy was shown to Schmidt and his Government – a prevailing view in the outside world was that young German terrorists were showing a somewhat uncouth way of trying to expiate the sins of their Nazi fathers. Paul Oestreicher, who indeed evinced sympathy, drew an awkward moral – "Something, somewhere, has gone badly wrong when a nation allows itself to be held to ransom by a group of desperados." So far, so good; but he added: "The roots of alienation in modern society will not be eradicated by police with automatic weapons and computers. They lie deeper in us all."[42] For Schmidt, such moralizing did not help. What became known as "The great terrorism debate" was under way.[43] Laws, by the end of 1977, had been passed to outlaw terrorist associations, to secure scrutiny of correspondence between defence counsel and accused, to question the affidavits of defence counsel, to tighten up remand and to prevent contact between defence counsel and their clients – under special circumstances. Did these laws already go too far? What would be left of a liberal society, if it were subjected to everlasting scrutiny, surveillance and even police search? These were questions which became linked with the overall powers of the state, with steps which had been taken long before to defend its security, and with the modernization of methods which could make surveillance of the citizen universal and complete.

The new security laws, arising from the threat of terrorism, were far-reaching. Thus, from the beginning of 1978, check-points could be set up on roads and wherever police were conducting searches.[44] The police could ask anybody for proof of identity. Those who could not prove their identity could be taken to a police station and held until identity had been established. If anyone was regarded as a suspect, photographs and fingerprints could be taken, and such people could be searched. Whole buildings could be searched by the police, and not just single apartments. Finally, lawyers could be barred from the trials of suspected terrorists. In April 1978, there was fresh legislation, enabling police to hold suspects for up to twelve hours and to install screens in prison visiting-rooms, to prevent objects being passed between prisoners and their visitors.

There is nothing very unusual about such legislation; suspects can be just as easily arrested or detained in countries like Britain and France, while lawyers guilty of complicity with their clients' criminal activities would be disbarred.[45] But the measures taken in the Federal Republic to counter terrorism have become part of the wider debate about security in general. This debate includes, in particular, the so-called *Berufsverbot*, under which political extremists may be barred from the public service.

Schmidt has denied that any such thing as a *Berufsverbot* – or ban on employment – exists.[46] He claimed that the word itself is a piece of Communist propaganda, used to discredit the Federal Republic, and he based his stance on established practice in other western democracies. According to one Government publication,[47] the Basic Law of the Federal Republic provided safeguards to ensure that democratic liberties should not be abused. Among these safeguards were provisions to ensure the loyalty of public servants to a free and democratic order. These were regarded as normal, until the appearance of the "new left" around 1968, and the controversy which has since arisen has involved an international campaign against the State, which ignores the Federal Republic's observance of human rights but castigates retention of its right to employ only people regarded as suitable.

Every State, of course, has this right. In Britain, for instance, candidates for posts in Government service are most carefully screened. Thus prospective entrants into the Foreign Service have to produce acceptable "referees", who answer questions relating to their personal and political suitability – one standard question is whether the candidate has had any affiliation with a communist or other subversive organization. But what is normal practice in Britain is regarded as rank oppression when similar regulations are enforced in Germany. In the view of the Federal President, Walter Scheel, the regulations admittedly "were from time to time implemented in a way which did not reflect a true liberal spirit".[48] But, the President went on, it was a mistake to treat "this very difficult subject as *the* test of democratic convictions" – the "opponents of the regulations deliberately overlooked the fact that the way we appoint members of the public service compares favourably with every other democracy", and "the fact that the regulations should safeguard not merely the security of the state but everyone's freedom to apply for jobs".

The President concluded that "false slogans", like *Berufsverbot*, had created a feeling of insecurity among the young and had made them unnecessarily afraid of the State. The two sides of this pointless debate, he suggested, ought to learn to understand each other. Pointless or not, the debate may have been overdone. According to one published figure, only 287 applicants were turned down on security grounds in 1976–7, out of 745,000 who sought employment in state service.[49] In one *Land*, the Saar, hundreds of investigations over a period of five years failed to uncover a single "subversive" applicant.[50] While, at the end of the day, there were at least 2,300 Communists in state employment but, presumably, regarded as politically harmless.[51] To a great many Germans, nothing could have been more irritating than the arrival in their country of the well-meaning busy-bodies of the Russell Tribunal, based in Britain and making a habit of poking their noses into the affairs of other countries. The members of the Tribunal claimed that the so-called *Berufsverbot* was a serious threat to human rights, and created the utterly false impression that the investigation of applicants for state employment was something quite new as well as sinister.

Schmidt was necessarily concerned that accusations of the repressive nature of the West German State went far beyond the *Berufsverbot*. One book published in Britain in 1978 produced an exhaustive list of allegedly repressive actions.[52] The author sought to show that even ostensibly "good democrats" were the enemies of true freedom. Thus Willy Brandt had proclaimed an "immediate programme to modernize and intensify crime prevention" in 1969, and the SPD Mayor of Bremen was quoted as saying: "Dear comrades, give us a chance to find a way ... to take in hand the defence of our own state, now, while we have time and not when the next explosion is upon us." The author claimed that government statements about "increases in security offences" and "political crimes" were offensive and played on the fears of the bourgeoisie, while a paper like the *Frankfurter Allgemeine* was contributing to the scare campaign by writing that "to defend freedom against unusually dangerous enemies, unusual means are required".[53] Other complaints were that the authorities used too much electronic equipment, that files were opened against people who had been investigated but found guiltless, that the State claimed "a monopoly of violence", that criminal law was based on Nazi precepts, and that the law courts were "in the plot". Finally: "West Germany is on the way to becoming a Big Brother police state", with political prisoners, in particular, "sealed off until you suffocate".[54]

So far from trying to create a police state, Schmidt's government had been at pains to explain that security regulations should be essentially designed to protect rather than pursue the citizen. In January 1979, the Cabinet decided to recommend that routine inquiries to the security authorities should cease, and should only be made when there were genuine grounds for suspecting an applicant for a state job. Such inquiries should be made only when all other credentials of an applicant had been checked, so that there should be no question of compiling lists of "undesirables" for the sake of doing so. Applicants under eighteen years would be regarded as juveniles, and no enquiries should be made – the very liberal assumption being that people so young should not be regarded as potentially dangerous politically. The exception would be young people who had already been involved in criminal proceedings, and whose names would therefore already be in police files.[55]

The Schmidt Government is aware that the debate on the alleged undue power and inquisitiveness of the State will go on. Security regulations, intimately linked with the activities of the Baader-Meinhof gang, have been only one of many factors contributing to a nation-wide uneasiness of mind which might seem strange in a people so inherently hardy, so patently successful, so increasingly "normal" – compared with fathers and grandfathers badgered by events over which they had no control, or dedicated in missionary service of their country. In 1979, the people of the Federal Republic were, on average, living better than any of their fellow Europeans, except the Swiss, and very much better than the citizens of the other large European countries. But material well-being does not necessarily bring real happiness, or peace of mind; there are perils, even, derived from plenty. In Switzerland, these take the form of an introspective melancholy and claustrophobia; and the Swiss have no ulterior reason for sadness. It remains otherwise with the Federal Republic.

In 1978, at long last, there was a rash of industrial strikes –
involving 85,000 metal workers, 32,000 printing workers and,
finally, 87,000 people in the steel industry. The strikes were
answered by massive lock-outs, and *The Times*[56] reported the
worsening of the industrial climate under the headline "Is it the
British disease?", and with an undertone of satisfaction. In 1978,
too, came major political scandal, in the "Filbinger Affair".
Hans Karl Filbinger was the Prime Minister of that most orderly
and decently genteel *Land*, of Baden-Wurtemberg. It was
discovered that, as a judge and prosecutor in the German Navy,
he had passed death sentences during the last months of the war.
He was forced to resign, but only after months of controversy
during which he stubbornly refused to admit that he might have
been, if not wrong in a truly pejorative sense, merely mistaken.
One critic wrote:

> In the twelve years that Filbinger was Prime Minister in
> Stuttgart, Baden-Wurtemberg became the most intensively-
> industrialized, economically powerful region in the country.
> It had more foreign workers and fewer jobless than any
> other *Land*. As Prime Minister, Filbinger achieved great
> things, but never the greatest, to acknowledge his
> shortcomings and draw the right conclusions at the right
> time.[57]

The past, it seems, has fastened onto the body politic of
Germany with the proverbial tenacity of the bull-dog. In
November 1978, it asserted itself embarrassingly. The Federal
President, Walter Scheel, was prepared to run for a second term
in 1979 (he subsequently withdrew). He was successful and
popular; moreover, he was only 59 years old and there was an
obvious virtue in the head of state being a man with his wits still
very much about him. The CDU produced an excellent
candidate to oppose him, Dr Karl Carstens, the Speaker of the
Bundestag. He was an alert, informed, integrated 64.

It transpired that both men had been members of the Nazi
Party. The President said that he had never applied for
membership and was a serving officer in the German Air Force
when he was enrolled. He agreed that he was notified, late in
1942. He had been de-Nazified after the war, had never had a
"membership book", and so had felt that the matter was closed.
Dr Carstens had a slightly more complicated story to tell. He had
belonged to the student branch of the brown-shirted SA from
1933 to 1935, when he returned his membership card. In 1937 he

had applied to join the Nazi Party; bureaucratic delays had resulted in his application being rejected only in 1939. But in 1940, after being called up for military service, he was notified that he had been accepted after all as a member of the Party. He, too, was denazified in 1948, when he had applied for a post in the public service. The denazification court paid him a parting compliment, in commending him for having done what he could to oppose Nazi oppression.

Scheel and Carstens were men who have made valuable contributions to post-war German democracy. But the Nazi past will not leave them alone, any more than it will leave more than 62 million West German citizens alone – although well over 60 per cent of them are too young to have contributed one iota to Nazism's evil record. The Nazi past is a spectre which rises up, predictably or totally unexpectedly, to haunt Germans who have tried to build and maintain democracy in the "rump state" of the Federal Republic. Now yet another, lingering problem re-emerged into the political limelight in 1978 – that of Nazi war-criminals.

Under the existing Federal "Statute of Limitations", investigations into murder may not be started if 30 years have passed since the crime was committed. The special problem of dealing with murders perpetrated by the Nazis arose in 1965, when the existing 20 year period was extended. This was done by a strategem: the starting-date was brought forward to 1949, when the Federal Republic was established and West German law-courts first put war-criminals on trial. In 1969, then, the Bundestag had to think again; it extended the period to 30 years, hoping that this would be enough.

Up to 1978 about 85,000 Germans were tried for crimes committed during the Nazi era, and 6,500 were sentenced. By 1979, trials were still going on of about 3,000 people. Up to 1964, 10 per cent of alleged Nazi war-criminals were found guilty; since then, the rate dropped to well under 2 per cent.[58] Witnesses can no longer identify the accused; new evidence simply is not available; the East Germans, with a vast amount of documentation at their finger-tips, refuse to disgorge it – they prefer to reserve the option of disclosing "scandals" of supposed West German complacency or ineptitude.

The West Germans have, of course, done far more than bring people to trial and sentence some of them. They have collected information assiduously, and have filed cases against all *known* war-criminals, including many who have sought refuge in foreign countries or who have disappeared altogether. All such people can be charged, the moment they set foot on German soil. But the problem of extending the Statute of Limitations, or revising it, or simply leaving it as it is, needed to be settled before the end of 1979. Although there were no exactly defined "party lines", the SPD were in favour of abolishing the Statute, in all cases of murder; most of the CDU would abide by the Statute, as it stood; so would the bulk of Schmidt's FDP coalition partners. A small, but very convinced group of CDU members of the Bundestag favoured indefinite possibility of prosecution for murder. So did Chancellor Schmidt.

Right and wrong are liable to be submerged in the welter of legalistic or moralizing argument. A more immediately operative thought is that the Federal Republic was saddled with this problem, too, in addition to all those others passed down by history. A democracy must maintain a legal system and a rule of law, and the protagonists and opponents of revising or maintaining the Statute of Limitations cannot be divided into sheep and goats. It is axiomatic to talk of justice being done, and being *seen* to be done; but sometimes the two concepts do not coincide.

Schmidt himself must be well aware that the perils of plenty are not, uniquely, a problem for today's Federal German Republic. Other countries, in the past, have become sated and smug. It could even be argued that the *malaise* afflicting the Federal Republic today is, in fact, a healthy reaction – against a self-satisfaction which other Europeans would regard as understandable. But this *malaise* posed really difficult psychological problems for the government of the day, and for Helmut Schmidt. He has faced them with the candour and commonsense to be expected of a man born and bred so close to the Hamburg water-front.

1. R. B. Telford and R. J. C. Preece. *Federal Germany. Political and Social Order.* London, 1970.
2. Helmut Wolfgang Kahn. *Helmut Schmidt.* Hamburg, 1971.
3. Ibid.
4. Ibid.
5. Ibid.
6. Clyde Farnsworth. *New York Times* magazine. 2 May 1976.
7. Helmut Wolfgang Kahn, op. cit.
8. Ibid.
9. Ibid.
10. Ibid.

11. Walter Nelson. *Germany Rearmed.* New York, 1972.
12. *The Economist*, 29 October 1977.
13. Walter Henkels. *Bonner Koepfe.* Düsseldorf, 1968.
14. Helmut Wolfgang Kahn, op. cit.
15. Helmut Schmidt. *The Balance of Power.* London, 1971.
16. Ibid.
17. Ibid.
18. Ibid.
19. Caroline Moorhead. The London *Times*, 8 May 1978.
20. Ibid.
21. Helmut Schmidt, op. cit.
22. The London *Times*, 21 October 1977.
23. Malcolm Crawford. *Sunday Times*, 11 September 1977.
24. Michael Hornsby. The London *Times*, 10 March 1978.
25. James Poole and Malcolm Crawford. *Sunday Times*, 12 March 1978.
26. Bulletin of the Federal German Press Office, 11 October 1978.
27. *Frankfurter Rundschau*, 4 April 1979.
28. Claus Wettermann. *Nordwest Zeitung*, 22 December 1978.
29. Klaus Dreher. *Sueddeutsche Zeitung*, 13 September 1978.
30. Report of the Federal Minister of the Interior, Gerhart Baum, to the Bundestag, 13 October 1978.
31. German Press Agency (DPA), summary, 22 January 1979.
32. Federal Ministry of the Interior statement. Quoted by the *Sunday Telegraph*, 21 January 1979.
33. David Shears. *Daily Telegraph*, 9 March 1979.
34. Erhard Becker. *Handelsblatt*, 12 April 1977.
35. Wolfgang Wagner. *Hannoversche Allgemeine Zeitung*, 14 October 1978.
36. Jillian Becker. *Hitler's Children.* London, 1977.
37. Ibid.
38. Jonathan Carr. *Financial Times*, 24 October 1977.
39. Rev Paul Oestreicher. The London *Times*, 12 September 1977.
40. Günter Grass. *Der Aktuelle Artikel.* Inter Nationes service, 12 December 1977.
41. "J. C.". *Financial Times*, 24 October 1977.
42. Rev Paul Oestreicher. The London *Times*, 12 September 1977.
43. Marion Doenhoff. *Die Zeit*, 17 February 1978.
44. German Press Agency (DPA), report, 17 February 1978.
45. Walter Nelson. *The Tablet*, 27 May 1978.
46. Ibid.
47. Inter Nationes report. *Berufsverbot and Human Rights*, February 1978.
48. Walter Scheel, in speech at Bonn University, 13 December 1978.
49. David Shears. *Daily Telegraph*, 17 January 1979.
50. *The Spectator*, 16 December 1979.
51. Friedrich Karl Fromme. *Frankfurter Allgemeine Zeitung*, 28 December 1978.
52. Sebastian Cobler. *Law, Order and Politics in West Germany.* London, 1978.
53. *Frankfurter Allgemeine Zeitung*, 7 March 1975.
54. Sebastian Cobler, op. cit.
55. Ulrich Lueke. *Die Welt*, 18 January 1979.
56. Peter Norman. The London *Times*, 27 June 1978.
57. Erich Ruckgabe. *Hannoversche Zeitung*, 8 August 1978.
58. *Frankfurter Allgemeine Zeitung*, 28 October 1978.

CHAPTER ELEVEN

Towards Leadership in Europe?

Just as Helmut Schmidt inherited from Willy Brandt a Federal Republic so materially prosperous that to European neighbours it appeared to be bursting at the seams, so a foreign policy was passed on to him which seemed quietly and sensibly satisfactory. The Federal Republic, it was confidently assumed, would remain a loyal partner in NATO and the EEC. It would continue to subscribe to a policy of East–West détente, even though the "spirit of Helsinki" would turn out to be a disappointment and the division of Germany would remain as absolute as before. The Federal Republic would play its full part, too, in the North–South dialogue between the industrialized nations and the Third World – rather more than its full part, for Willy Brandt soon showed that he would make this his particular interest and responsibility. Two things seemed fairly sure at the outset of Schmidt's Chancellorship; there was no real scope for any sort of independent West German foreign policy, and the Federal Republic would need to remain content with the relatively modest role of supporting American leadership in NATO, and French in the EEC.

Schmidt quickly established standard good relations with President Gerald Ford, whom he visited in Washington in December 1974. His relationship with France's President, Valéry Giscard d'Estaing, became far more intimate – there was talk of the "Helmut and Valéry show"[1] which produced remarkable unanimity until the French–German "axis" began to fall apart over EEC farm prices in the summer of 1978. The French did not want farm subsidies; the Germans did; and both were blamed for "displaying all the national self-interest ... often ascribed to the British".[2] Schmidt's personal friendship with Giscard was not impaired. By 1979 their governments were rediscovering common ground, and were partners in the European Monetary System which Britain had refused to join.

Relations with Britain, indeed, remained a worry – however cordial they appeared to be on the surface. Schmidt was exasperated by the proposal of Mr Harold Wilson, made when he was still Prime Minister, that Britain should have a separate seat at the world energy conference. The Chancellor was beginning to develop a new asperity in the endless, fruitless discussions over the future of the EEC. He asked that German contributions, now four-fifths of the "net transfer" within that organization, should be used to further economic integration, and not to finance the extravagances of the less viable members among the Nine. He was referring to Britain in particular, and he had little sympathy with the British argument that too much money was being spent on helping European farmers and not enough on helping British industry.

Nor did he get on any better with James Callaghan, when the latter succeeded Wilson as Prime Minister. Schmidt, blunt and direct, has always prided himself on his commonsense, straight approach to problems; he could not be expected to relish Callaghan's brand of avuncular, bland joviality. Allegedly, the Chancellor called Callaghan's Foreign Secretary, Dr David Owen, a "brash lout".[3] Allegedly, too, the reason was Dr Owen's reference, in a newspaper interview, to "Franco-German idylls which never last long".[4] There was a lame official denial in Bonn; later it was stated that Schmidt had "only" said that Dr Owen was "a bit young" and sometimes "hyper-active".[5] A gentle reproof was added to the more abrasive one which may well have preceded it.

Once again, there was a sad awareness, on the German part, that British Governments – instead of being the best partners in Europe – tended to be the most awkward.

The change of government in Britain in May 1979 brought, paradoxically, a more relaxed atmosphere in Anglo-German relations – paradoxically, because Schmidt now had to deal with a Conservative administration, instead of a Labour Government represented along with his own SPD on all international socialist occasions. At his first meeting with the new British Prime

Minister, Mrs Margaret Thatcher, Schmidt found himself being sincerely complimented on the German tax system. He countered, smiling, with "You mustn't make me unpopular with my own party".

There were troubles with other allies. A Belgian television programme compared civil liberties in the Federal Republic with those in Spain, Chile and the Argentine. In the summer of 1977 there was harsh criticism of Schmidt's government for not extraditing Herbert Kappler, an aged and ailing former Nazi police chief in war-time Italy, who escaped from a prison-hospital in Rome while serving a life sentence for war-crimes. In November, Schmidt went to Rome for talks with the Italian Premier, Giulio Andreotti; afterwards he said that "the irritations of the past" were best forgotten. In March 1979, it was France's turn again; unkind words came from both the Gaullist leader, Jacques Chirac, and Georges Marchais of the Communist Party, who claimed that his country was being subjected to the domination of a Federal Republic which was economically and militarily too strong, and which was selling more arms than France was – a strange complaint indeed, this, coming from an apostle of European disarmament![6]

Sometimes Schmidt's patience snapped. Shortly before his meeting with Andreotti he gave an interview to the Italian paper, *La Reppublica*.[7] In it, he explained that "because I am sensitive, and want to remain so, I understand some of the preoccupations about us. What I find totally incomprehensible, however, is that such preoccupations are expressed always and only about the Federal Republic, and never about the communist dictatorship of the German Democratic Republic." He believed that this was due, quite simply, to envy, because the Federal Republic was so patently prosperous. In these critical European countries "Germany becomes a substitute for their own internal enemies".

There was plenty of reason for Schmidt's occasional display of irritation. Many Germans have become convinced that, whatever they say or do, they will be found to be in the wrong. Are they seeking a leadership role – for example, in the economic field? One finds a leading British economist proclaiming that "Germany won't lead Europe's revival".[8] Why not? His answers, coming from a Britain strike-ridden and industrially stagnant for years past, were truly astounding: German industry was "beginning to suffer from ageing equipment and an inability to deliver", there was "a severe shortage of skilled labour", the German "surplus in goods is already shrinking and has to pay for their holidays in the sun and their deficit in other services", and "the mark is so high that they cannot make a decent margin in export markets". And this came from the representative of a country which, but for North Sea oil, might have been very near economic and social collapse!

Then there was that persistent, agonizing problem of Nazi war-criminals. As the time approached for a final decision on prosecuting them – the Federal Government and Parliament had to decide by the end of 1979 if fresh prosecutions could be made possible by amending the Statute of Limitations – attacks on the Schmidt Government came from the most surprising quarters. The *Daily Telegraph* has generally been steadily sympathetic to German needs and hopes. Yet an editorial, in March 1979, claimed that the ruling Social Democrats had "created an opportunity to parade as uncompromising anti-Nazis, casting by imputation a totally unjustified slur on the Opposition". They were also "cashing in on German remorse" aroused by the television film of the "Holocaust", and were "encouraging an endless and sordid witch-hunt for scapegoats" and so "damaging Germany's image".[9] Here, truth was being stood on its head. The amending of the 1851 Statute, which laid down that criminals should go free if no charges were brought over a period of 20 years, was in no sense a "popular" measure; most Germans were proud of any liberal traditions which survived the Bismarckian as well as the Nazi era. Schmidt's Government was doing no more than organize a free vote in Parliament on this highly controversial and vexing issue. Had it done otherwise, it would surely have been accused of failing in its duty and its obligations to millions who were murdered by the Nazis, and millions more who survived bitter and brutal persecution.

One finds the Bonn correspondent of another leading British paper[10] comparing German democracy to "fried snowballs" and opining that "One morning, democracy will fail to appear at breakfast" (it would make, according to his analogy, a curious breakfast-dish). The same writer claimed that the Germans were all wrong to talk about a "Hitler wave" of literature about Nazism; it was "a healthy development" and Germans should not behave "like a giant searching for fleas" – nothing wrong, then, about books extolling Nazi Party hacks and Nazi war-heroes, or explaining that Hitler never knew about the concentration camps? This article carried a very long headline. It read: "Because they are afraid that at any moment it might kick

the bucket, the West Germans cosset their democracy, protect it
... They have brought it up like an only child, and now that it is
nearly thirty it is neurotic ..." British journalism used to be more
concise than this.

Schmidt and his Government may have been less worried by
this sort of thing than by difficulties with the United States. These
were pleasing to his ultra-left European critics, busily depicting
the Social Democrats as "new Nazis". The Federal Government
did indeed avoid open criticism of the United States after the final
fiasco of Vietnam; there were fears in Germany of a "Vietnam
situation" in Central Europe, not so much due to the Federal
Republic being a thirty year-old "neurotic" as to the sombre fact
of being in the front line of the Western Alliance. There was
some minor American concern over the supply of German
nuclear reactors, to be used for purely peaceful purposes by
Brazil. Schmidt was in Washington in July 1977, and listened to
American objections; in the event, the deal was still on.

But the Chancellor was concerned about President Carter's
stand on human rights; there was always the chance, as he saw it,
that this might increase repression in the Soviet Bloc. The Federal
Republic had a special interest in this question. In 1977, 55,000
ethnic Germans were allowed to leave East European countries,
against a total of 63,000 in the previous two years combined.
Here was a problem upon which the rest of the Western world
wasted next to no thought; the general reaction has been that if
"Hitler's War" left Germans stranded on the wrong side of the
post-war frontiers created by the Soviet Union, this was
unfortunate, possibly even sad. That was all. Schmidt signed an
agreement with Poland in October 1975 under which the Federal
Republic produced 2,300 million marks, in part a loan and in
part down-payment as restitution for victims of Nazism. In
return, Poland agreed to release more ethnic Germans; only
58,000 had been allowed to return to their mother-country
during the previous five years. Another 284,000 ethnic Germans
had applied to leave Poland, using the West German Red Cross
as intermediary. Poland now expected to be able to send back
125,000 in four years. Here, for Schmidt, was another small trick
won in the poker-game of European détente.

Poland was the main repository of ethnic Germans. Other East
European countries, like Rumania, Hungary and to a lesser
extent the Soviet Union, had speeded them on their way west,
after war ended in 1945. Poland had two reasons for keeping
Germans back. There were many thousands working in the coal

mines, a high proportion of them skilled and therefore valuable. There were others who were relatively well-educated and who could do all sorts of useful jobs; often, they were singletons who had been completely cut off from their families, which had sought refuge after 1945 in the Federal Republic. These people were stranded for up to thirty years; they could have safely been allowed to go, at any time. Poland suffered unbelievable misery from Nazi occupation, but the sadness of these isolated Germans should have been avoided.[11]

Schmidt's view has been that the problem of the ethnic Germans still in Eastern Europe can be resolved, within the limits and laborious workings of East–West détente. President Carter's stand on human rights, however, went far indeed beyond the question of isolated remnants of once thriving German communities in Eastern Europe. He was involved in implementation of the Helsinki Agreement, in seeking some relaxation of Soviet oppression of dissidents as well as of racial minorities, in making human rights a major political issue, all for good reasons. For Schmidt, too, the issue was broadened; the inhabitants of the East German Republic were part of the problem. Any government in Bonn must strive to help those who want to leave. How can this be done? By tact, combined with persistent pressure?

One is immediately embarked on the complicated subject of détente and East–West relations. Schmidt did not want to strike out a new line into this diplomatic minefield, although the Wehner-Bahr group in his own party was apparently pressing him to do so. In 1974, indeed, he had high hopes of expanding economic cooperation with the Soviet Union, and so obtaining concessions in the field of human relations in return. He met Brezhnev in Moscow in October, and discussed a grandiose concept with him; the West Germans would construct a major nuclear power station for the Russians at Kaliningrad (once upon a time, ironically, Koenigsberg and the pride of East Prussia), in return for a supply of nuclear power from it to West Berlin. And West Germany would supply gas pipes, in return for Soviet natural gas. Schmidt and Brezhnev certainly hit it off together, in a personal sense, but these plans had to be drastically revised, and in the next year Schmidt caused the leaders in the Kremlin some concern when he went to Peking at the end of October, and had a lengthy conversation with Chairman Mao. Through diplomatic channels he assured the Russians that this in no way indicated diminished interest in East–West détente in Europe.

Nor did it, although some voices were being loudly raised in criticism of the Soviet performance. One leading writer[12] pointed out that the Russians were holding up cultural exchanges between the two countries and were not honouring the Four Power Agreement on Berlin – they refused to have anything to do with non-political bodies in West Berlin like the Office for the Protection of the Environment and the Federal Archaeological Office, and protested when Berliners were included in West German delegations. Schmidt was philosophical; Brezhnev was in Bonn in May 1978, and Schmidt paid a return visit to Moscow. In his "State of the Nation" speech he made plain that East–West relations still left much to be desired.[13] But trade, at least, was pushed ahead; in 1978 the Federal Republic was the Soviet Union's best Western trading partner, with two-way trade worth over £10,000 million in a generally fair and useful exchange of Russian raw materials for West German industrial products.[14] The Federal Republic, for that matter, was East Germany's only worthwhile western trading partner, with two-way trade running at about £2,300 million a year.[15]

Rumours of continuing differences between Schmidt and President Carter proliferated during the first few months of 1979, but there was not much concrete evidence that relations were deteriorating. Carter's decision to defer production of the neutron bomb caused a shock in some quarters, and Franz Josef Strauss commented that, for the first time since the war, an American President had "openly knuckled under to a Russian Czar". For their part, the Federal Government refused to be the only European NATO country to house the new generation of American medium-range missiles. Willy Brandt warned that the "arms-race, in which everyone acts in the interest of national security, has brought about a situation in which the destruction of mankind is no longer an unrealistic prospect."[16] There were differences over the Chinese invasion of Vietnam in February 1979; Schmidt praised the Soviet reaction as restrained and "almost wise". There were differences, too, over the urgency of a conservationist energy policy; in Bonn, alarm mingled with contempt over Carter's endless procrastinations over curbing oil consumption and taking this first, essential step to strengthen the dollar. Schmidt, personally, made his impatience plain.

There were manful efforts to bridge these growing differences. President Carter was in Berlin in the summer of 1978, and exerted his simple but considerable charm – among other things, he pronounced that "Was immer sei, Berlin bleibt frei"

(Whatever happens, Berlin remains free). But the Berliners were much less impressed than when President Kennedy declared "Ich bin ein Berliner", fifteen years earlier. Schmidt emphasised that his government trusted in "the protective role and the leadership" of the United States "in both the economic and military spheres".[17] He promised full support of the United States in the meandering "Strategic Arms Limitation Talks" (SALT 2), which (remembering what Brandt had said a week earlier) he called "a matter of life and death". But, once again, he praised Brezhnev – this time for suggesting a non-aggression pact to be signed by the 35 signatories of the sadly inoperative Helsinki Agreement. And, once again, Europe's diplomatic corridors hummed with talk of the new, special relationship between Schmidt and Brezhnev. It was much less than that; Schmidt's ease in dealing with the Soviet leader stemmed from his innate self-confidence – perhaps a little, too, from personal recall of the superiority of German arms in the Second World War.

What was becoming plain early in 1979 was that the Federal Republic's somewhat ambivalent allies were eyeing Bonn with two very different thoughts in their minds. The first was that West German foreign policy was entering a new phase, in which the Federal Republic would espouse the old, pre-1959 Social Democratic philosophy of movement towards German reunification, even if this involved neutralization between East and West. The second thought was that the Federal Republic might shortly bid for leadership in Europe. These two opposed views were subtly complementary; for the second school of thought assumed that an unsuccessful West German bid for leadership in Europe would result in a switch to neutralization, by opting out of the Western Alliance. At this stage of history, these suspicions deserve only brief attention.

First, the thought that the Federal Republic will desert the West, and embark upon an "all-German" course of its own, is unworthy. But it is more relevant that it is absurd. "Neutralization" of the Federal Republic would leave it pitifully isolated, a fragment of the free world, seeking to come to terms with the whole gigantic might of the Soviet Bloc. Any West German statesman who knowingly contemplated the creation of such a situation would be a madman, or moron. Past German attempts to steer Europe – like a "bent" croupier at the roulette-wheel – have always ended in abject failure.

But there should be an emphasis on the word "knowingly"; any Federal Government, honestly wishing to push détente ahead, could lapse into grievous error. Two articles in the *Daily Telegraph*, by Robert Moss, are worth study in this context. Moss pointed out that the *eminence grise* of the Social Democratic Party, Egon Bahr, had talked very plainly ten years ago of the possibility of liquidating the Warsaw Pact and NATO, in order to create a new system of "collective security" in Central Europe.[18] This would have entailed the military neutralization of Poland, Czechoslovakia, Hungary and the East German Republic on one side of the Iron Curtain, and of Denmark, and the three little Benelux states and the Federal German Republic on the other.[19] Moss believed that Bahr had never given up his plans for this kind of "German solution" in Central Europe, and that Bahr had been in constant, and recent touch with the Russians – which could lead to a Soviet guarantee of a "bloc-free" Federal Republic similar in some respects to the Soviet guarantee of isolated West Berlin.

The same writer claimed[20] that the Social Democrats were bending, under left-wing pressures, towards accommodation with Moscow. Thus Egon Bahr, now secretary-general of the SPD, had declared that he favoured "liberation movements in Africa, but not in Eastern Europe" – where they might constitute "a threat to world peace".[21] Then Schmidt himself had, allegedly, persuaded other Western leaders to accept the revolutionary regime which had just ousted the Shah of Iran. Another straw in the wind was a statement by Herbert Wehner, chairman of the Parliamentary party of the SPD, that the Soviet Union's military might was essentially "defensive", and that East–West détente might, some day, lead to "confederation" between the two German states.[22] Nobody, of course, could contemplate such a confederation coming into existence, unless the Federal Republic left NATO. But Wehner, on this as on other occasions, was abrupt in his refusal to explain himself – a school of thought was growing up which believed that his short temper was becoming a real liability to Schmidt.

Here, then, was one current of suspicion of German intentions. The second was that the Federal Republic was about to bid for leadership in Western Europe. An American magazine quoted "a Schmidt adviser" as saying that "Schmidt is a man who cannot live in a vacuum. If there is a leadership gap in the West, he is ready to help fill it ... he clearly sees himself as No. 1 in Europe".[23] German commentators have confirmed this view; one leading West German newspaper believed that "West Germany has joined Britain, France and the United States as leaders of the West. Bonn, an acknowledged economic giant and political dwarf since the sixties, has assumed a new role".[24] Part of this role was to avert another Cold War, to maintain ties with the Soviet Bloc as a whole, and in particular improve relations with the East German State.

In the Bundestag, Schmidt said that Europe was now the second safest continent in the world, after Australia,[25] and the Federal Republic had never been more secure. On more than one occasion, he insisted that the Federal Republic was "no more than a medium-sized power".[26] He repeated his view that the Soviet Union was behaving responsibly and did not want war, and suggested that there was more to East–West equilibrium than the balance of military power. He urged the need for continuing progress towards disarmament, through the SALT 2 talks, which had just been roundly denounced by the House of Representatives Armed Services Committee in Washington.[27] His words were doubtless intended to comfort, but was his confidence justified?

The Warsaw Pact summer manoeuvres in 1978 showed an increased concentration on attack, rather than defence. They showed that new Soviet aircraft and tanks were specifically designed for an offensive role; "back-up" exercises indicated that full mobilization could be effected in a period of from four to six weeks, instead of the previously accepted ten. A NATO conference in Bonn confirmed that the present level of Warsaw Pact forces far exceeded the requirements of defence, and constituted a direct threat to the Federal Republic and Western Europe.[28] The Inspector-General of the Bundeswehr, General Harald Wust, was quoted as saying that "in the mutual balanced force reduction talks in Vienna, Moscow's objective is basically to consolidate by treaty its conventional forces' superiority and the corresponding military disparity in Central Europe".

This disparity was obvious enough. A survey of February 1979 gave these figures:[29]

The Soviet Bloc maintains 58 battle-trained divisions in East Germany, Poland and Czechoslovakia as its potential strike-force against Western Europe. NATO has 28 divisions (some of them under-strength). The Soviet Bloc forces can be reinforced, within a few days, by 33 more Soviet divisions, giving a total of 91 divisions. The United States is currently considering planning reinforcement, by 6 divisions, of NATO forces in Europe. They would be flown across the Atlantic in a period of sixteen days, and would bring NATO strength up to 34 divisions.

The Warsaw Pact has 19,000 tanks in the front line, and another 8,500 Soviet tanks could be made immediately available. NATO has 6,500 tanks. The Warsaw Pact has 2,800 combat aircraft; another 1,100 could be flown at once from the Soviet Union. NATO has a maximum of 2,230 combat aircraft available, which would include French planes which are not in fact under NATO command. The disparity in artillery is just as great: the Warsaw Pact has 5,800 guns and 1,200 multiple rocket-launchers, against NATO's 2,600 guns and 220 rocket-launchers.

In 1978 alone the Soviet Union built 7,000 tanks, including more than 2,000 of the improved and now ultra-modern T.72s. This brought the Soviet tank force up to about 50,000. Two new long-range Soviet weapons have been developed which could be used in Europe – their latest "Backfire" aircraft, with a range of 1,800 miles, and the 2,500 mile SS.20 missiles, which can be fitted with nuclear warheads. Perhaps of even greater concern for NATO is the Warsaw Pact submarine fleet, estimated at over 260 immediately available and 380 in all. For Western military experts are arguing that strategic planning is entering a new phase, in which access to raw materials is as operative a factor as military strength.[30] The Soviet Union has, in addition, over 80 cruisers and destroyers, equipped with nuclear missiles; two aircraft-carriers in service and a third under construction; and an ocean-going merchant marine of 4,500 vessels, many of which are used for spying, shadowing and military transport.

NATO, moreover, has become chronically short of money. When the NATO Defence Ministers met in Brussels in December 1978, they failed to pass the infrastructure budget for the next five years, totalling £3,000 million.[31] The West German Defence Minister, Hans Apel, said that his country's defence budget was already fully allocated – and the Federal Republic was the most solvent of the principal contributors! It was revealed that at least five NATO members – Denmark, Italy, Greece, Holland, Turkey – had failed to honour the 1977 NATO agreement to increase defence expenditure by a minimum of 3 per cent. In addition, Canada and Portugal were asking to be allowed to reduce their expenditure. In February 1979 came another blow to NATO: its south-eastern flank was deprived of the limited "cover" supplied by the Central Treaty Organization (CENTO). Iran and Pakistan quitted the organization and Turkey, in a state of near-bankruptcy, was left as its isolated and sole surviving regional member. Western defence now ended at Mount Ararat. In Bonn, the Federal Minister of Defence, Hans Apel, admitted that

NATO's southern flank was now a serious problem for the alliance, and that European interests in the Middle East were becoming dangerously exposed.[32]

It would not be unnatural for any government in Bonn – given the frightening weakness of NATO – to "reinsure" by seeking to develop better relations with its Eastern neighbours and, very particularly, with the Soviet Union. The picture of Western impotence and disunity (one should not forget the petty squabbles within the EEC and the sad lack of cooperation between the Nine and the United States) is becoming alarming. One opinion was: "Western deterrence is being dangerously reduced. Europe is that much closer to the awful alternatives, submission or destruction – with or without American intervention. And America is being brought closer to the risk of devastation for an ally that cannot be persuaded to make the necessary effort to defend herself, although this is well within her capabilities."[33] Submission or destruction – these alternatives must loom very large in the minds of West German Ministers. For their country is in the front line, and will inevitably be hit first, and hardest.

The history of the next years will probably show that sympathy for the special situation of the Federal Republic will be well-founded, but that suspicions of West German good faith will be unjustified. The overwhelming majority of West Germans believe in the Western Alliance and in indissoluble bonds between the Federal Republic and the rest of Western Europe. The same is true of an overwhelming majority of members of the political parties in the Bundestag. Once upon a time, there were German right-wing nationalists ready to play off Russia against the West, and left-wing Communists who wanted alliance with the Soviet Union unequivocally, for ideological reasons. Extremists of right and left can no longer secure a single seat in Parliament. The left-wingers in the SPD will not mount a challenge to the community as a whole, but their preoccupation with a policy of closer relations with Eastern Europe does, indeed, merit continuing study, and some concern. Adenauer believed in operating, where East–West relations were concerned, from a position of strength. NATO possessed such strength in Adenauer's day. His successors, Erhard, Kiesinger and Brandt, evolved the concept of "small steps", which could ease the lot of the people of Berlin and of the DDR. But NATO's condition is such that it would be unwise to embark on a more grandiose policy of movement towards German "confederation" at this moment in time. Nothing would be gained, and Western solidarity could be destroyed.

Still, one should not forget that Willy Brandt developed his own concept of détente, partly as a result of the failure of his Western allies to do anything to stop the building of the Berlin Wall. Western failure today is on an alarming scale, covering defence planning within NATO, economic planning within the EEC, political cooperation among the European powers and between them and the United States. Could a successor to Willy Brandt draw his conclusions from all this, and evolve an amended version of détente which would lead to German neutralization? German "confederation", perhaps leading to full reunification, seems a tempting bait.

One observer who felt that it was such a bait was Conor Cruise O'Brien, the former Irish Cabinet Minister who is now Editor of the *Observer* newspaper. After attending a conference of the Aspen Institute in West Berlin, he had this to say:[34]

> Beneath all, though in a perspective of many years ahead, lay the will towards the reunification of Germany: "the division of our country is not acceptable". It was "not a topical question", but remained alive "as a moral issue". If the West refused to play the reunification card – an opposition politician thought – "the Russians might play it". The same speaker warned against "suicidal appeasement" of the Russians, but thought that "suicide is none the less possible" ... The prevailing and authoritative view was that unification was a real though "sleeping" issue, that one day it would wake up, and that even in its sleep it had a powerful bearing on the formation of German policy.

Sometimes, indeed, it looks as if the chances of the two Germanys drawing closer together are improving. In November, 1978, new "transit" agreements were signed in East Berlin. On the face of it, they looked promising. A new autobahn is to be built from West Berlin to Hamburg, costing £325 million (of course, the Federal Republic will foot the bill). The canal network round Teltow, in south Berlin, will be reopened, and will cut the turnaround of ships by over 24 hours (Bonn will pay for this too; the bill will be £25 million). There will be improvements to East German roads and canals, linking West Berlin with West Germany; to finance these, Bonn will pay road tolls of £142 million in 1979, against £122 million in 1978. The Federal Republic also agreed to pay about £50 million to offset the blocked accounts in East Germany of East German old-age pensioners who have been allowed to settle in West Germany. All of this might seem to add up to negotiated blackmail, costing the Federal Republic at least £420 million. But the Schmidt Government was pleased; it had the money, and it was prepared to use it to improve communications with its East German neighbour.

That neighbour remains outwardly as unattractive as ever. There are over one million mines strewn along its interzonal border with the Federal Republic, and in 1978 only 186 East Germans managed to escape across it, against over 300 in the previous year. Another 200 East Germans somehow found their way into West Berlin, in spite of the grim, forbidding barrier of the Wall; but that compared with over 400 in 1977. Nearly 3,000 more East Germans left the country, usually absconding from holidays on the Black Sea or Baltic coasts via neutral countries. One writer has euphemistically explained that East Germans suffer "from a lack of travel opportunities".[35] What he contrived to avoid saying in plain language has been better expressed: "East Germans are able to spend their holidays anywhere from Ulan Bator to Havana, but are denied access to the West except under the most pressing family circumstances, or if they are old-age pensioners."[36]

More than 50,000 East Germans a year are courageous enough to apply for emigration visas. Helsinki and human rights mean nothing to their rulers, but money does and they are prepared to "trade" human bodies. In 1978 about 1,000 East German citizens were bartered for sums ranging from £8,000 for an ordinary industrial worker to £32,000 for a scientist or well-qualified doctor.[37] Many of them had been serving prison sentences for alleged "political crimes". Since 1964, over 14,000 East Germans have been ransomed in this way, and the cost has been estimated at more than £350 million. The Chairman of the ruling Socialist Unity Party has justified this system by claiming that "a crime must be assessed by the damage done to the state" – so the Federal Republic has merely been paying swingeing fines for the men released from East German gaols.[38]

The East German authorities have introduced military training into their schools, beginning with fourteen year-olds. The Christian churches have protested, and in some places young people have tried to help, by distributing leaflets carrying the texts of sermons on this subject. In September 1978 a Protestant pastor, Rolf Guenther, burnt himself to death in protest in front of a congregation of 400 in his Dresden church.[39] He was the second to do so. Other clergy have been arrested; so have a number of East Germans who have demanded that human rights should be respected within the terms of the Helsinki Agreement. The DDR remains a police state, only of a more genteel kind than before. Significantly, visitors notice the total lack of animation; East Germans creep about their business, unsmiling, and their cities "look grim and neglected" with "the air polluted with the stink of low quality petrol and the smoke from an L. S. Lowry landscape, of high, smoking chimneys".[40]

East Germany's rulers are determined that their system shall survive. They have built up a surprisingly strong industrial state, with cheap housing and basic foodstuffs, sports, state educational and health services, a new and efficient technocracy, and so many men in uniform that another rising of the kind that took place in 1953 is out of the question. But the East German State can only survive with Soviet approval, and this is the reason why it so often plays the part of jackal to the Russian bear. Along with Cubans, the Germans act as the principal agents of the Soviet Union in seeking to disrupt Western democracy and Western influence in the Third World. The East Germans have collaborated in the training of Palestinian terrorists. They have been active in Angola and Mozambique, and have helped to organize attacks on Rhodesia, South-West Africa and Zaire. Their "advisers" are present in Ethiopia, Afghanistan, Iran, and the South Yemen (Aden); in the last, they have established a secret police force along Gestapo lines. It is not surprising that most West Germans, particularly the young, have come to regard the DDR as a strange, unfriendly, foreign country, and that the number of visits by West Germans – still increasing up to 1978 – is expected to drop in the years ahead. In spite of détente, increased trade and those "small steps" to which both Brandt and Schmidt have attached so much importance, Germany looks like becoming more divided than before.

The division of their country may be one of the less palpable reasons for a nation-wide feeling of fear. "Fear" may, indeed, be too strong a word; the German *Angst* is more expressive, denoting an amalgam of fear, anxiety and uneasiness. A study at the Munich University Institute of Psychology showed that a general anxiety-neurosis was a principal symptom of the millions of people with psychological problems (the figure could be as high as eight million).[41] A disturbing common factor was acceptance that psychological stress was altogether natural. This seems strange, indeed, in a country so obviously prosperous and successful. Yet this nation-wide *Angst* was a fact.

This was forcibly indicated in the spring of 1979 when the "Three Mile Island" nuclear near-disaster occurred at Harrisburg in Pennsylvania. The Federal Republic is the biggest producer of nuclear energy in Europe, with a dozen nuclear power plants and an installed capacity of 9,000 megawatts. The Federal Government has invested £8,000 million in nuclear research and development, and capacity was due to be doubled by the end of 1981.

Even before Harrisburg, a major campaign was launched by environmentalists to block further nuclear development. There was particular opposition to the creation of a "graveyard" for nuclear waste near Gorleben in Lower Saxony, close to the East German border. Orders for the installation of 10,000 megawatts' capacity were held up, partly by legal action. Harrisburg caused a gut-reaction of alarm, and made the building of any more nuclear power plants unlikely, although foundations had been laid and much money spent. This could mean a serious energy problem in the future: the Federal Republic has an expanding highly-industrialized economy, no oil of its own and the price of oil is bound to rise, perhaps sensationally.

West German youth has been much involved in the nuclear power controversy, and is in a general sense at least as much affected by the overall *Angst* complex as any other section of society. One writer felt that Germany was in process of producing a "lost generation" of young people, who "believe they are living in a society where all is not well, where the values of human life are disdained ... with which they cannot identify".[42] He went on: "There are tens of thousands with no ambition to be integrated into this society, for whom external forms mean as little as inner discipline, and who demonstrate their infinite contempt for capitalist society ... They are the alienated." Some of them sought "a kind of anarchic freedom"; most accepted "their university years as a more or less desolate period of stress, which one goes through as a valley of tears".

A Swiss professor went so far as to suggest that the Federal Republic was breeding "a generation of cowards" (*Duckmauesern*), with a "kindergarten mentality".[43] But there was one good reason for apprehension on the campuses: since 1975, nearly half of the unemployed have been under the age of 30, and there is a likelihood of increased unemployment among the young in the years ahead. From 1980 onwards, the number of school-leavers will be exceptionally high; they were born during a period of buoyant optimism and economic expansion. By 1982, perhaps only 50 per cent of even the best qualified school-leavers may be assured of employment.[44]

Nothing is so unsettling for the young as the thought that their educational certificates and university degrees, however good, may not bring a worthwhile job. What, then, is the point of all the work done for their examinations? A former Bonn Correspondent of *The Times*, returning to Germany ten years after leaving it, found "economic anxiety" among all sections of the community: "The most striking phenomenon for me on returning to Bonn was the discovery of wide-spread concern about the country's economic future, when it is envied everywhere abroad as a shining example of stability and strength."[45] Put in crude terms, the Federal Republic was, in a mechanical sense, too successful. An expanding economy was able to absorb three million foreign workers as "the hewers of wood and drawers of water", then managed to modernize, to rationalize means of production, and to save labour. In this continuing process, the labour force is in a state of perpetual uncertainty about its terms of existence. Over-efficiency, improbable as it may sound, is seen as one of the perils of an age of plenty. Even civil servants and other well-established employees must worry about their future; *Angst* afflicts all, or nearly all.

One view is that the almost frenzied activity of the present-day Germans is a form of escapism, from the uncertainties of the present, the fears of the future – and, as in the rest of Europe, inflation has become one of the most potent of these – and the menacing shadows of the past. Up until very recently, the general tendency has been to ignore those shadows, or pretend they never existed. Among the young a degree of resentment was beginning to show itself – why should they, the young, feel responsible for the crimes of their grandfathers? Even among Chancellor Schmidt's generation it was felt that the time had come to banish the past.

Somewhat sensationally, the showing of the television film *Holocaust* changed the opinions of a great many Germans overnight. The film was shown on Channel 3 of West German television from 22 to 26 January 1979. There was careful preparation for this; on 11 January, all West German networks ran a 45-minute documentary on pre-1933 anti-semitism in

Germany and Austria and, on 18 January, they showed a 90-minute documentary of Hitler's "Final Solution" for the destruction of European Jewry. Such films had been shown before; there was complete uncertainty as to what impact *Holocaust*, with its human story, would make on the German public.

In the event, 32 per cent of viewers tuned in on 22 January, and the number climbed steadily. Just on half of all viewers saw one or more of the five episodes, or roughly 20 million people. Two-thirds of them declared themselves deeply moved; 35 per cent of people writing or phoning in were afraid that the film would do harm to present-day Germany; 14 per cent thought the film misleading or even "disgusting". All television stations opened special telephone-lines for enquiries, which poured in; there were 30,000 calls to Cologne alone. Three per cent of those who telephoned were anti-semitic.[46]

In the Bundestag, Schmidt said that the film would force people to re-examine their moral attitudes.[47] This was indeed what a great many Germans were doing. Many who telephoned were in tears; many who wrote in explained that they were at last able to understand "what it was all like" – hitherto they had been given cold facts and figures, now they were able to identify with those who had suffered. The Chancellor had drawn his own moral from the story of Nazi persecution in an earlier speech (he had, as it happened, already seen *Holocaust* in America). Speaking in the Cologne Synagogue, to mark the fortieth anniversary of the 1938 "Reich Crystal Night" pogrom, Schmidt said that Nazi persecution began:

> with the search for scapegoats ... with the use of force against books and property. The use of force against human beings was then a natural consequence. It began with contempt for the dignity of our fellow-men, with the shouting-down of people voicing a different opinion. It continued with the sweeping condemnation of the whole democratic system. The natural consequence was finally murder itself.[48]

The moral which he drew was that the dignity and inviolability of the citizen and of his opinions was the "yardstick of freedom"; self-discipline was needed to safeguard freedom, but the evil of anarchism would not be combated with the evil of an anti-liberal State. Subtly, Schmidt linked the story of Nazi persecution with the need for the Federal Republic to defend its democratic freedoms today, whether the enemy was a dyed-in-the-wool neo-Nazi or an idealistic but misguided young terrorist.

Schmidt, it seems, generally has the right word for the right occasion. His popularity-rating, among his own people, has never been higher. Abroad, he has taken his place among the "Big Four" (the Presidents of the United States and France, and Britain's Prime Minister) as a matter of course, and his "image" is that of a man whose occasional crudeness of diction detracts little from the fact that he knows exactly where he is going. Early in March 1979 there were forebodings of trouble in his coalition Government. Willy Brandt was only just taking up his duties again, after a long illness. The Foreign Minister, Hans-Dietrich Genscher, had suffered a recurrence of heart trouble. Herbert Wehner's views on East–West relations were causing concern, and there was even talk of a rift in the coalition.

One critic thought that resignation was spreading, and "though the party still remains in power, it does so increasingly with a bad conscience".[49] There was no real planning for the future; constituency parties were suffering most from this. There was a dearth of talent, and too much depended on the Schmidt-Brandt-Wehner triumvirate. There were doubts whether this triumvirate was as united as it had been, and the SPD was perhaps relying too much upon it. Even before mid-1979, Schmidt was much exercised by the problem of holding the SPD together, and giving all possible encouragement on the side to his Free Democratic allies. He had to compete with a paradoxical situation. Normally, a political party seeks votes for itself; it does not have to dissipate its energies in keeping another party in being. Schmidt, an experienced campaigner, must know that the failure of the FDP to beat the "five per cent clause" would put the CDU into power – perhaps for a long time.

Still, early in 1979, the SPD emerged unshaken from two key *Land* elections, in Berlin and the Rhine-Palatinate, actually gaining 4 per cent more votes in the latter while the CDU lost over 6 per cent. More important, the Free Democrats more than held their own, uncomfortably aware that they must survive in the *Laender* if they are to continue as the "third force" in Bonn. There, the Government majority was down to eight, but the coalition could survive up to the next Federal elections and retained the chance of winning once more in them.

Schmidt, then, is fifth in a line of Federal Chancellors who have ruled with determination and sense – it is almost comical to reflect that he was called, six years ago, "historically outdated" and was even compared to Kaiser Wilhelm II as egotist and autocrat![50] His five years in office have been unspectacular; and how should this be otherwise? There have been no dramatic decisions to take, although one at least may lie only a short way ahead – Schmidt has himself forecast an early, major step forward in creating a more united European community.[51] What a German head of government most needs to offer today is rational thinking, sound administration, moderation, commonsense, toleration. Schmidt used not to be a tolerant man; he has progressed.

Adenauer won back for his people sovereignty and self-respect. His Chancellorship achieved a truly remarkable breakthrough, but it should not be allowed to dwarf the achievements of his successors. Erhard gave the Federal Republic an economic philosophy which, paradoxically, arouses some contempt at home today, but only admiration and envy abroad. His Chancellorship was undistinguished, for his best work had already been done during his long tenure of the post of Minister of Economics. But he developed the practices of Cabinet solidarity and Cabinet responsibility to Parliament, and Kiesinger carried Parliamentarianism a stage further in bringing Social and Christian Democrats into coalition. There will always be tough talking at election-time, but the old, deep animosities between different social classes, and their representatives, may have gone for ever.

Brandt gave social democracy its first chance in 40 years to determine Germany's future. He helped, indeed, to frame a new sort of social democracy in his country, middle-of-the-road, representing the whole people and not a section of society. He built on the beginnings of Ostpolitik which had taken place under Erhard and Kiesinger, and at least pushed the door to better East–West relations ajar. Schmidt has continued to build on the foundations created by his predecessors. After its first 30 years as a State, one can only say that the Federal Republic has been fortunate indeed in its rulers, all men of intelligence, understanding and dedication to duty. And there has been another break-through in the last decade of German post-war history. Schmidt once said: "I don't think much of the term 'world prestige' and I don't wish to use it. It reminds me of bygone days up to the time of Wilhelm II. I don't think we Germans should wear a helmet with feathers on top. I'll stick to the cap I've been wearing for ten years or more."[52] Schmidt's small, peaked cap is very much "of the people". So is Schmidt; so was Brandt. With the horrible exception of Hitler, it has almost always been patricians or comfortably established members of the middle class who have ruled Germany in the past. Men "of the people" have a special chance of consolidating German democracy.

Naturally, problems remain. Those of a material nature will be solved, whether it is the future of the isolated and forlorn foreign workers, the combating of unemployment which hovers round the million mark, the housing of perhaps half a million homeless – in spite of a remarkable record of building, the expansion of the population creates a permanent shortage of homes. One writer called the Federal Republic "one of the most successful societies in Europe":

> West Germany has all but buried the fanatical excesses of the thirties. It is a society that avoids the pernicious class antagonism of the British, the almost cyclical revolutionary fury of the French, the ruinous competition between big business and big labor of the Italians – and that is becoming more detached about its own cult of *Vaterland.* Germany, Schmidt has said repeatedly, does not seek political leadership in Europe. But the role may be thrust upon it by the weakness of other Governments and the irrepressible energy of the German economy.[53]

Certainly, no other European country can rival the Federal Republic's material economic and social progress.

Its psychological problems will be more difficult to deal with. Recently, the eminently level-headed Federal President, Walter Scheel, touched on this subject.[54] He said that Germans turned discussion of every problem, however small, into a wrangle over principles which was never resolved: "We fight so long and so hard for the outward forms of democracy that we scarcely have time and energy left for democratic content." One writer put this down to an ingrained German fear of their own history – this brought "alarmist arguments and language" in Parliament and the political parties, and this was why "the whole tone of debate is shrill".[55] A particular feature of this debate is self-criticism – an extreme example was provided by the playwright, Erich Kuby, who called the Federal Republic "a boring and dangerous state", whose citizens were intellectually the most isolated in the world, interested only in their material needs and the victims of a sated stupefaction.[56]

The Nazi past is perpetually obtrusive. One finds so competent an observer as the writer Eugen Kogon writing confidently, three years ago, that the "ugly German" has become a mere cliché – for young Germans have been growing up uninhibited by the "burden of the past" and uninterested in the accusation of collective guilt which the Allies mistakenly laid at the door of the whole German people.[57] This sounds convincing, but the image of the "ugly German" remains very much alive. In 1978 it became, once again, a matter of obsessive interest in the Federal Republic, and those Germans who objected to *Holocaust* early in 1979 were mainly concerned with the possibility of yet another wave of anti-German feeling in the outside world. One paper even produced a major article for the fifteen million German holiday-makers, dealing with the "anti-German prejudices they are most likely to encounter" and suggesting answers to the sort of allegations they could expect.[58] Anti-German feeling, indeed, tends to come in waves, provoked by the written word, or the spoken word on radio and television. It is cyclical, and it will continue, for the Nazi era produced dimensions of destruction, suffering and residual bitterness which cannot be forgotten for a long time to come. The "ugly German" remains the symbol of non-acceptance. This can, in turn, breed a new resentment, among generations of guiltless Germans who want only to get on with being good citizens of their country and of Europe.

It is presumptuous to try to "strike a balance" in the affairs of other nations. There is an obvious temptation to do this with the Germans, and a particular reason. Whether they like it or not, the Germans became the problem-children of Europe, after their part in two world wars and a Nazi era. All sorts of other nations, therefore, are acutely interested in what the "new Germany" is, and what it is likely to become. To them, the Germans have brilliant, or nightmarish potentialities; nobody would think in quite the same way about, for instance, the British or the French.

The dangers which threaten the Federal Republic (which remains the only legitimate representative of the German people as a whole) have been outlined in this book. There is the danger of it being drawn into the Soviet orbit, of "Finlandization" and the loss of true independence and identity. There is the danger of frustration, resulting from the division of a great people by a world dominated by two rival super-powers, building up into a destructive explosion of feeling – with too many possible consequences to be analysed here. There is the danger of a fruitless German search for its own soul. Then there are all the other, conventional dangers which threaten other Western democracies: stark materialism, inflation, waning self-confidence, political stagnation bringing mental atrophy, envy, malice and resentment against all established authority.

Such dangers should not be ignored, but a book about the thirty years of the Federal Republic is a book about hope. Five Federal Chancellors have consolidated Parliamentary democracy and the rule of law. They have defended human freedoms, and the independence of the press and other media may have been the most important of these. They have eradicated militarism, and kept political extremism under close control. They have encouraged popular participation in the affairs of the nation – of course, as in other countries, this has not gone far enough, but the West German citizen today goes to the polls, values his own opinions and even asserts them through the columns of the press. How different, indeed, from the Nazi or even the Wilhelmian eras! Then, the great mass of citizens were mere units, digits, in the State.

Under these five Chancellors, the Federal Republic has been a loyal ally and partner within NATO and the European Community. It has made what restitution it could for Hitler's crimes. Its people show an increasing patience and forbearance, which used to be less apparent among their forefathers. It is revealing that, with the Baader-Meinhof terrorists at their deadly work, there has been no real campaign for the re-introduction of the death penalty. In spite of fear and uncertainty, the Germans of today are grateful for what has been done for them, with their own help; public opinion polls show that a big majority consider the present to be the best period in German history.

Perhaps the most important achievement of all has been what – for lack of a better definition – might be called the "new normality". One French historian noted that "West German society is becoming increasingly similar to that of other societies, like that of France. Take an article on unemployment among the young, for instance, get rid of two or three local references, translate it into French and publish it in a French newspaper. Nobody will notice that it is a translation from German."[59] Or take this description of the German young:

> They are not saddled with the burden of the past that their parents bear. They are not inappropriately nationalistic in their outlook. In common with young people in other industrialized countries, they are

international in outlook, keen on individual and group friendships, inclined towards peace and friendship. They are not unduly demanding in their expectations. They are cheerful in their own company, and in that of others of their age. They are unconventional in their choice of clothing and behaviour. They are sporting. They are critical or even sceptical about the Establishment. At all events, they are not comformist in the way that young people in Germany once were.[60]

And one short, telling statement of fact: "I looked from the Swiss border to that of Denmark, and couldn't find a single, 'typical', arrogant, monocled 'Prussian officer' in the Bundeswehr".[61] How many grisly phantoms of past German history are disposed of in that one sentence!

The Germans, in short, have become very much like their European counterparts, in their habits and interests, their fears, loves and hates, their way of thinking and of expressing themselves. They are much as we are, belong with us, and have been accepted by us – back into a European fold which needs them badly. They should be made welcome there, without reservation. Their "new normality" is normality re-won; and that, maybe, is the biggest achievement of all of the 30 year-old Federal Republic.

1. John Palmer. *The Guardian*, 21 December 1978.
2. Ibid.
3. *Der Spiegel*, 17 February 1979.
4. Siegfried Buschschluter. *The Guardian*, 20 February 1979.
5. Ibid.
6. Michael Field. *Daily Telegraph*, 15 March 1979.
7. *La Reppublica*, 7 October 1977.
8. Sir Frederick Catherwood. *Sunday Times*, 24 September 1978.
9. *Daily Telegraph*, 16 March 1979.
10. James Fenton. *The Guardian*, 30 October 1978.
11. The author, on one visit to Poland, stayed at a hotel in Wroclaw (formerly Breslau). He complimented one of the staff on her excellent German, and she promptly burst into tears. She was German, one of the half-million or so stranded in Poland and not allowed to leave.
12. Guenther von Well. *Journal of the West German Society of International Affairs*, October 1976.
13. Helmut Schmidt, in speech to the Bundestag, 13 March 1978.
14. *Newsweek*, 12 March 1979.
15. Helmut Schmidt, in speech to the Bundestag, 13 March 1978.

16. Report of the Brandt International Commission on Development Affairs, 1 March 1979.
17. Helmut Schmidt, in speech to the Bundestag, 8 March 1979.
18. Robert Moss. *Daily Telegraph*, 18 September 1978.
19. Moss pointed out that the "Bahr Plan" was explained to the American strategist, Walter Hahn, in 1969, but first published in the magazine *Orbis* in 1973.
20. Robert Moss. *Daily Telegraph*, 19 March 1979.
21. Ibid.
22. David Shears. *Daily Telegraph*, 20 March 1979.
23. *Newsweek*, 12 March 1979.
24. Erich Hauser. *Frankfurter Rundschau*, 19 January 1979.
25. Helmut Schmidt, in speech to the Bundestag, 9 March 1979.
26. Thus, most recently, Peter Jenkins, in *The Guardian*, 6 April 1979.
27. This Committee reported that the SALT 2 proposals favoured the maintenance, and even increase of existing Soviet military superiority in Europe.
28. Bonn Correspondent of the London *Times*, 11 August 1978.
29. Berlin newspaper, *Der Tagesspiegel*, 21 February 1979.
30. Thus Dr Christoph Bertram, Director of the International Institute of Strategic Studies, in the London *Times*, 11 August 1978.
31. Clare Hollingworth. *Daily Telegraph*, 14 March 1979.
32. Hans Apel on the Second German Television Programme, 21 January 1979.
33. R. H. C. Steed. *Daily Telegraph*, 28 February 1979.
34. Conor Cruise O'Brien. *The Observer*, 4 March 1979.
35. Jonathan Steele. *Socialism with a German Face*. London, 1977.
36. Anthony Robinson. *Financial Times*, 21 March 1979.
37. Leslie Colitt. *Financial Times*, 11 December 1978.
38. Michel Meyer. *Freedom Purchase-Trade in People in Germany*. Paris, 1977.
39. The London *Times*, 20 September 1978.
40. Anthony Robinson. *Financial Times*, 21 March 1979.
41. Karl Stankiewicz. *Frankfurter Neue Presse*, 22 June 1978.
42. Kurt Sontheimer. *Deutsche Zeitung*, 7 July 1978.
43. Professor Hansjuerg Steinlin, speaking to journalists in Bonn, 10 January 1978.
44. Georg Benz. *Frankfurter Hefte*, 1976 (No. 4).
45. Charles Hargrove. The London *Times*, 18 August 1978.
46. Summary in *Association of Jewish Refugees* monthly magazine, London, March 1979.
47. Helmut Schmidt, in speech to Bundestag, 24 January 1979.
48. Helmut Schmidt, in speech in Cologne Synagogue, 9 November 1978.
49. Wolfgang Manersberg. *Koelner Stadt-Anzeiger*, 7 March 1979.
50. Helmut Wolfgang Kahn. *Helmut Schmidt*. Hamburg, 1973.
51. Helmut Schmidt, in article in the *Financial Times*, 2 January 1979.
52. Helmut Schmidt, in interview on West German Television, 30 July 1976.
53. Clyde Farnsworth. *New York Times Magazine*, 2 May 1976.
54. Walter Scheel, in speech at Bonn University, December 1978.
55. Günter Gillessen. *Frankfurter Allgemeine Zeitung*, 28 February 1978.
56. Erich Kuby. *Frankfurter Hefte*, 1976 (No. 4).
57. Eugen Kogon. *Frankfurter Hefte*, 1976 (No. 11).
58. Helmut Herles. *Frankfurter Allgemeine Zeitung*, 3 August 1978.

59. Professor Alfred Grosser. *Welt der Arbeit*, 14 December 1978.
60. Eugen Kogon. *Frankfurter Hefte*, 1976 (No. 11).
61. Walter Henry Nelson. *Germany Rearmed*. New York, 1972.

Bibliography

ABSHAGEN, Karl-Heinz. *Schuld und Verhaengnis*. Stuttgart, 1961. Union Verlag.

ADENAUER, Konrad. *Memoirs*.
  Vol. 1. London, 1966. Weidenfeld & Nicolson.
  Vol. 2. Stuttgart, 1966. Deutsche Verlagsanstalt.
  Vol. 3. Stuttgart, 1967. Deutsche Verlagsanstalt.
  Vol. 4. Stuttgart, 1968. Deutsche Verlagsanstalt.

ALEXANDER, Edgar. *Adenauer and the New Germany*. New York, 1957. Farrar, Straus & Cudahy.

ALLEMANN, Fritz René. *Bonn ist nicht Weimar*. Cologne, 1956. Kiepenhauer & Witsch.

ALTMANN, Rudiger. *Das Erbe Adenauer's*. Munich, 1963. Kindler Verlag.

ARNTZ, Helmut (Editor). *Regierung Adenauer, 1949–1963*. Wiesbaden, 1963. Franz Steiner Verlag.

ASHKENAZI, Abraham. *Reformpartei und Aussenpolitik*. Cologne, 1968. Westdeutscher Verlag.

AUGSTEIN, Rudolf. *Konrad Adenauer*. London, 1964. Secker & Warburg.

BALFOUR, Michael & MAIR, John. *Four Power Control in Germany and Austria*. London, 1956. Oxford University Press.

BARING, Arnulf. *Aussenpolitik in Adenauer's Kanzler-Demokratie*. Munich, 1969. Oldenbourg.

BAUER, Otto. *Die illegale Partei*. Paris, 1939.

BECKER, Jillian. *Hitler's Children*. London, 1977. Michael Joseph.

BERGHAHN, V. R. *Germany and the Approach of War in 1914*. London, 1973. Macmillan.

BERHANDT, Jan Peter. *Willy Brandt*. Hanover, 1961. Verlag fuer Literatur.

BINDER, David. *Willy Brandt. A German Life*. New York, 1969. New York Times publication.

BOLESCH, Hermann Otto & LEICHT, Hans-Dieter. *Willy Brandt*. Tuebingen, 1971. Horst Erdmann Verlag.

BOLESCH, Hermann Otto (Editor). *Typisch Brandt*. Munich, 1972. Bertelsmann.

BRANDT, Willy.

Verbrecher und andere Deutschen. Oslo, 1946. Aschehong.

Norwegen's Freiheitskampf. Hamburg, 1948. Auerdruck.

My Road to Berlin (as told to Leo Lania). London, 1960. Peter Davies.

Berlin, Israel and the Jews. Berlin, 1961. Berlin Press Office.

Pladoeyer fuer die Zukunft. Frankfurt, 1961. Europaeische Verlagsanstalt.

Mit Herz und Hand. Hanover, 1962. Verlag fuer Literatur.

The Ordeal of Coexistence. Cambridge (Mass), 1963. Harvard University Press.

Begegnungen mit Kennedy. Munich, 1964. Kindler Verlag.

Friedenssicherung in Europa. Berlin, 1968. Berlin Verlag.

Aussenpolitik, Deutschlandpolitik, Europapolitik. Berlin 1968. Berlin Verlag.

In Exile. London, 1971. Oswald Wolff.

People and Politics. London, 1978. Collins.

BRANT, Stefan. *The East German Rising*. London, 1955. Thames & Hudson.

BRAUN, Otto. *Von Weimar zu Hitler*. New York, 1940. Europa Press.

BRAUNTHAL, Julius. *Need Germany Survive?* London, 1943. Gollancz.

BRENTANO, Heinrich von. *Germany and Europe*. London, 1964. André Deutsch.

BROWN, George (later Lord). *In My Way*. London, 1971. Gollancz.

BURKE, Arleigh. *NATO after Czechoslovakia*. Washington, 1969. Centre for Strategic and International Studies, Georgetown.

BUTLER, Ewan. *City Divided*. London, 1955. Sidgwick & Jackson.

CATE, Curtis. *The Ides of August*. London, 1979. Weidenfeld & Nicolson.

CHALMERS, Douglas A. *The Social Democratic Party of Germany*. New Haven, 1964. Yale University Press.

CHAMBERLIN, William Henry. *The German Phoenix*. London, 1963. Robert Hale.

CHILDS, David. *From Schumacher to Brandt. The Story of German Socialism*. London, 1966. Pergamon.

CHURCHILL, Winston. *The World Crisis*. London, 1927. Butterworth.

CLAY, General Lucius. *Decision in Germany*. New York, 1953. Doubleday.

COBLER, Sebastian. *Law, Order and Politics in West Germany*. London, 1978. Penguin.

COLLIER, Richard. *Bridge across the Sky*. London, 1978. Macmillan.

CONNELL, Brian. *Watcher on the Rhine*. London, 1959. Weidenfeld & Nicolson.

CONZE, Werner. *Die Zeit Wilhelm II und die Weimarer Republik*. Tuebingen, 1964. Verlag Hermann Leins.

CRAIG, Gordon. *From Bismarck to Adenauer*. Baltimore, 1958. John Hopkins.

CRAWLEY, Aidan.
De Gaulle. London, 1969. Literary Guild.
The Rise of Western Germany. London, 1973. Collins.

DAHRENDORF, Ralf. *Fuer eine Erneuerung der Demokratie in der Bundesrepublik*. Munich, 1968. Piper Verlag.

DALBERG, Thomas. *Franz Josef Strauss*. Guetersloh, 1968. Bertelsmann.

DAVIDSON, Basil. *Germany. What Now?* London, 1950. Frederick Muller.

DE GAULLE, Charles. *Memoirs of Hope*. London, 1971. Weidenfeld & Nicolson.

DEHIO, Ludwig. *Germany and World Politics in the Twentieth Century*. London, 1959. Chatto & Windus.

DILL, Marshall. *Germany*. Ann Arbor, 1961. University of Michigan Press.

DOLLINGER, Hans. *Willy! Willy!*. Munich, 1970. Wilhelm Heyne.

DRECHSLER, Hanno. *Die Sozialistische Arbeiterpartei Deutschlands*. Meisenheim, 1935. Anton Hain.

DULLES, Eleanor Lansing. *Berlin. The Wall is not Forever*. Chapel Hill, 1967. University of North Carolina Press.

ECKARDT, Felix von. *Ein Unordentliches Leben*. Duesseldorf, 1967. Econ Verlag.

EDEN, Sir Anthony. *Full Circle*. London, 1960. Cassell.

EDINGER, Lewis J.
Kurt Schumacher. Stanford, 1965. Stanford University Press.
German Exile Politics. Berkeley, 1956. University of California Press.

EINSIEDEL, Heinrich von. *The Shadow of Stalingrad*. London, 1953. Allan Wingate.

ERDMANN, Karl-Dieter. *Adenauer in der Rheinlandpolitik nach dem ersten Weltkrieg*. Stuttgart, 1966. Ernst Klett Verlag.

ERHARD, Ludwig. *The Economics of Success*. London, 1963. Thames & Hudson.

ESCHENBURG, Theodor. *Zur politischen Praxis in der Bundesrepublik*. Munich, 1963. Piper Verlag.

FEST, Joachim. *The Face of the Third Reich*. London, 1970. Weidenfeld & Nicolson.

FEUCHTWANGER, E. J. (Editor). *Upheaval and Continuity*. London, 1973. Oswald Wolff.

FLACH, Karl Hermann. *Erhard's schwerer Weg*. Stuttgart, 1964. Seewald Verlag.

GATZKE, Hans W. *Stresemann and the Rearmament of Germany*. Baltimore, 1954. John Hopkins.

GERARD, James W. *My Four Years in Berlin*. London, 1917. Hodder & Stoughton.

GOLDMANN, Nahum. *Memoirs*. London, 1970. Weidenfeld & Nicolson.

GOLLANCZ, Victor. *In Darkest Germany*. London, 1947. Gollancz.

GOYKE, Ernst. *Willy Brandt, Der Bundeskanzler*. Bonn, 1971. Ergo Verlag.

GRASS, Günter. *Speak Out!* New York, 1969. Harcourt Brace.

GREBING, Helga. *The History of the German Labour Movement.* London, 1969. Oswald Wolff.

GROSSER, Alfred.
Die Bundesrepublik Deutschland. Tuebingen, 1967. Rainer Wunderlich Verlag.
Western Germany from Defeat to Rearmament. London, 1955. Allen & Unwin.

GUMBEL, J. *The American Occupation of Germany.* Stanford, 1968. Stanford University Press.

HARPPRECHT, Klaus. *Willy Brandt. Portraet und Selbstportraet.* Munich, 1970. Kindler Verlag.

HAYTER, Sir William. *The Diplomacy of the Great Powers.* London, 1960. Hamish Hamilton.

HECK, Bruno (Editor). *Konrad Adenauer und seine Zeit.* Stuttgart, 1976. Deutsche Verlagsanstalt.

HEIDENHEIMER, Arnold.
Adenauer and the CDU. The Hague, 1960. Martinus Nijhoff.
The Governments of Germany. New York, 1964. Thomas Crowell.

HENDERSON, Sir Nevile. *Failure of a Mission.* London, 1940. Hodder & Stoughton.

HENKELS, Walter.
Gar nicht so Pingelig. Duesseldorf, 1965. Econ Verlag.
Bonner Koepfe. Duesseldorf, 1969. Econ Verlag.

HEUSS, Theodor.
Bilder meines Lebens. Tuebingen, 1964. Rainer Wunderlich Verlag.
Wuerdigungen. Tuebingen, 1955. Rainer Wunderlich Verlag.

HILDEBRANDT, Rainer. *It happened at the Wall.* Berlin, 1967. Gruenewald Verlag.

HISCOCKS, Richard. *Democracy in Western Germany.* London, 1957. Oxford University Press.

HOEHNE, Heinz & ZOLLING, Hermann. *Network.* London, 1972. Secker & Warburg.

HORNE, Alistair. *The Price of Glory.* London, 1962. Macmillan.

IHLEFELD, Heli.
Kiesinger. Anekdoten. Munich, 1967. Bechtle Verlag.
Willy Brandt. Anekdotisch. Munich, 1968. Bechtle Verlag.

KAHN, Helmust Wolfgang. *Helmut Schmidt.* Hamburg, 1973. Holsten Verlag.

KAISER, Karl. *German Foreign Policy in Transition.* London, 1968. Oxford University Press.

KENNAN, George. *Realities of American Foreign Policy.* London, 1954. Oxford University Press.

KIEP, Walther. *A New Challenge for Western Europe.* New York, 1974. Mason & Kipscomb.

KIESINGER, Kurt Georg. *Schwaebische Kindheit.* Tuebingen, 1964. Rainer Wunderlich Verlag.

KING-HALL, Sir Stephen & ULLMANN, Richard. *German Parliaments.* London, 1954. Hansard Society.

KIRKPATRICK, Sir Ivone. *The Inner Circle.* London, 1959. Macmillan.

KITZINGER, Uwe. *German Electoral Politics.* Oxford, 1960. Clardendon Press.

KNICKERBOCKER, H. R. *Germany. Fascist or Soviet?* London, 1932. Bodley Head.

KOHN, Hans.
German History. Some New German Views. London, 1954. Allen & Unwin.
The Mind of Germany. London, 1961. Macmillan.

LAMM, Fritz. *Die grosse Koalition und die naechsten Aufgaben der Linken.* Frankfurt, 1967. Verlag Neue Kritik.

LEMMER, Ernst. *Manches war doch anders.* Frankfurt, 1968. Verlag Heinrich Scheffler.

LEONHARDT, Wolfgang. *This Germany.* Greenwich (Conn), 1955. New York Graphic Society.

LEVY, Richard. *The Downfall of the Anti-Semitic Political Parties of Imperial Germany.* New Haven, 1975. Yale University Press.

LINDLAU, Dagobert (Editor). *Gedanken ueber einen Politiker.* Munich, 1972. Kindler.

LOEWENTHAL, Richard. *Hochschule fuer die Demokratie.* Cologne, 1971. Markusverlag.

LUKOMSKI, Jesse. *Ludwig Erhard. Der Mensch und der Politiker.* Duesseldorf, 1965. Econ Verlag.

McBRIDE, Will & FINCKENSTEIN, Hans Werner, Graf von. *Adenauer. Ein Portraet.* Starnberg, 1965. Joseph Keller Verlag.

McDERMOTT, Geoffrey. *Berlin. Success of a Mission?* London, 1963. André Deutsch.

MACMILLAN, Harold. *Tides of Fortune.* London, 1969. Macmillan.

MANDER, John. *Berlin. Hostage for the West.* London, 1962. Penguin.

MARRIOTT, J. A. R. *The Evolution of Prussia.* Oxford, 1917. Oxford University Press.

MEINHARDT, Guenther. *Adenauer und der rheinische Separatismus.* Recklinghausen, 1962. Kommunal Verlag.

MENDE, Erich. *Die FDP.* Stuttgart, 1972. Seewald Verlag.

MEYER, Michel. *Freedom Purchase – Trade in People in Germany.* Paris, 1977.

MOMMSEN, Wilhelm. *Deutsche Parteiprogramme.* Munich, 1951. Isar Verlag.

MOWAT, R. C. *Ruin and Resurgence.* London, 1966. Blandford Press.

MUMM, Reinhard. *Der Christlich-Soziale Gedanke.* Berlin, 1933. Mittler Verlag.

NELSON, Walter Henry.
Germany Rearmed. New York, 1971. Simon & Schuster.
The Berliners. New York, 1969. David McKay.
The Soldier Kings. New York, 1970. Putnam.

NETZER, Hans-Joachim (Editor). *Adenauer und die Folgen.* Munich, 1965. Beck'sche Verlag.

NEVEN-DUMONT, Juergen. *After Hitler*. London, 1970. Penguin.

OPPEN, Beate von (Editor). *Documents on Germany, 1945–55*. London, 1955. Oxford University Press.

PAKENHAM, Lord. *Born to Believe*. London, 1953. Jonathan Cape.

PECK, Joachim. *Dr Konrad Adenauer 1917–1952*. Berlin, 1952. Verlag der Nation.

PERRIS, G. H. *Germany and the German Emperor*. London, 1914. Andrew Melrose.

PIRKER, Theo. *Die SPD nach Hitler*. Munich, 1965. Ruetten Verlag.

POLTERING, Hans Gert. *Adenauer's Sicherheitspolitik*. Düsseldorf, 1975. Econ Verlag.

POPPINGA, Anneliese. *Meine Erinnerungen an Konrad Adenauer*. Stuttgart, 1970. Deutsche Verlagsanstalt.

PRITTIE, Terence.
  Germany Divided. Boston, 1960. Little Brown.
  Germans against Hitler. London, 1964. Hutchinson.
  Adenauer. A Study in Fortitude. London, 1972. Tom Stacey.
  Willy Brandt. New York, 1974. Schocken.

REUTHER, Helmut. *Adenauer. Bildnis und Deutung*. Bonn, 1963. Komm mit Verlag.

ROWSE, A. L. *All Souls and Appeasement*. London, 1961. Macmillan.

RUGE, Friedrich. *Politik, Militaer, Buendnis*. Stuttgart, 1963. Deutsche Verlagsanstalt.

RUMMEL, Alois (Editor). *Konrad Adenauer 1876–1967*. Bonn, 1975. Bonn Aktuell Verlag.

SCHAEFER, Emil. *Von Potsdam bis Bonn*. Lahr, 1950. Verlag Schauenburg.

SCHALLUECK, Paul (Editor). *German Cultural Developments since 1945*. Munich, 1971. Heuber Verlag.

SCHILLER, Karl. *Berliner Wirtschaft und Deutsche Politik*. Stuttgart, 1964. Seewald Verlag.

SCHLABRENDORFF, Fabian von. *The Secret War against Hitler*. London, 1966. Hodder & Stoughton.

SCHMIDT, Helmut. *The Balance of Power*. London,1971. William Kimber.

SCHREIBER, Hermann & SIMON, Sven. *Willy Brandt – Anatomie einer Veraenderung*. Düsseldorf, 1970. Econ Verlag.

SCHROEDER, Georg (Editor). *Konrad Adenauer, Eine Bilddokumentation*. Guetersloh, 1966. Bertelsmann.

SCHROEDER, Gerhard. *Decision for Europe*. London, 1964. Thames & Hudson.

SCHULZ, Gerhard. *Die CDU: Merkmale ihres Aufbaues*. Stuttgart, 1955. Ring Verlag.

SCHUMACHER, Kurt. *Der Auftrag des demokratischen Sozialismus*. Bonn, 1972. Neue Gesellschaft (2nd ed.).

SCHUTZ, Wilhelm Wolfgang. *Rethinking German Policy*. New York, 1967. Praeger.

SCHWARZ, Hans-Peter. *Konrad Adenauer. Seine Deutschland-und-Aussenpolitik*. Mainz, 1971. Beck'sche Verlag.

SCHWERING, Leo. *Fruehgeschichte der Christlich-Demokratische Union*. Recklinghausen, 1963. Kommunal Verlag.

SEALE, Patrick & McCONVILLE, Maureen. *French Revolution, 1968*. London, 1968. Heinemann.

SEIFERT, Juergen. *Die Spiegel Affaere*. Olten, 1966. Walter Verlag.

SETTEL, Arthur (Editor). *This is Germany*. New York, 1950. William Sloane.

SHEARS, David. *The Ugly Frontier*. London, 1970. Chatto & Windus.

SHIRER, William L. *The Rise and Fall of the Third Reich*. New York, 1960. Simon & Schuster.

SONTHEIMER, Kurt. *The Government and Politics of West Germany*. London, 1972. Hutchinson.

SPAAK, Paul Henri. *Why NATO?* London, 1959. Penguin.

SPRINGER, Axel. *Von Berlin aus gesehen*. Stuttgart, 1971. Seewald Verlag.

STEELE, Jonathan. *Socialism with a German Face*. London, 1977. Jonathan Cape.

STEGERWALD, Adam. *Deutsche Lebensfragen*. Berlin, 1921. Verlag fuer Politik und Wirtschaft.

STEINERT, Marlis. *Capitulation 1945*. London, 1969. Constable.

STERN, Carola. *Ulbricht*. London, 1965. Pall Mall Press.

STRAUSS, Franz Josef. *The Grand Design*. London, 1965. Weidenfeld & Nicolson.

THAYER, Charles. *The Unquiet Germans*. London, 1958. Michael Joseph.

TILFORD, R. B. & PREECE, R. J. C. *Federal Germany. Political and Social Order*. London, 1970. Oswald Wolff.

TIRPITZ, Grand Admiral Alfred von. *My Memoirs*. Vol. 1, 2. London, 1919. Hurst & Blackett.

TOLAND, John. *Adolf Hitler*. New York, 1976. Doubleday.

TREVOR-ROPER, H. R. *The Last Days of Hitler*. London, 1946. Macmillan.

VOGEL, Rolf. *The German Path to Israel*. London, 1969. Oswald Wolff.

WALSER, Martin (Editor). *Die Alternative*. Hamburg, 1961. Rowohlt.

WATT, D. C. *Britain Looks at Germany*. London, 1965. Oswald Wolff.

WEYMAR, Paul. *Konrad Adenauer*. London, 1957. Andre Deutsch.

WHEELER-BENNETT, Sir John. *The Nemesis of Power*. London, 1953. Macmillan.

WHITE, Theodore. *Fire in the Ashes*. New York, 1953. William Sloane.

WIGHTON, Charles. *Adenauer. Democratic Dictator*. London, 1963. Frederick Muller.

WILLIS, F. Roy. *France, Germany and the New Europe*. Stanford, 1965. Stanford University Press.

WILSON, Rt Hon Harold. *The Labour Government 1964–1970*. London, 1971. Weidenfeld.

WINDSOR, Philip.
City on Leave. London, 1963. Chatto & Windus.

Germany and the Management of Detente. London, 1971. Chatto & Windus.
German Reunification. London, 1969. Paul Elek.
WISKEMANN, Elizabeth. *Germany's Eastern Neighbours*. London, 1956. Oxford University Press.
ZINK, Harold. *The United States in Germany*. Princeton, 1957. Van Nostrand.

Index